Suicide

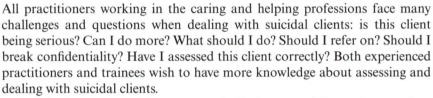
All practitioners working in the caring and helping professions face many challenges and questions when dealing with suicidal clients: is this client being serious? Can I do more? What should I do? Should I refer on? Should I break confidentiality? Have I assessed this client correctly? Both experienced practitioners and trainees wish to have more knowledge about assessing and dealing with suicidal clients.

Suicide: Strategies and Interventions for Reduction and Prevention examines myths about suicide, explores facts and statistics at national and international levels, and uses client cases to uncover thoughts leading to suicidal behaviour. The editor offers an insight into what can be done in the community, and within therapeutic settings when working with this challenging client group. Contributions are divided into four parts covering:

- suicide: statistics, research, theory and interventions
- personal experience of suicide
- three therapeutic approaches to prevent suicide
- group interventions.

Featuring chapters from a range of experienced practitioners, this book provides a wealth of information on strategies and possible interventions. The addition of a Self-Harm Management Plan, assessment checklists, and list of useful organizations makes it essential reading for both mental health professionals, and those in training.

Suicide

Strategies and interventions for reduction
and prevention

Edited by Stephen Palmer

Routledge
Taylor & Francis Group

LONDON AND NEW YORK

First published 2008 by Routledge
27 Church Road, Hove, East Sussex BN3 2FA

Simultaneously published in the USA and Canada
by Routledge
270 Madison Avenue, New York, NY 10016

*Routledge is an imprint of the Taylor & Francis Group, an Informa
business*

Typeset in Times by RefineCatch Limited, Bungay, Suffolk
Printed and bound in Great Britain by TJ International Ltd,
Padstow, Cornwall
Paperback cover design by Jim Wilkie

British Library Cataloguing in Publication Data
A catalogue record for this book is available from the British Library

Library of Congress Cataloging-in-Publication Data
Suicide : strategies and interventions for reduction and prevention /
edited by Stephen Palmer.
      p. ; cm.
Includes bibliographical references and index.
ISBN 978–1–58391–994–1 (hbk.) – ISBN 978–1–58391–995–8
(pbk.). 1. Suicide. 2. Suicidal behavior. 3. Suicide–Prevention.
4. Suicide–Psychological aspects. I. Palmer, Stephen, 1955–
[DNLM: 1. Suicide. 2. Psychotherapy–methods. 3. Suicide–prevention
& control. WM 165 S9485 2007]
RC569.S9369 2007
362.28–dc22   2007007860

ISBN: 978–1–58391–994–1 (hbk)
ISBN: 978–1–58391–995–8 (pbk)

To RH

Contents

Illustrations and tables

Figures

Tables

Notes on the editor
and contributors

Stephen Palmer, PhD, is Honorary Professor of Psychology and Director of the Coaching Psychology Unit at City University, London, and Director of the Centre for Stress Management, London. He is Honorary President and Fellow of the Association for Coaching, Honorary Vice-President of the Institute of Health Promotion and Education, Honorary Vice-President of the International Stress Management Association (UK), a director of the Association for Rational Emotive Behaviour Therapy and Consultant Director of the New Zealand Centre for Cognitive Behaviour Therapy.

He was the first chair of the British Psychological Society Special Group in Coaching Psychology for 2004–2005, and was chair of the Scientific Awards Committee of the British Psychological Society Division of Counselling Psychology from 1997 to 1999. He is co-editor of *The Rational Emotive Behaviour Therapist*, editor of the *International Journal of Health Promotion and Education* and UK coordinating editor of the *International Coaching Psychology Review*.

He was the academic consultant on the Surrey Police Deepcut Investigation Final Report and in April 2004 he was appointed as a specialist advisor to the House of Commons Defence Select Committee on the Duty of Care Inquiry into the initial training establishments in all three services of the armed forces. He is a member of the International Association for Suicide Prevention and the American Foundation for Suicide Prevention. He is an award-winning psychologist and psychotherapist.

Yvonne Bergmans is the suicide intervention consultant at the Arthur Sommer Rotenberg Chair in Suicide Studies in Toronto, Canada. She has developed and continues to coordinate and facilitate intervention groups for individuals who are at high risk for suicide.

David Cooke has a BA in Business and Management from Northumbria University, UK. He spent his childhood in a small Cornish town and is currently living in London working as a property consultant.

Berni Curwen works at the Primary Care Counselling and Psychology Department, Dartford, Kent, as a UKCP registered psychotherapist. She is co-author of *Brief Cognitive Behaviour Therapy* (2000, with Stephen Palmer and Peter Ruddell).

Melissa Darmody is a counselling psychologist with a doctorate in counselling psychology. She has developed employee assistance programme (EAP) services since 1997 in Ireland and other countries and has particular expertise in working with victims of abuse and trauma. She has written several articles incorporating solution-focused brief therapy into work with adult survivors of abuse and trauma. She is the clinical director of an EAP based in Ireland.

Wayne Froggatt, Dip.Soc.Wk, CQSW, MANZASW, Certified REBT Supervisor, Executive Director, New Zealand Centre for Rational Emotive Behaviour Therapy and Centre for Cognitive Behaviour Therapy, Consultant Director, UK Centre for REBT, is the author of *Choose to be Happy, GoodStress, FearLess, Relaxation for the Real World, The Rational Treatment of Anxiety, Learning to use Rational Emotive Behaviour Therapy, Learning to use Cognitive-Behaviour Therapy.*

Ginette Goulard, MD, FRCP(C), is Director of Education, Centre Hospitalier Pierre-Janet, Gatineau Assistant Professor, Department of Psychiatry, University of Ottawa, Canada.

Anopama Kapoor is a chartered counselling psychologist, registered with the British Psychological Society. She trained at City University, London, and has worked with people suffering from a range of mental health problems, for many years. She has also worked as a tutor for City University.

John Lees is a BACP senior registered practitioner who runs the Masters in Therapeutic Counselling at the University of Greenwich, London. He has a small private practice and is interested in research methods based on the principles of counselling and psychotherapeutic practice.

Paul S. Links, MD, is Arthur Sommer Rotenberg Chair in Suicide Studies, Professor of Psychiatry, Department of Psychiatry, St Michael's Hospital, University of Toronto, Canada.

Brendan Madden, MA, MIACP, works as a psychotherapist, brief therapy trainer and EAP consultant. A co-founder of the Brief Therapy Group, he has published several articles and co-authored *Becoming a Solution Detective* (2001, with John Sharry and Melissa Darmody) on solution-focused brief therapy interventions.

Rory C. O'Connor has been conducting research in suicidology since 1995. He has published many articles on suicidal behaviour and psychological distress as well as co-authoring *Understanding Suicidal Behaviour* (2000, with Noel Sheehy). He is a member of the International Association for Suicide Prevention, American Association of Suicidology and International Academy for Suicide Research.

Minna Pietilä has an academic background in sociology and social constructionism. She has studied various health and social welfare related issues in Finland. Her PhD concerned moral meaning-making of suicide and bereavement in the family.

Peter Ruddell is the Clinical Director of the Centre for Stress Management, London. He is a UKCP registered psychotherapist and a director of the Association for Rational Emotive Behaviour Therapy. He is co-author of *Brief Cognitive Behaviour Therapy* (2000, with Berni Curwen and Stephen Palmer).

Monique Séguin, PhD, is professor in the Department of Psychology, Université du Québec en Outaouais, McGill Group on Suicide Studies, McGill University Douglas Hospital, Canada.

John Sharry is principal social worker at the Mater Hospital and co-founder of the Brief Therapy Group in Dublin. He is author of *Solution Focused Groupwork* (2001) and *Counselling Children, Adolescents and Families* (2004) and co-author of *Becoming a Solution Detective* (2001, with Brendan Madden and Melissa Darmody).

Noel Sheehy is Professor of Psychology, Liverpool John Moores University, Liverpool. He is an applied social psychologist who has worked on issues to do with the perception and management of risk behaviours since 1997. He is editor of the North American journal *Current Psychology* and co-authored *Understanding Suicidal Behaviour* (2000, with Rory C. O'Connor).

Cameron Stark is a consultant in public health with NHS Highland, and an honorary clinical senior lecturer at the Centre for Rural Health of the University of Aberdeen, Scotland. He trained in psychiatry before moving to public health. His research interests include self-harm, rural health and risk theory.

Quentin Stimpson is a psychotherapist and supervisor in private practice. He also supervises practitioner research, and has edited *Clinical Counselling in Voluntary and Community Settings* (2003). Currently, he is co-writing 'Words and Symbols' (to appear in the Open University Press, Core Concepts in Therapy Series).

Susan Walen was formerly an associate professor in the Department of Psychology at Towson State University, and clinical faculty at the Department of Psychiatry, Johns Hopkins Hospital, Baltimore, MD. She has published extensively on cognitive therapy, lectured internationally and maintained an active private practice. Retired in January 2007, she is currently pursuing her second passion, quilting arts.

Foreword

Darkness visible: strategies and prevention

Cary L. Cooper, CBE

The author William Styron, in his book *Darkness Visible: A Memoir of Madness* (New York, 1992), describes his own experiences of being clinically depressed:

> Depression is a disorder of mood, so mysteriously painful and elusive in the way it becomes known to the self ... as to verge close to being beyond description. It thus remains nearly incomprehensible to those who have not experienced it in its extreme mode, although the gloom, 'the blues' which people go through occasionally and associate with the general hassle of everyday existence are of such prevalence that they do give many individuals a hint of the illness in its catastrophic form.
>
> (p. 7)

We are seeing a rise in depression in society generally since the mid-1990s because of the increases in pressures and insecurities of people in the workplace, in the family and in almost all walks of life, backed by the break-up of the extended family and the communities who were once the 'natural counsellors' to help us through life's problems. With these increasing stresses and strains manifesting themselves through depression, we are also seeing an increase in suicide attempts, as individuals cry for help or look for what they think is the easy solution to what they perceive to be intractable personal problems. This book helps us all understand the issues surrounding the socially taboo topic of suicide. It highlights not only the extent and costs of it to society but also what strategies work and how we might prevent suicides in the future, from leading researchers and practitioners in the field. It explores the definitions, statistics and interventions for suicides internationally, explores personality and cognitive styles of suicidal behaviour, assessing the risks and the various therapeutic approaches available to prevent it (e.g. cognitive behavioural therapy (CBT), rational emotive therapy, psychodynamic approaches, solution-focused approaches).

This book will help to take away the veil of mystery and suspicion about a topic that now permeates all of society in times of constant and unremitting change and stress, suicides. The editor has done a magnificent job in demystifying this subject, and deserves our wholehearted support and gratitude. We need to help and support people who are desperate and depressed, to see that <u>life is a gift to cherish</u>. As Leonard, in the film *Awakenings* (1990), suggests, having awakened from his psychotic state, when first reading a newspaper:

> Read the newspaper. What does it say? All bad. It's all bad. People have forgotten what life is all about. They've forgotten what it is to be alive. They need to be reminded – they need to be reminded about what they have and what they can lose . . . what I feel is the joy of life, the gift of life, the freedom of life, the wonderment of life!

Cary L. Cooper, CBE, is Professor of Organizational Psychology and Health at Lancaster University, and President of the British Association of Counselling and Psychotherapy.

Preface

The World Health Organization (WHO), mental health bodies and governments around the world are attempting to reduce suicide rates by the establishment of suicide prevention programmes. Although in some countries suicide rates are gradually reducing, in others they have either reached a plateau or are still rising.

What can be done to reduce or prevent suicide? Many possible answers have been provided in the published literature although their implementation is often more problematic. In this book we consider a number of these interventions at an international, national and individual level and provide insight into what can be done in the community and within therapeutic settings.

Assessment of suicidal risk, personal experience of suicide, three therapeutic approaches and group interventions are included which will provide counsellors, psychotherapists, psychologists and other health practitioners with an insight into helping suicidal clients or patients.

With the advent of the internet, obtaining information about suicide has become easier for both the professional and layperson. There are even macabre websites which have photos of people who have committed suicide. The number of web pages devoted to 'suicide' appears to be on the increase and a quick *Yahoo!* search in 2007 provided 122,000,000 results (with numerous repeated pages). Although the democracy of the internet allows anybody to upload websites, fortunately many suicide-related sites do provide helpful information. Therefore in Appendix 3 there is a list of useful suicide prevention, support and research related websites and organizations.

For many health professionals this book, written by nineteen contributors from Europe, North America and New Zealand, may be the first text they have read on suicide prevention and reduction. It is hoped that this book may act as the springboard leading the reader to move on to other publications or websites which focus on different aspects of suicidology. In Appendix 4, a booklist has been included to help this process.

Working in this field or with suicidal clients is often challenging but it can have rewards too when the interventions have proved successful or we make significant findings in our research. It is important for mental health professionals to look after themselves. We owe it to ourselves, our families, our colleagues, our profession, society and to our clients who may be reliant upon us.

Stephen Palmer

Acknowledgements

This book was possible due to the hard work and dedication of the nineteen contributors. Many chapters were written specifically for this book and a number are updated articles and papers. I would like to thank the editors and publishers of the *British Journal of Guidance and Counselling* for giving us permission to use revised or updated articles which were published in a special suicide symposium issue I edited.

Sheehy, N. and O'Connor, R.C. (2002) Cognitive style and suicidal behaviour: implications for therapeutic intervention, research lacunae and priorities. *British Journal of Guidance and Counselling*, 29(3), 353–362.

Ruddell, P. and Curwen, B. (2002) Understanding suicidal ideation and assessing for risk. *British Journal of Guidance and Counselling*, 29(3), 363–372.

Lees, J. and Stimpson, Q. (2002) A psychodynamic approach to to suicide: a critical and selective review. *British Journal of Guidance and Counselling*, 29(3), 373–382.

Sharry, J., Darmody, M. and Madden, B. (2002) A solution-focused approach to working with clients who are suicidal. *British Journal of Guidance and Counselling*, 29(3), 383–399.

Pietilä, M. (2002) Support groups: a psychological or social device for suicide bereavement? *British Journal of Guidance and Counselling*, 29(3), 401–414.

Walen, S. (2002) It's a funny thing about suicide: a personal experience. *British Journal of Guidance and Counselling*, 29(3), 415–430.

Chapter 8 is based on an article revised by the author. It has been reproduced with the kind permission of the British Psychological Society (BPS) and The Editor of *Counselling Psychology Review*.

Kapoor, A. (2004) Suicide: the effect on the counselling psychologist. *Counselling Psychology Review*, 1(3), 28–36.

I thank the World Health Organization for permission for the use of its data and figures in Chapter 1. This important data allows us to look at suicide on a global level.

I thank Bruce Whyte of the Scottish Public Health Observatory and of Choose Life for his assistance and for giving us permission to use the data and graphs in Chapter 2. My thanks also goes to the Choose Life Marketing and Communications Manager, Nicola Hughes, for permission to use data and examples from the Choose Life publications and local action plans.

Professor Keith Hawton and his team at the Centre for Suicide Research in Oxford are thanked for giving permission to use Figures 2.4, 2.5 and 2.6 taken from the report, *Deliberate Self-harm in Oxford 2005*. The data were based on those produced by the Office for National Statistics (ONS), UK. This report was co-written by Keith Hawton, Deborah Casey, Elizabeth Bale, Anna Shepherd, Helen Bergen and Sue Simkin and is available from the Centre's website: http://cebmh.warne.ox.ac.uk/csr/

Staff at Routledge have been very supportive in the commissioning and production of this book. Particular thanks go to Joanne Forshaw and Kate Moysen for their hard work and patience.

I would like to thank our clients and ex-clients whose case studies contributed to the chapters in this book. Their support in sharing their experiences with us in books helps health professionals to increase their understanding of events or clinical conditions that trigger suicidal ideation and behaviour and the subsequent suicide prevention and management. Due to confidentiality we are unable to name them individually.

Finally, I am extremely grateful to Susan Walen, David Cooke and Anopama Kapoor for sharing with us their personal experiences of suicide from the view of the client, the friend and the therapist respectively. This personal material gives us an insight into how they felt and thought during a difficult period of their lives.

Introduction

Suicide

Strategies and interventions for reduction and prevention: an introduction

Stephen Palmer

> To be or not to be: that is the question.
> Whether 'tis nobler in the mind to suffer
> The slings and arrows of outrageous fortune,
> Or take arms against a sea of troubles,
> And by opposing end them. To die; to sleep;
> No more; and by a sleep to say we end
> The heart-ache and thousand natural shocks
> That flesh is heir to, 'tis a consummation
> Devoutly to be wish'd. To die, to sleep
> Shakespeare, *Hamlet*, Act 3, Scene 1

For thousands of years, people have written about suicide. The early Roman culture accepted and sometimes even recommended *mors voluntaris* as long as you were a free citizen, i.e. not a slave (De Leo et al., 2006). In the sixteenth and seventeenth centuries, William Shakespeare was probably one of the leading untrained suicidologists and psychologists with a great insight into the human condition. His understanding came from observation and experience and he was able to successfully convey that in his plays such as *Hamlet* without any formal psychological study.

In the twentieth century health professionals have undertaken research in an attempt to understand both suicide and psychology. Suicidology covers the theory, research, prevention, reduction, management, assessment, strategies and interventions associated with understanding and managing suicidal behaviour. This is a vast undertaking and is currently directed at international, national and local levels by many government and non-governmental organizations (NGOs) and individuals. This book covers a number of areas relating to suicidology.

How is the book organized?

The book is divided into five main parts:

I   Suicide: statistics, research, theory and interventions
II   Personal experience of suicide
III Three therapeutic approaches to prevent suicide
IV   Group interventions
V   Appendices

Part I Suicide: statistics, research, theory and interventions

The first chapter by Stephen Palmer is on 'Suicide: definitions, statistics and interventions at the international level' and is an orientation chapter which brings together some of the relevant statistics, research and interventions at a global level. In Chapter 2, Stephen Palmer focuses on 'Suicide statistics for the UK and the National Suicide Prevention Strategy'. This provides comparisons of the suicide rates across the UK and then information about the suicide prevention strategies for England and Scotland. In Chapter 3, Cameron Stark focuses on 'Suicide in rural areas'. He notes that the relationship between rurality and health is not straightforward and questions the public image of the rural idyll. He quotes one older woman in the Western Isles of Scotland in a conversation with a health worker, 'It may be beautiful scenery, but it's all I've got'. Young people and children may be isolated, paradoxically within a rural community that may be perceived by outsiders as close knit. Stark notes that death by firearms may be over-represented in some areas such as the Highland National Health Service (NHS) Board area, Devon and Yorkshire. Research into suicide by farmers has highlighted factors such as mental health problems but also living alone and lacking close friends. Again, firearms were over-represented and easy access to firearms seems to be a suicide factor in rural areas across the world, for example, USA and Australia. In Chapter 4, Noel Sheehy and Rory C. O'Connor focus on 'Cognitive style and suicidal behaviour'. It is suggested that suicide is associated with a constriction in cognitive style which leads to decrements in problem-solving and information-processing. Stress may be a triggering factor which interacts with vulnerability and buffering factors such as social support. Research is highlighting the relevance of socially prescribed perfectionism and self-oriented perfectionism in suicidal behaviour. O'Connor has found evidence to support Mark Williams' cry of pain model and believes that it affords a meaningful representation of the suicidal process. The implications of the research for counselling and therapy would point to the need of teaching cognitive thinking skills especially to counter social perfectionism, and problem-solving in individual or group therapy settings to help the client to deal with life issues and reduce their suicidal ideation. The last chapter in Part I is by Peter Ruddell and Berni Curwen, who cover 'Understanding suicidal ideation and assessing for risk'. Over 90 per cent of people who commit suicide have suffered from a psychiatric illness. The chapter includes a list of the common myths associated with suicide, assessment issues, questionnaires and interview techniques. The question that is left unanswered is:

do counselling and psychotherapy training courses adequately cover these topics and are therapists aware of the key risk factors? To reduce the incidence of client suicide these topics may be essential.

Part II Personal experience of suicide

Part II looks at three personal experiences of suicide which may inform our understanding of suicide and the aftermath. Chapter 6 by Susan Walen is titled 'It's a funny thing about suicide'. She describes her personal experience of depression with suicidal ideation. This is a case study with a difference as Susan Walen is an experienced psychologist and psychotherapist writing about her own experience. During this episode of her life she kept a diary of how she felt thus her personal experience comes alive in the text. As a psychologist who practised rational emotive behaviour therapy, she was aware of the techniques that she '*should*' have been able to use on herself. This case study demonstrates how theory and practice may not always be in harmony when a person is depressed. It also highlights the vulnerability of health professionals who may be as fallible as their clients and patients. In Chapter 7, 'A friend's view of suicide', David Cooke describes how he felt when his close childhood friend committed suicide. He shares with us his mixed emotions and the anger he had towards his friend and also the difficulties he had leading up to and during the funeral. He had experienced the death of other friends but it was not the same as a friend committing suicide. Chapter 8 by Anopama Kapoor on 'Client suicide and its effect on the therapist' is another personal experience, where the therapist explores the impact upon her when one of her clients committed suicide. Not surprisingly, her initial reaction was shock. She felt hurt and her confidence was shattered. She also felt angry towards her client and wished that her training institution had prepared her for such an event. Later she read the research literature and discovered that her response was similar to many other therapists who had experienced client suicide. The rest of her chapter focuses on this research. We are indebted to Susan Walen, David Cooke and Anopama Kapoor for sharing their experiences with us. Part II of this book can be seen as a preparation for Part III by obtaining an insight into the personal experiences of suicide from three viewpoints and then moving towards therapeutic interventions.

Part III Three therapeutic approaches to prevent suicide

Part III covers three therapeutic approaches and how they are applied in helping suicidal clients. It was decided to include two established therapeutic approaches, i.e. cognitive behavioural and psychodynamic and also the solution-focused approach which evolved more recently in the 1980s. In Chapter 9, Wayne Froggatt and Stephen Palmer focus on the 'Cognitive behavioural and rational emotive management of suicide'. Their unified model combines the key elements from both cognitive behavioural and rational emotive behavioural therapeutic approaches. It describes a range of assessment procedures and also cognitive, imaginal and behavioural interventions and techniques. This is an extended chapter as the approach uses many different methods. Case examples are provided. In Chapter 10, John Lees and Quentin Stimpson explore the Freudian and post-Freudian view of suicide and relate clinical practice to these theoretical notions. Their reflections on the ethical issues involved in working with suicidal clients includes whether the therapist should allow the client to commit suicide. They provide two case examples in which one client did commit suicide. In Chapter 11, the 'Solution-focused approach' advocated by John Sharry, Melissa Darmody and Brendan Madden, takes a practical approach working on therapeutic goals and helping the client to envision a positive future. Clients are invited to discuss alternative perspectives about the problems they are facing. However, they recommend caution as there is a lack of empirical evidence for solution-focused therapy with clients who are suicidal and/or at risk of harming themselves and wisely suggest that traditional approaches to risk assessment and management should not be abandoned.

Part IV Group interventions

Part IV focuses on group interventions. Coming to terms with the suicide of a family member is not easy. In Chapter 12, Minna Pietilä describes one area of support. It is an ethnomethodological research study consisting of sixteen interviews with bereaved parents and adult children, half of whom had attended a bereavement support group after a family member's suicide. Half the interviewees appreciated talking in support groups as a therapeutic measure as sharing what they were going through with 'fellow sufferers' had validated their own experience as normal, with the additional benefit of group members forming a 'safety net' among themselves. In an 'anonymous' group, they could talk to each other without taking into account the emotions and experiences of their intimate circle. In Chapter 13, Monique Séguin, Ginette Goulard, Yvonne Bergmans and Paul S. Links look at 'A group intervention for adolescents and young adults with recurrent suicide attempts'. This chapter is underpinned by research they undertook when developing the approach in Canada.

Part V Appendices

In Part V, the appendices include the Personal Self-Harm Management Plan, suicide assessment checklist, useful organizations and websites, and useful books on suicidology from 2000 onwards.

A short caveat

This book has been edited so that chapters can be read independently of each other, allowing the reader to dip into different sections. However, it is recommended that the theories, strategies and techniques taken from the therapeutic chapters in Part III should not be read in isolation and then applied without seeing them in the context of the whole chapter. The authors of the therapeutic chapters recommend that clinical supervision from qualified practitioners is obtained when in practice as a therapist, especially when working with suicidal clients.

Reference

De Leo, D., Burgis, S., Bertolote, J.M., Kerkhof, A.J.F.M. and Bille-Brahe, U. (2006) Definitions of suicidal behavior: lessons learned from the WHO/EURO Multicentre Study. *Crisis*, 27(1), 4–15.

Part I

Suicide

Statistics, research, theory
and interventions

1   Suicide

Definitions, statistics and interventions at the international level

Stephen Palmer

This chapter provides a general overview to suicide definitions and global suicide statistics, and covers a number of issues, strategies and initiatives that are currently being undertaken to prevent suicide at an international level.

Definitions of suicide, parasuicide and deliberate self-harm

In attempting to assess whether or not suicide prevention strategies and interventions are working, it is important for researchers and statisticians to share a common definition of suicide and for the reporting of death by suicide in countries and by their national bodies such as prison and health services, to be identical or similar. However, this is not the case. De Leo et al. (2006) point out that the areas of terminology and definitions in suicidology are confusing. They state that 'a satisfactory nomenclature of suicide should be applicable and usable both within and across all domains in which it is to be employed, whether the focus is research, clinical practice, public health, politics, or the law' (De Leo et al., 2006, p. 5). O'Carroll (1989) highlights that it is not always clear that the death was self-inflicted or intended. Thus the process of death certification can bias mortality rate statistics (Brooke, 1974; Atkinson et al., 1975). However, studies have found that regardless of possible social influences upon the recording of suicide mortality rates, there is still a level of consistency across countries and regions (e.g. see Sainsbury and Jenkins, 1982). When it comes to the finer details, Linehan (1997) has raised the issue of definitional obfuscation and how it has made research more difficult when attempting to compare studies.

So what is suicide? It was in 1642 when a physician, Sir Thomas Browne, first coined the term 'suicide' in *Religio Medici*. The word 'suicide' is believed to derive from the Latin words *sui* – of oneself, and *caedere* – to kill; in other words, to kill oneself. However, this description is too simplistic for the purposes of research. In 1897 Durkheim defined suicide as, 'All cases of death resulting directly or indirectly from a positive or negative act of the victim himself, which he knows will produce this result' (1897/1951, p. 44). This is a sociological perspective.

In 1986 for research purposes across different sites, the WHO Working Group developed the following definition:

> Suicide is an act with a fatal outcome which the deceased, knowing or expecting a fatal outcome, had initiated and carried out with the purpose of provoking the changes he desired.
>
> (WHO/EURO, 1986)

This multicentre study was going to focus on non-fatal suicidal behaviour and initially used the term 'parasuicide' to describe this behaviour. The term 'parasuicide' was first introduced by Kreitman et al. in 1969 and subsequently was used in different ways by researchers and practitioners. Generally parasuicide and attempted suicide have been used interchangeably although often attempted suicide was seen as a subcategory of parasuicide and denotes a strong intention to die. The WHO/EURO Group decided that parasuicide could be described as follows:

> An act with nonfatal outcome in which an individual deliberately initiates a non-habitual behaviour that, without intervention from others, will cause self-harm, or deliberately ingests a substance in excess of the prescribed or generally recognized therapeutic dosage, and which is aimed at realizing changes which the subject desired, via the actual or expected physical consequences.
>
> (WHO/EURO, 1986)

In the 1990s, to overcome the definitional problems, the WHO/EURO Multicentre Study on Parasuicide decided the terms 'parasuicide' and 'attempted suicide' could be used interchangeably. However, this was still unsatisfactory and later the terms 'fatal' and 'non-fatal' suicidal behaviour were proposed (De Leo et al., 1999). It is worth noting that this contributed to the group being renamed the WHO/EURO Multicentre Study on Suicidal Behaviour.

This definitional debate has continued and in an attempt to overcome the particular problems inherent with the existing definitions, De Leo et al. (2006) have developed the following:

> Suicide is an act with fatal outcome, which the deceased, knowing or expecting a potentially fatal outcome, has initiated and carried out with the purpose of bringing about wanted changes.
>
> (De Leo et al., 2006, p. 12)

This definition would not include dangerous sports or other risk-taking activities as this behaviour is not intended to bring about 'changes'.

De Leo et al. (2006, p. 14) have proposed a comprehensive category of 'non-fatal suicidal behaviour, with or without injuries'. The definition becomes:

A nonhabitual act with nonfatal outcome that the individual, expecting to, or taking the risk to die or to inflict bodily harm, initiated and carried out with the purpose of bringing about wanted changes.

(De Leo et al., 2006, p. 14)

This should overcome the problems previously associated with the term parasuicide. However, in parallel with the above process, a number of organizations use different definitions or descriptions of suicide-related terms. This is illustrated by an American Psychiatric Association (APA, 2003) publication which has described a number of the key terms:

Suicide: Self-inflicted death with evidence (either explicit or implicit) that the person intended to die.

Suicidal ideation: Thoughts of serving as the agent of one's own death. Suicidal ideation may vary in seriousness depending on the specificity of suicide plans and the degree of suicidal intent.

Suicide attempt: Self-injurious behaviour with a nonfatal outcome accompanied by evidence (either explicit or implicit) that the person intended to die.

Suicidal intent: Subjective expectation and desire for a self-destructive act to end in death.

Deliberate self-harm: Wilful self-inflicting of painful, destructive, or injurious acts without intent to die.

In the UK, Choose Life, the National Strategy and Action Plan to Prevent Suicide in Scotland, uses the following definitions:

Suicide: an act of deliberate self-harm which results in death

Deliberate self-harm: an act which is intended to cause self-harm, but which does not result in death. The person committing an act of deliberate self-harm may, or may not, have an intent to take their own life.

(Scottish Executive, 2002, p. 12)

Thus, when referring to the suicide research or statistics over a period of time it is important to clarify which suicide-related definition(s) are or were being used to ensure that the study outcomes can be compared without further adjustment. In the following chapters of this book, the WHO's International Classification of Diseases ICD-10 codes (see Appendix 5) for self-harm and suicide are occasionally referred to although the data may also refer to ICD-9 codes if taken over a period of time.

International suicide statistics

If we look beyond the health and caring professions, we could argue that governments and international bodies such as the World Health Organization have a responsibility to act on behalf of the public to reduce the incidence of suicide or non-fatal suicidal behaviour. Reducing the high level of reported suicides has become an incentive for the relevant authorities and bodies to take a proactive approach. But how much of a problem is suicide? In 1995 about 900,000 suicides were reported worldwide. According to the World Health Organization, future estimates based on current trends for the year 2020, approximately 1.53 million people will successfully commit suicide. Between ten and twenty times more people will attempt suicide. These figures are not precise but they do provide a frightening picture if nothing is done to prevent suicide. Table 1.1 provides the reported suicide rates per 100,000 of the population for countries across the world as of December 2005 published by the World Health Organization (WHO, 2005).

Some countries report a very high number of suicides for males per 100,000 of the population: Belarus: 63.3; Cuba: 24.5; Estonia: 47.7; Hungary: 44.9; Japan: 35.2; Kazakhstan: 50.2; Latvia: 45.0; Lithuania: 74.3; Russian Federation: 69.3; Slovenia: 45.0; Sri Lanka: 44.6. The Eastern Europe grouping have shared similar sociocultural and historical experiences which may partially explain the high suicide rate (see Bertolote and Fleischmann, 2002). A common factor with the majority of them is that they have experienced a period of political upheaval and change since the early 1990s. This has had an impact upon the population, jobs and support structures. Unemployment is a key factor with suicide in many countries. However, Cuba, Japan and Sri Lanka may have different causes and share the common factor of being island countries.

Although the rates of suicide per 100,000 of the population in some Eastern European countries are very high, due to the high population numbers in Asia, approaching 30 per cent of suicides occur in China and India.

Figure 1.1 (adapted WHO, 2004a) highlights the evolution of the global suicide rates between 1950 and 2000.

For males there has been a gradual but substantial increase of suicides since 1950 whereas there has been only a slight increase with female suicide in the same period. However, these figures do not provide a clear picture of what is exactly happening. In 1950 the data was based on eleven countries. Figure 1.2 (WHO, 2004b) highlights the shift in the distribution of suicides by age over the same period. In 1950 more people committed suicide in the 45 plus age group whereas in 2000 more people committed suicide in the 5–44 age range.

Additional countries were included in the 2000 assessment so the distribution shift should be treated with caution. The distribution of suicide rates, by

Table 1.1 Suicide rates (per 100,000) by country, year and gender, December 2005

Country	Year	Males	Females
Albania	03	4.7	3.3
Antigua and Barbuda	95	0.0	0.0
Argentina	96	9.9	3.0
Armenia	03	3.2	0.5
Australia	01	20.1	5.3
Austria	03	27.1	9.3
Azerbaijan	02	1.8	0.5
Bahamas	95	2.2	0.0
Bahrain	88	4.9	0.5
Barbados	95	9.6	3.7
Belarus	03	63.3	10.3
Belgium	97	31.2	11.4
Belize	95	12.1	0.9
Bosnia and Herzegovina	91	20.3	3.3
Brazil	95	6.6	1.8
Bulgaria	03	21.0	7.3
Canada	01	18.7	5.2
Chile	94	10.2	1.4
China (selected rural and urban areas)	99	13.0	14.8
China (Hong Kong SAR)	02	20.7	10.2
Colombia	94	5.5	1.5
Costa Rica	95	9.7	2.1
Croatia	03	31.4	8.4
Cuba	96	24.5	12.0
Czech Republic	03	27.5	6.8
Denmark	00	20.2	7.2
Dominican Republic	94	0.0	0.0
Ecuador	95	6.4	3.2
Egypt	87	0.1	0.0
El Salvador	93	10.4	5.5
Estonia	02	47.7	9.8
Finland	03	31.9	9.8
France	01	26.6	9.1
Georgia	01	3.4	1.1
Germany	01	20.4	7.0
Greece	02	4.7	1.2
Guatemala	84	0.9	0.1
Guyana	94	14.6	6.5
Honduras	78	0.0	0.0
Hungary	03	44.9	12.0
Iceland	01	19.6	5.6
India	98	12.2	9.1
Iran	91	0.3	0.1
Ireland	01	21.4	4.1
Israel	00	9.9	2.7
Italy	01	11.1	3.3
Jamaica	85	0.5	0.2
Japan	02	35.2	12.8
Jordan	79	0.0	0.0

(Continued overleaf)

Table 1.1 Continued

Country	Year	Males	Females
Kazakhstan	02	50.2	8.8
Kuwait	02	2.5	1.4
Kyrgyzstan	03	16.1	3.2
Latvia	03	45.0	9.7
Lithuania	03	74.3	13.9
Luxembourg	03	18.5	3.5
Malta	03	8.6	1.5
Mauritius	00	18.8	5.2
Mexico	95	5.4	1.0
Netherlands	03	12.7	5.9
New Zealand	00	19.8	4.2
Nicaragua	94	4.7	2.2
Norway	02	16.1	5.8
Panama	87	5.6	1.9
Paraguay	94	3.4	1.2
Peru	89	0.6	0.4
Philippines	93	2.5	1.7
Poland	02	26.6	5.0
Portugal	02	18.9	4.9
Puerto Rico	92	16.0	1.9
Republic of Korea	02	24.7	11.2
Republic of Moldova	03	30.6	4.8
Romania	02	23.9	4.7
Russian Federation	02	69.3	11.9
Saint Kitts and Nevis	95	0.0	0.0
Saint Lucia	88	9.3	5.8
Saint Vincent and the Grenadines	86	0.0	0.0
Sao Tome and Principe	87	0.0	1.8
Seychelles	87	9.1	0.0
Singapore	02	11.4	7.6
Slovakia	02	23.6	3.6
Slovenia	03	45.0	12.0
Spain	02	12.6	3.9
Sri Lanka	91	44.6	16.8
Suriname	92	16.6	7.2
Sweden	01	18.9	8.1
Switzerland	01	26.5	10.6
Syrian Arab Republic	85	0.2	0.0
Tajikistan	01	2.9	2.3
Thailand	02	12.0	3.8
TFYR Macedonia	03	9.5	4.0
Trinidad and Tobago	94	17.4	5.0
Turkmenistan	98	13.8	3.5
Ukraine	02	46.7	8.4
United Kingdom	02	10.8	3.1
United States Of America	01	17.6	4.1
Uruguay	90	16.6	4.2
Uzbekistan	02	9.3	3.1
Venezuela	94	8.3	1.9
Zimbabwe	90	10.6	5.2

Source: World Health Organization, 2005. Reproduced with permission.

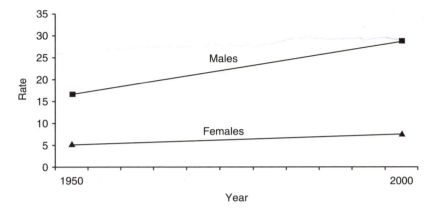

Figure 1.1 Evolution of global suicide rates (per 10,000), 1950–2000.

Source: adapted from World Health Organization, 2004a. Reproduced with permission.

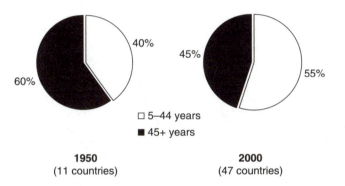

□ 5–44 years
■ 45+ years

1950
(11 countries)

2000
(47 countries)

Figure 1.2 Changes in the age distribution of cases of suicide between 1950 and 2000.

Source: adapted from World Health Organization, 2004b. Reproduced with permission.

age and gender in 2000 (see Figure 1.3), highlight the peaks for males in the 45–54 and 75 plus age ranges (WHO, 2004c). This is a cause for concern. Females also have an increase in suicide rates in the 75 plus range. One of the causes of suicide in this age group for both males and females is likely to be unbearable physical pain due to illness, although in many societies, loneliness, depression, alcohol abuse and complicated grief may also be factors (DeVries and Gallagher-Thompson, 2000). Often in older people depression goes unrecognized by family and health professionals as the focus is on the physical illness and not the associated psychological distress that such pain and/or an illness can trigger. Compared to younger people, older adults are more likely to achieve their goal of death by suicide and use more lethal methods. This suggests that they are less likely to be attention-seeking, and are more

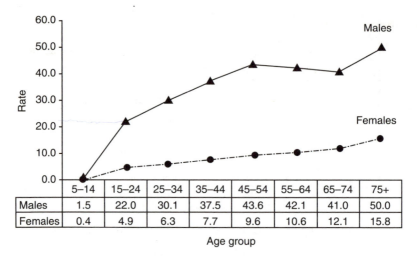

	5–14	15–24	25–34	35–44	45–54	55–64	65–74	75+
Males	1.5	22.0	30.1	37.5	43.6	42.1	41.0	50.0
Females	0.4	4.9	6.3	7.7	9.6	10.6	12.1	15.8

Age group

Figure 1.3 Distribution of suicide rates (per 100,000) by gender and age, 2000.

Source: adapted from World Health Organization, 2004c. Reproduced with permission.

focused on completing suicide. The common methods used include firearms, hanging, gas and poison methods (Alexopoulos, 1996).

However, taken at a global level, fewer older people commit suicide due to the age distribution factors, i.e. there are fewer older people, especially in the age band of 65 years and above. Thus 55 per cent of suicides are in the 5–44 years age band (see Figure 1.3).

Overall, Figure 1.3 highlights that there is a positive relationship between age and suicide rates for both males and females although there is a small reduction in suicide rates for males in the 55–74 age bands.

China

There is one anomaly in the statistics. In rural districts of China more women commit suicide than men. For Chinese mainland and selected rural districts in 1999, 6672 females and 5783 males respectively committed suicide (see WHO, 2003). There are a number of sociocultural-economic factors involved, as noted by Phillips et al. (1999). The pressures on young single women not to become a financial burden on their families appear to be a factor in the rural districts. Unplanned pregnancy for single women living in rural districts is another pressure. Telephone hotlines have been set up to help people in both rural districts and the cities of China to obtain support if they are feeling depressed or suicidal (Palmer, 1997; Palmer et al., 1998). However, telephone counselling services are unable to deal with the multifaceted external causes that may trigger suicidal feelings and mainly support callers during a crisis.

When considering the link between culture and suicide there are a number of key intervening variables (Wendler and Matthews, 2006, p. 161):

- degree of acculturation
- differences in cultural attitudes towards suicide
- variations in the prevalence of risk factors such as unemployment, poverty, and alcohol and drug abuse
- differences in religious views of suicide
- differences in the lethality of the methods used for suicide in that culture
- genetic differences in susceptibility to depressive disorders
- international differences in detecting and reporting suicide
- issues in the therapeutic alliance between individuals of different cultures.

Cultural and religious factors

Bertolate and Fleischmann (2002) discussed the differences between suicide rates of Islamic countries and with other countries that had predominantly different religions. In Islamic countries committing suicide is unacceptable and the total suicide rates are generally very low. In Kuwait, the rates are just above zero. If we revisit the WHO suicide rates for countries with predominantly different religions, these differences can be observed in Table 1.2 in ascending order from Muslim, Jewish, Christian, Hindu, Buddhist to ex-communist/atheist (including Russian Orthodox).

Overall, if an average is taken of Christian countries, they have a higher suicide rate than Hindu countries, and atheist countries have the highest levels of suicide. However, when data is selected in this manner or countries are banded together by religion, there are countries that do not fit neatly into this descriptive analysis. For example, suicide rates in France are relatively high for a predominantly Christian country and France is placed higher than Buddhist countries on average. In the mid–1980s when President Gorbachev launched an anti-alcohol campaign in Russia by increasing prices and reducing production, the overall decrease in alcohol consumption paralleled a 40 per cent reduction in suicide rates and as the campaign was later phased out the suicide rates started to rise again (Pridemore and Spivak, 2003). This simple behavioural version of stimulus control had a dramatic effect upon the suicide rates regardless of being a communist state. Thus findings

Table 1.2 International suicide rates by religion, 2004

	Male	*Female*
Iran (Muslim)	0.3	0.1
Kuwait (Muslim)	2.5	1.4
Israel (Jewish)	9.9	2.7
Italy (Christian)	11.1	3.3
India (Hindu)	12.2	9.1
Japan (Buddhist)	35.2	12.8
Russian Federation (ex-communist, atheist?)	69.3	11.9

Source: adapted from World Health Organization, 2005. Reproduced with permission.

just based on religion can be contradictory and other factors may be relevant too.

If we take another example, despite the suicide rate in Japan, Buddhist beliefs do not generally support suicide, although researchers have suggested that some religious groups such as Buddhists and Confucianists have no strong prohibitions against committing suicide (Kok, 1988). In fact, about 90 million people in Japan report being Buddhists but the religion does not directly affect their everyday life to any great extent (see Japan Guide, 2006). However, another factor is that the Japanese also practise Shinto (the way of the Gods), which is the indigenous religion of Japan. The two religions coexist and are seen to complement each other. To view Japan as a Buddhist country overlooks the adherence to Shinto, a flexible religion with no absolute rights and wrongs and an acceptance that people are not perfect. Therefore weddings may be in Shinto style but as death is viewed in Shinto as a source of impurity, funerals are held in Buddhist style. There is also another culturally important factor in Japan; traditionally it is acceptable to commit suicide for issues associated with shame. Tseng (2001) asserts that in highly interpersonally orientated cultures, claiming bankruptcy may shame the family for many generations so that severe financial debt is more likely to lead to suicide, whereas in western societies bankruptcy is seen as an acceptable solution (Wendler and Matthews, 2006). A new factor regarding Japan is that there have been occurrences of small groups of strangers meeting up to commit suicide together. With the advent of internet chat rooms, there has been a general increase in Japan of internet suicide pacts. In the first four weeks of 2005, fifty-nine people died in internet suicide pacts (British Psychological Society (BPS), 2005).

Neeleman and Lewis (1999) highlighted the difficulties of undertaking research across cultures and religions and suggested that socioeconomic confounders and the levels of religiosity need to be considered. They found strong negative linear associations between aggregate levels of religion and suicide rates, and males are more sensitive than females to suicide acceptance being dependent on the personal and contextual levels of religious belief.

Suicide bombers or martyrs

Understandably there has been a lot of public anxiety and media coverage given over to suicide bombers and martyrs. Suicide bombers have become an international problem knowing no boundaries. In fact, more suicide attacks have occurred from 2002 to 2004, than in the previous twenty-five years (Atran, 2004). The tragic death of so many people at the World Trade Center in 2001 highlighted on a global scale the phenomenon of suicide martyrs. However, the origins of the suicide bomber go back to November 1980 when a 13-year-old child, Hossein Fahmideh, strapped rocket-propelled grenades to his chest and blew himself up under an Iraqi tank. He became a national hero for the Iranian Ayatollah Khomeini regime with street posters and children's knapsacks showing his heroic sacrifice (Baer, 2006).

Regardless of the media and political portrayal, it could be seen as an oversimplication to suggest that religious fanaticism or extreme Islamist beliefs are the simple cause of suicide bombings (Marsden and Attia, 2005). The majority of suicide bombings occurring in the 1980s and 1990s were in Sri Lanka by the Tamil Tigers, who are mainly from the Hindu culture (Pape, 2003). Silke (2003) highlights that most suicide bombers are psychologically normal. Marsden and Attia (2005) suggest that,

> when we abandon the idea of suicide bombers as mentally ill individuals acting out individual death wishes, and see suicide bombing as a coordinated community response that fits a context of violence, aggression and revenge, then much of the incomprehensibility of suicide bombing dissolves.
>
> (Marsden and Attia, 2005, p. 153)

Examples of a 'coordinated community response' could include Gaza. The implication is that simple interventions are not going to dissuade willing volunteers from joining up with groups to become martyrs. Understandably the major international concern regarding suicide bombers is far less the suicidal aspect but far more the homicidal aspect of their death. Realistically, dealing with suicide bombers or martyrs may be outside the remit of international suicide prevention strategies due to the complexity of the many diverse issues involved.

World Health Organization strategy for the prevention of suicides: SUPRE

With the increasing rates of suicide around the world and it being the third largest cause of death among those aged between 15 and 44 (both sexes), understandably the World Health Organization decided to take a proactive approach to suicide. In 1999 WHO launched an international initiative called SUPRE for the prevention of suicide. In this section we will briefly cover its objectives and strategies taken from the information documents available from its website (adapted from WHO, 2000).

SUPRE objectives

The main objective is to reduce mortality and morbidity due to suicidal behaviours; breaking the taboo surrounding suicide and bringing together national authorities and the public in an integrated manner to overcome the challenges.

The specific objectives are:

1   To bring about a lasting reduction in the number of suicides and suicide attempts, with emphasis on developing countries and countries in social and economic transition.
2   To identify, assess and eliminate at early stages, as far as possible, factors that may result in young people taking their own lives.
3   To raise the general awareness about suicide and provide psychosocial support to people with suicidal thoughts or experiences of attempted suicide, and to their relatives and close friends, as well as to those of people who committed suicide.

Strategy

The following basic elements are envisaged, along the lines of the Primary Health Care strategy:

- Organization of global, regional and national multisectoral activities to increase awareness about suicidal behaviours and their effective prevention.
- Strengthening of countries' capability to develop and evaluate national policies and plans for suicide prevention. The following activities, adapted to countries' particular needs, will be developed:

  ○ support and treatment of populations at risk (e.g. people with depression, elderly, youth)
  ○ reduction of availability of and access to means of suicide (e.g. toxic substances, handguns)
  ○ support/strengthening of networks of survivors of suicide
  ○ training of primary health care workers and other sectors

- Countries in which overall suicide rates are particularly high (e.g. China, Cuba, Lithuania, Mauritius, Marshall Islands, Russian Federation, Sri Lanka), the age distribution is skewed towards young people or women, or the prevention of suicide is already of special concern, will be considered as priorities for launching the project's activities.
- The SUPRE project will be managed and evaluated in close collaboration with regional offices and governments concerned, and assisted by a task force.

Management

The programme is managed by the WHO Department of Mental Health and Substance Abuse. The work is conducted in coordination with different clusters and departments at Headquarters (i.e. Health Systems, Child and Adolescent Health and Development, Chemical Safety), WHO Regional Offices, sister UN agencies (e.g. UN, ILO, UNICEF and UNESCO), relevant non-governmental organizations (NGOs) and WHO Collaborating Centres.

Will SUPRE work?

WHO with its partners has a difficult task as each country may need an individual strategy and each country needs to take an active interest in tackling suicide. Some of the countries with the highest rates of suicide have gone through political and social upheaval and war. However, the intervention focusing on training primary health care professionals may be easy to implement.

In addition, WHO (2000) has a downloadable document on its website that contains the components and instruments (SUPRE-MISS: Multisite Intervention Study on Suicidal behaviours) for the international research study. Tools include the WHO Well-being Index; Beck Depression Inventory; Hopelessness; alcohol and drug related questions; Trait Anger Scale; Social Support; Social Role Performance/Psychiatric Disability Assessment Schedule; community stress and problems; plus socio-demographic information and current episode history. The research data will be extensive especially if the optional biological (blood samples) and impulsiveness scale are undertaken.

WHO has developed a series of internet downloadable guidelines available in different languages for health workers, general physicians, teachers, media professionals, prison officers and survivors of suicide. Of particular interest are the guidelines on Preventing Suicide: How to start a Survivors' Group (WHO, 2000). Apart from the educational aspect describing the impact of suicide, it covers the sources of help for bereaved people, how to initiate a self-help support group, identifying the need, preparation for the first meeting, developing the operational framework for the group including aims and objectives, membership criteria, the format for meetings, roles and responsibilities, codes of ethics, identifying and gaining access to resources to support the group, and gauging success. Importantly it also covers some of the potential risk factors and their management. Empowering people to set up and run these support groups is important as it does not limit them to just health professionals. However, health professionals and others may find these relatively simple guidelines very helpful in setting up of groups within their communities.

WHO takes part in the annual World Suicide Prevention Day. This event brings suicide prevention to the attention of the public, world governments and other bodies. The WHO press releases also remind others that they have developed a series of guidelines and other material. Each annual event focuses on an aspect of suicidology. Working in collaboration with the International Association for Suicide Prevention and the World Federation for Mental Health, the theme for World Suicide Prevention Day in 2006 was 'With Understanding, New Hope'. It focused on the importance of 'translating the knowledge and understanding of suicide into the development of effective suicide prevention strategies and programmes' (International Association for Suicide Prevention (IASP), 2006, p. 1).

To answer the question, 'Will SUPRE work?' we need to reconsider the objectives. The ongoing work of WHO will assist those agencies interested in suicide prevention although WHO does not directly tackle unemployment and other external factors that may trigger depression, suicidal ideation and behaviour. But by encouraging governments and relevant bodies to put and keep suicide prevention on their agenda, where policies have been put into action, there is already a decrease in some countries in their suicide rates. SUPRE will add to the international commitment to suicide prevention and can be seen as a positive start down a long difficult path.

Conclusion

The suicide mortality rates taken from around the world vary considerably. International organizations such as WHO, NGOs and governments are attempting to reduce the number of suicides by a variety of strategies and interventions. This is an enormous task but essential if the WHO estimates for the year 2020 of approximately 1.53 million people successfully committing suicide are to be kept as low as possible.

References

Alexopoulos, G.S. (1996) Affective disorders, in J. Sadavoy, L. Lazarus, L.F. Jarvik and G.T. Grossberg (eds) *Comprehensive Review of Geriatric Psychiatry II* (2nd edn). Washington, DC: American Psychiatric Press.

American Psychiatric Association (2003) Practice guideline for the assessment and treatment of patients with suicidal behaviors. *American Journal of Psychiatry*, 160(supplement), 1–60.

Atkinson, M.W., Kessel, N. and Dalgaard, J.B. (1975) The comparability of suicide rates. *British Journal of Psychiatry*, 127, 247–256.

Atran, S. (2004) Mishandling suicide terrorism. *Washington Quarterly*, 27(3), 67–90.

Baer, R. (2006) The making of a suicide bomber. *Sunday Times*, News Review, 4 September, 7.

Bertolote, J.M. and Fleischmann, A. (2002) A global perspective in the epidemiology of suicide. *Suicidologi*, 7(2), 6–8.

British Psychological Society (2005) Suicide concerns. *The Psychologist*, 18(12), 723.

Brooke, E. (ed.) (1974) *Suicide and Attempted Suicide*, Public Health Papers 58. Geneva: World Health Organization.

De Leo, D., Bertolote, J.M., Schmidtke, A., Bille-Brahe, U. and Kerkhof, A.J.F.M. (1999) Definitions in suicidology: the evidence-based and the public health approach. *Twentieth World Congress of the International Association for Suicide Prevention Proceedings*. Athens.

De Leo, D., Burgis, S., Bertolote, J.M., Kerkhof, A.J.F.M. and Bille-Brahe, U. (2006) Definitions of suicidal behavior: lessons learned from the WHO/EURO Multicentre Study. *Crisis*, 27(1), 4–15.

DeVries, H.M. and Gallagher-Thompson, D. (2000) Assessment and crisis intervention with older adults, in F.M. Dattilio and A. Freeman (eds) *Cognitive-behavioural strategies in crisis intervention* (2nd edn). New York: Guilford.

Durkheim, E. (1897) *Suicide: A study in sociology*. Trans. J.A. Spaulding and G. Simpson, 1951. Glencoe, IL: The Free Press.

IASP (2006) Press release for World Suicide Prevention Day, 10 September. *IASP News Bulletin*, August, 1.

Japan Guide (2006) Basic information, Shinto. http://www.japan-guide.com/e/e2056.html (accessed 19 August 2006).

Kok, L.P. (1988) Race, religion and female suicide attempters in Singapore. *Social Psychiatry and Psychiatric Epidemiology*, 23, 236–239.

Kreitman, N., Philip, A.E., Greer, S. and Bagley, C.R. (1969) Parasuicide. *British Journal of Psychiatry*, 115, 746–747.

Linehan, M.M. (1997) Behavioral treatments of suicidal behaviors: definitional obfuscation and treatment outcomes, in D.M. Stoff and J.J. Mann, *The Neurobiology of Suicide: From the bench to the clinic*. Annals of the New York Academy of Sciences, 836, pp. 302–328. New York: New York Academy of Sciences.

Marsden, P. and Attia, S. (2005) A deadly contagion. *The Psychologist*, 18(3), 152–155.

Neeleman, J. and Lewis, G. (1999) Suicide, religion, and socioeconomic conditions: an ecological study in 26 countries, 1990. *Journal of Epidemiology and Community Health*, 53, 204–210.

O'Carroll, P.W. (1989) A consideration of the validity and reliability of suicide mortality data. *Suicide and Life-Threatening Behavior*, 19, 1–16.

Palmer, S. (1997) Telephone counselling in China. *Counselling Psychology Quarterly*, 10(4), 473–479.

Palmer, S., Wang, X. and Xiaoming, J. (1998) Counselling in China: telephone hotlines. *Counselling Psychology Review*, 13(2), 21–25.

Pape, R. (2003) The strategic logic of suicide terrorism. *American Political Science Review*, 97, 343–361.

Phillips, M., Liu, H. and Zhang, Y. (1999) Suicide and social change in China. *Culture, Medicine and Psychiatry*, 23(1), 25–50.

Pridemore, P. and Spivak, A. (2003) Patterns of suicide mortality in Russia. *Suicide and Life-Threatening Behavior*, 33, 132–150.

Sainsbury, P. and Jenkins, J.S. (1982) The accuracy of officially reported suicide statistics for purposes of epidemiological research. *Journal of Epidemiology and Community Health*, 36, 43–48.

Scottish Executive (2002) *Choose Life: A national strategy and action plan to prevent suicide in Scotland*. Edinburgh: Scottish Executive.

Silke, A. (2003) *Terrorists, Victims and Society: Psychological perspectives on terrorism and its consequences*. Chichester: Wiley.

Tseng, W-S. (2001) *Handbook of Cultural Psychiatry*. San Diego, CA: Academic Press.

Wendler, S. and Matthews, D. (2006) Cultural competence in suicide risk assessment, in R.I. Simon and R.E. Hales (eds) *Textbook of Suicide Assessment and Management*. Washington, DC: American Psychiatric Publishing.

World Health Organization (1986) *Summary Report, Working Group in Preventative Practices in Suicide and Attempted Suicide*. Copenhagen: WHO Regional Office for Europe.

World Health Organization (2000) *Multisite Intervention Study on Suicidal Behaviours – SUPRE-MISS: Components and instruments*. Geneva: World Health Organization.

World Health Organization (2003) *Suicide Rates per 100,000 by Country, Year and Sex*, http://www.who.int/mental_health/prevention/suicide_rates/en/index.html

World Health Organization (2004a) *Evolution of Global Suicide Rates*, http:www .who.int/mental_health/prevention/suicide/evolution/en/index.html

World Health Organization (2004b) *Changes in the Age Distribution of Cases of Suicide*, http:www.who.int/mental_health/prevention/suicide/changes/en/index.html

World Health Organization (2004c) *Distribution of Suicide Rates by Gender and Age*, http.www.who.int/mental_health/prevention/suicide_rates_chart/en/index.html

World Health Organization (2005) *Suicide Rates per 100 000 by Country, Year and Sex, December 2005*, http://www.who.int/mental_health/prevention/suicide_rates/ en/index.html

2 Suicide statistics for the UK and the National Suicide Prevention Strategy

Stephen Palmer

This chapter focuses on UK suicide statistics and the UK National Suicide Prevention Strategy, which is divided into countries. An earlier suicide prevention strategy in Scotland will be considered.

Comparative suicide statistics for the United Kingdom from 1950 to 2004

The highest rates of suicide occurred in the early 1930s during the Depression, when rates for the older age groups were significantly higher than the lower age groups. Interestingly, in the nineteenth century, the trends for suicide rates in North America and the UK were similar with an average of 12.5 per 100,000. The changes in age distribution have been similar too, especially with the recent percentage increase in the 15–24 age group and decrease by suicide deaths by people over 45 years (Williams, 2001). In the period from 1993 to 2002 more people committed suicide on Mondays compared to any other day and on 1 January 2000 the largest number of suicides occurred (Johnson et al., 2005) suggesting the possible effect of entering a new time period.

In 1950 the intentional self-harm mortality rates for all persons aged 15–74 years was about the same for Northern Ireland and Scotland; it was about twice as high for England and Wales. But in the early 1970s Scotland overtook the other parts of the UK and the trend continued steadily upwards. This is illustrated in Figure 2.1. Since 1950 the intentional self-harm mortality rate in Scotland has remained higher than Northern Ireland apart from a couple of years.[1]

The intentional self-harm mortality rates for males in England and Wales dropped by the mid-1970s and then started rising again, peaking again in the early 1990s. Whereas for Scotland and Northern Ireland the overall trend has been a substantial rise from under 10 per 100,000 of the population in 1950 to over 20 per 100,000 from the later part of the 1980s onwards although Northern Ireland did drop below this figure for the 1990s (see Figure 2.2). However, since 2000 there has been a steep rise in the male intentional self-harm mortality rate in Northern Ireland although a slight decline in Scotland.

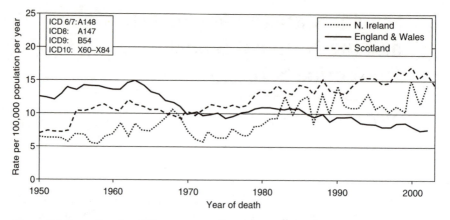

Figure 2.1 Intentional self-harm mortality (age standardized rates) for all UK persons aged 15–74.

Source: WHOSIS (December 2004).

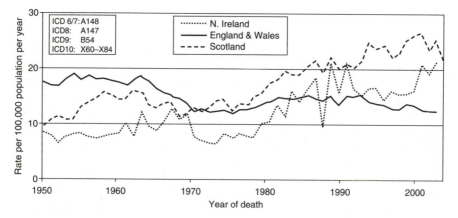

Figure 2.2 Intentional self-harm mortality (age standardized rates) among UK men aged 15–74, 1950–2003.

Source: WHOSIS and General Register Office for Scotland.

The intentional self-harm mortality rates for females in England and Wales was higher in 1950 than Scotland, and approximately twice as high as Northern Ireland. However, overall the rate for Scotland has become worse between 1950 and 2003 peaking in the late 1970s. The rate for Northern Ireland has had a number of peaks going between 10 and 20 per 100,000, since the 1960s, although it has now dropped below 10 since 2000 (see Figure 2.3).

The most recent comparative figures at time of writing from the Office for National Statistics (ONS, 2006) found that in 2002–2004 the suicide rate

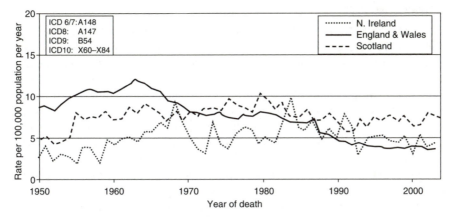

Figure 2.3 Intentional self-harm mortality (age standardized rates) among UK women aged 15–74, 1950–2003.

Source: WHOSIS and General Register Office for Scotland.

among men in Scotland was 30.0 per 100,000 compared with 22.4 in Wales, 18.3 in Northern Ireland, and 16.7 in England. Among women, the rate in Scotland was 10.0 per 100,000, compared with 6.0 in Wales, 5.6 in Northern Ireland and 5.4 in England. Some of their key findings were as follows (ONS, 2006):

- The UK suicide rate for men peaked in 1998 but has since fallen, while the suicide rate for women was stable between 1991 and 2004.
- Men had higher suicide rates than women throughout the period. In men, the highest suicide rates were seen in men aged 15–44 from 1998 onwards and in women the highest rates were in those aged 75 and over across the period.
- Analysis of suicides in England and Wales between 1999 and 2003 showed rates in the most deprived areas were double those in the least deprived.

Suicide statistics for England, Wales and Scotland

In this section we will consider the suicide statistics for England, Wales and Scotland, which have their regional differences. Due to the higher mortality rates per 100,000 of the population by intentional self-harm and undetermined intent in Scotland, more information is provided below for that country.

England and Wales

The Office for National Statistics and other bodies such as the National Institute for Mental Health in England and the Centre for Suicide Research in Oxford regularly compile statistics on a variety of indices including deaths by suicide and undetermined deaths whether accidentally or purposefully inflicted. In England and Wales all potential suicides are subject to a public inquest in a coroner's court. Proof 'beyond all reasonable doubt' is required before the coroner will return a verdict of suicide. Therefore in reality some suicides are given 'open' verdicts and are included in the mortality statistics as 'undetermined' deaths.

Figure 2.4 looks at the mortality from suicide and open verdicts in people aged 10 years and over in England and Wales by gender, from 1968 to 2005. It can be seen that suicide rates have been gradually declining in England and Wales in recent years although rates diverged during the mid-1970s to the end of the 1980s. A major national concern was the particularly high increase in the suicide rates of males in the 15–24 age group in the late 1980s and early 1990s (see Figure 2.5). However, although this has now declined, the 25–44 and 45–64 age groups have the highest rates of suicide but again these are also decreasing apart from a recent upturn in the latter age group.

In the late 1960s the rates of suicide for females across the four different age groups was wide. However, these rates have remained relatively steady in recent years with a convergence of the three higher age groups (see Figure 2.6) and the lowest age group, 15–24, remaining relatively steady over a thirty-year period, unlike the males in the similar age group. This suggests that there may have been an external social or environmental factor triggering the increase in suicides among the males in that age group.

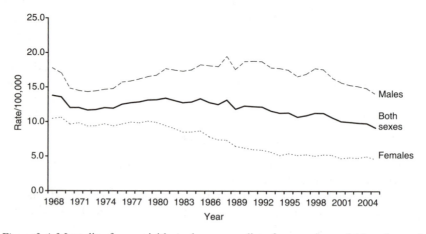

Figure 2.4 Mortality from suicide and open verdicts for people aged 10 and over in England and Wales, by gender, 1968–2005.

Source: Office for National Statistics. Reproduced with permission from the Centre for Suicide Research website: http://cebmh.warne.ox.ac.uk/csr/

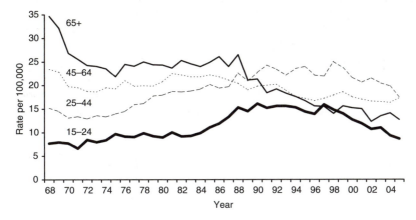

Figure 2.5 Rates of suicide and open verdicts for males in England and Wales, by age groups, 1968–2005.

Source: Office for National Statistics. Reproduced with permission from the Centre for Suicide Research website: http://cebmh.warne.ox.ac.uk/csr/

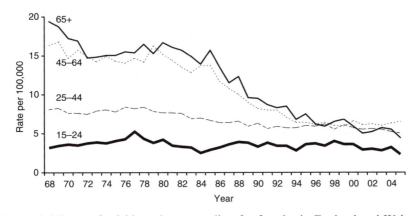

Figure 2.6 Rates of suicide and open verdicts for females in England and Wales, by age groups, 1968–2005.

Source: Office for National Statistics. Reproduced with permission from the Centre for Suicide Research website: http://cebmh.warne.ox.ac.uk/csr/

Scotland

By the early 1970s in Scotland the trend in intentional self-harm mortality in the 15–74 years age group overtook the rate for England and Wales and continued to rise until 2000. There has been a small reduction in intentional self-harm mortality since 2000 in Scotland.

In 1980 the intentional self-harm and undetermined intent mortality rates for the five main age groups from 15 to 55 years and above were divergent ranging from about 10 to 27 per 100,000 but by the late 1980s there was a convergence from about 15 to 21 per 100,000 approximately across the five age groups (still excluding 0 to 14 years of age). This is illustrated in Figure 2.7 (see Argyll and Bute Choose Life, 2005).

When looking at the data by gender as in Figure 2.8, it is easier to observe that the mortality rate for males has increased while that for women generally went down over the same period. However, this does mask the problem that certain age groups within these populations have much higher rates of suicide.

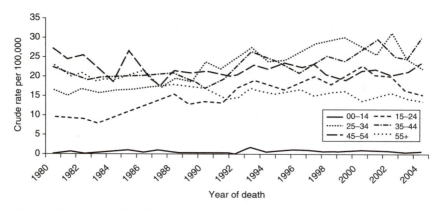

Figure 2.7 Intentional self-harm and undetermined intent rates for persons in Scotland, by age groups, 1980–2004.

Source: General Register Office for Scotland. Taken from http://www.chooselife.net/web/site/Statistics/ScottishTrends.asp. Reproduced with permission from Choose Life and Scottish Public Health Observatory.

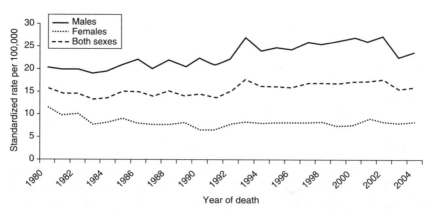

Figure 2.8 Intentional self-harm and undetermined intent rates in Scotland, 1980–2004.

Source: General Register Office for Scotland.

In Figure 2.9 the high rate for suicide in the 25–34 and 35–44 age groups is noticeable and has high peaks with the 25–34 year age group peaking over 50 per 100,000 during 2002–2004. Compared to England and Wales this is high.

Since 1980 the female suicide death rates have fallen overall but particular age groups still have high rates when compared to other parts of the UK (see Figure 2.10). Over this period there has been a gradual increase in suicides in the 15–24 age group but this is still lower than the age groups above. Over this period, the 55 years and higher age group has shown a gradual decline in suicides.

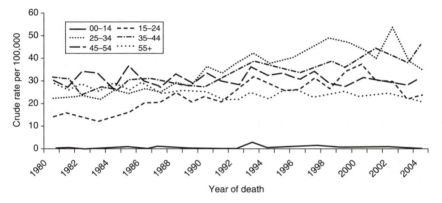

Figure 2.9 Intentional self-harm and undetermined intent rates for males in Scotland, by age groups, 1980–2004.

Source: General Register Office for Scotland.

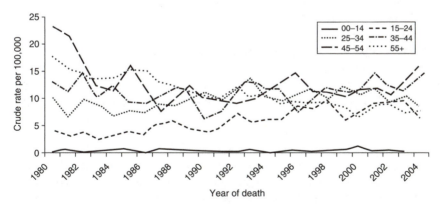

Figure 2.10 Intentional self-harm and undetermined intent rates for females in Scotland, by age groups, 1980–2004.

Source: General Register Office for Scotland.

Other Scottish suicide data from 2000 to 2004

For the years 2000 to 2004, in Scotland more people committed suicide on Mondays, sometimes known as the Monday Effect, and the suicide death rate peaks in the month of January, followed by August. The Scottish Public Health Observatory (SPHO) has noted that the risk of death by intentional self-harm and undetermined intent was significantly lower for Lothian and Forth Valley NHS Boards and was significantly higher for Greater Glasgow and Highland NHS Boards than for Scotland as a whole (SPHO, 2006a). If going by local authorities then the rate was significantly higher for West Dunbartonshire, City of Glasgow and Highland, and significantly lower for Angus, East Dunbartonshire, East Lothian, East Renfrewshire and City of Edinburgh, than for Scotland as a whole. For males the rate was significantly higher for West Dunbartonshire, City of Glasgow, Highland and Shetland Islands and significantly lower for Angus, East Lothian, East Renfrewshire, City of Edinburgh, Fife and South Lanarkshire, than for Scotland as a whole over this period. For females there was less variation across Scotland, with the risk of death by intentional self-harm and undermined intent being significantly higher for City of Glasgow and significantly lower for East Renfrewshire and Falkirk, than for Scotland as a whole (SPHO, 2006b).

In the following two sections the focus will be on suicide prevention in Scotland and England as these two countries have the highest and lowest suicide rates respectively in the UK (ONS, 2006).

Action in the United Kingdom to prevent suicide

Currently the UK is taking a proactive stance in suicide prevention. This is being driven by the ambitious target of reducing the death rate from suicide and undetermined injury by at least one-fifth by the year 2010 in the government's White Paper *Saving Lives: Our Healthier Nation* (Department of Health (DoH), 1999). The DoH is attempting to focus on a range of different areas of concern in England that may help this reduction.

The DoH (2002) issued a consultation document for all interested parties to comment on, including the Social Services, National Health Service, Prison Service, government departments and the voluntary sector. The National Director of Mental Health, Professor Louis Appleby, stated in the accompanying letter to the consultation document:

> The development of ways of reducing suicide is a major part of the Government's programme outlined in the White Paper, *Saving Lives: Our Healthier Nation*, which set out a challenging target to reduce the death rate from suicide and undetermined injury by at least a fifth by the year 2010, saving up to 4000 lives in total. The purpose of this strategy is to ensure that we are doing all we can to achieve this target.
>
> (DoH, 2002)

This message is reinforced in the Foreword, by Jacqui Smith, the Minister of State for Health, who stated:

> Although the rate of suicide in England is not high in comparison with other countries in the European Union, the figures remain disturbing. On average, a person dies every two hours in England as a result of suicide. It is the commonest cause of death in men under 35. It is the main cause of premature death in people with mental illness. . . . The factors associated with suicide are many and varied – they include social circumstances, biological vulnerability, mental ill-health, life events and access to means. A coherent, co-ordinated suicide prevention strategy therefore needs the collaboration of a wide range of organizations and individuals.
>
> (DoH, 2002, p. 3)

The *National Suicide Prevention Strategy for England* (DoH, 2002, pp. 5–6) targets reducing the death rate from suicide by at least 20 per cent by 2010 through the following six goals:

- Goal 1: To reduce risk in key high risk groups
  Local mental health services will be supported in implementing *Twelve Points to a Safer Service*; these aim to improve clinical risk management.

  - A national collaborative is being established for the monitoring of non-fatal deliberate self-harm.
  - A pilot project targeting mental health promotion in young men will be established and evaluated for national roll-out.

- Goal 2: To promote mental well-being in the wider population
  Actions to be taken include:

  - A cross-government network will be developed to address a range of social issues that impact on people with mental health problems, e.g. unemployment and housing.
  - The suicide prevention programme will link closely with the National Institute for Mental Health in England (NIMHE) substance misuse programme to:
    - improve the clinical management of alcohol and drug misuse among young men who carry out deliberate self-harm
    - make available training in suicide risk assessment for substance misuse services.

- Goal 3: To reduce the availability and lethality of suicide methods
  Actions to be taken include:

  - NIMHE will identify additional steps that can be taken to promote safer prescribing of antidepressants and analgesics.
  - NIMHE will help local services to identify their suicide 'hotspots' (e.g. railways, bridges) and take steps to improve safety at these.

- Goal 4: To improve the reporting of suicidal behaviour in the media
  Actions to be taken include:

  - A media action plan is being developed as part of the mental health promotion campaign, *Mind Out for Mental Health*, which will include:
    - incorporating guidance on the representation of suicide into workshops held with students at journalism colleges; round table discussion sessions with leaders in mental health and senior journalists
    - a series of road shows at which frontline journalists can discuss responsible reporting
    - a feature on suicide in media journals, e.g. *Press Gazette, Media Week, British Journalism Review*.

- Goal 5: To promote research on suicide and suicide prevention
  Actions to be taken include:

  - A national collaborative group will oversee a programme of research to support the strategy, including research on ligatures used in hanging and suicides using firearms.
  - Current evidence on suicide prevention will be made available to local services through NIMHE's website and development centres.

- Goal 6: To improve monitoring of progress towards the *Saving Lives: Our Healthier Nation* (DoH, 1999) target to reducing suicides
  Actions to be taken include:

  - A new strategy group of experts and other key stakeholders will be established.
  - The new strategy group will regularly monitor suicides by age and gender, by people under mental health care, by different methods and by social class.

The *National Suicide Prevention Strategy for England, Annual Report on Progress 2005* (NIMHE, 2006) highlighted the many different strategies that were being undertaken to achieve the above six goals at a national level and around the regions.

The target is to reduce the suicide death rate of 9.2 per 100,000 population in 1995/6/7 to a revised target of 7.3 deaths per 100,000 population in 2009/10/11. The target was originally 7.4 but this changed following a change in the methodology used by the ONS to record the cause of death.

This strategic approach has paralleled a reduction in the overall rate of suicide among the general population and is the lowest on record although a continued downward trend would provide more evidence to the success of the National Suicide Prevention Strategy (NIMHE, 2006).

Possible interventions

If an individual experiences the wish to kill themselves during an impulsive moment, then if ready means are not easily available, the wish may pass without any self-harm occurring. Therefore simple interventions may reduce the rate of suicide. Gunnell (1994) made a number of estimates regarding key interventions and concluded that a 4 per cent reduction in suicide rates may be achieved if general practitioners (GPs) prescribed safer antidepressants and the introduction of catalytic converters for vehicles would reduce it by 7 per cent. But the evidence for voluntary agencies reducing the suicide rate is limited. One study found that towns that had an established branch of the Samaritans did not differ in suicide rates from towns that did not have a branch (Jennings et al., 1974).

The change in the law in 1998 to reduce the amount of paracetamol and salicylate pack sizes available over-the-counter has reduced the number of deaths, liver damage and the size of the overdoses from this medication (Hawton et al., 2001). This is a good example of how the control of the amount of lethal self-prescribed medication available to a suicidal individual may reduce the suicide rate if the person is impulsive. The hoarding of medication (prescribed or self-prescribed) in preparation for a future suicide attempt is less of an impulsive act and control of pack sizes may have less influence in reducing the suicide rate in those cases. The withdrawal of the pain control medication, co-proxamol, in 2006 may also help to reduce the suicide or accidental death rates. Many patients did not realize that co-proxamol can sometimes be lethal at a low dosage. Obviously individuals wishing to commit suicide could use other means at their disposal but those who favour this method may be deterred. Another example is the Prison Service strategy. One of the most stressful times for prisoners is the initial period of incarceration. This period could be targeted for intervention by regular monitoring and the use of suicide screening. Currently the Prison Service has already started to take action regarding the design for safer prison environments. Risk assessment and possible interventions will include the reduction of ligature points and methods to prevent access to materials that could be used as ligatures (DoH, 2002).

Nelson (2002) raised a number of farming-related issues. Specific interventions with the farming communities are becoming more commonplace around the UK. The foot and mouth outbreak in 2001 had an adverse impact upon many farmers and in Devon, farmers' wives even asked the police to remove their partners' guns for their own safety. This highlights how concerned they were about their husbands' psychological state. Charities helped to feed farmers and their families. The Rural Stress Information Network received funds from the Addington Fund to provide financial help to the farmers. Unfortunately, the large amount of paperwork associated with any aspect of farming is also a stress factor.

Alcohol control may have an important impact upon suicide rates. As mentioned in Chapter 1, when President Gorbachev launched an anti-alcohol campaign in Russia in the mid–1980s, the overall decrease in alcohol consumption paralleled a 40 per cent reduction in suicide rates and as the campaign was later phased out, the suicide rates started to rise again (Pridemore and Spivak, 2003). The campaign involved increasing prices and reducing production. Yet, if we consider the changes in legislation in the UK in recent years, public houses and other venues can have more flexible opening times or even 24-hour opening times, making alcohol more easily available especially in town centres. As alcohol consumption can lead to more impulsive behaviour, its easier availability for social drinking in the UK may have an effect upon suicide rates.

Earlier initiatives in Scotland

If we look back to the end of the 1980s, the Highland Health Board (HHB), Scotland, also put the issue of suicide prevention on the agenda. In the period 1989–1991, mortality rates per 100,000 of the population were: Highland, 21.7; Scotland, 14.2; England, 11.0. This highlighted a considerable difference across the UK. During the period 1988–1992, twenty-four more people died by suicide than from road traffic accidents. After producing a report (Oates, 1994), the HHB made fifteen recommendations to reduce the high suicide rate when compared to the rest of Scotland. Below are some of the recommendations made in the document to illustrate the comprehensive approach (HHB numbering used):

1 There should be an educational programme for primary care staff on depression and suicide covering early detection and effective treatment in particular.
3 All junior medical staff, especially those in accident and emergency departments, should be informed of the necessity to refer all parasuicides for psychiatric assessment.
5 The development of the community psychiatric nursing service should be a major priority for the HHB over the next three years such that cover is provided throughout the area for twenty-four hours a day, seven days a week.
8 There should be liaison with the National Farmers Union and the Scottish Crofters Union to explore appropriate preventive measures within the farming community.
9 The Board should allocate £5000 to the Samaritans in Highland for each of the next three years.
13 A multidisciplinary group should be set up to develop a strategy for the promotion of mental health and the prevention of suicide.
15 Highland Health Board should raise the priority of mental illness and adopt the target from Health of the Nation.

(Oates, 1994)

The high suicide rate was due mainly to Highland males, mostly aged between 35 and 44, comprising 400 male (76 per cent), 126 female (24 per cent), and mean age 45 years (range 14–98). Most of the male deaths were due to carbon monoxide poisoning from vehicle exhausts (Oates, 1994). The commonest cause of death among women was poisoning by liquid or solid substances; in particular, analgesics, tranquillizers and psychotropics accounted for 62 per cent of all overdoses. The target was: 'To reduce the overall suicide rate by at least 15 per cent by the year 2000' (Oates, 1994). (The proposed suicide rate reduction from 19.1 per 100,000 of the population in 1990, to no more than 16.2, was derived from the Health of the Nation target.)

Although it is very difficult to attribute cause and effect, by the period 1997–1999, the suicide figure in the Highland had decreased by 15 per cent to 18.57 per 100,000. However, if a slightly different period had been observed then this decrease might not have been obtained so the result could be considered as a statistical anomaly. The suicide strategy had received a high profile and a number of interventions had been undertaken, which may have had a positive effect on suicide rates. For example, depression management training of general practitioners, the tightening up of gun licensing by the police, the work with the farming community and Samaritans may all have contributed to this reduction.

Scotland Choose Life strategy and action plan

In December 2002, Scotland launched the Choose Life strategy and action plan, which takes a national and local approach to prevent suicide in Scotland (Scottish Executive, 2002). It is a ten-year plan aimed at reducing suicides in Scotland by 20 per cent by 2013. It took an inclusive approach and drew on the expertise of family members of people who had attempted or completed suicide, suicide survivors, teachers, health and social care workers, young people, public health specialists, voluntary and community agencies, and others.

Choose Life objectives

The Choose Life objectives are as follows (Scottish Executive, 2002, p. 21):

- *Objective 1: Early prevention and intervention* providing earlier intervention and support to prevent problems and reduce the risks that might lead to suicidal behaviour.
- *Objective 2: Responding to immediate crisis* providing support and services to people at risk and people in crisis, to provide an immediate crisis response and to help reduce the severity of any immediate problem.
- *Objective 3: Longer-term work to provide hope and support recovery* providing ongoing support and services to enable people to recover and deal with the issues that may be contributing to their suicidal behaviour.

- *Objective 4: Coping with suicidal behaviour and completed suicide* providing effective support to those who are affected by suicidal behaviour or a completed suicide.
- *Objective 5: Promoting greater public awareness and encouraging people to seek help early* ensuring greater public awareness of positive mental health and well-being, suicidal behaviour, potential problems and risks among all age group and encouraging people to seek help early.
- *Objective 6: Supporting the media* ensuring that any depiction or reporting by any section of the media of a completed suicide or suicidal behaviour is undertaken sensitively and appropriately and with due respect for confidentiality.
- *Objective 7: Knowing what works* improving the quality, collection, availability and dissemination of information on issues relating to suicide and suicidal behaviour and on effective interventions to ensure the better design and implementation of responses and services and use of resources.

Priority groups

Choose Life priority groups include the following (Choose Life, 2006a):

- children (especially looked after children)
- young people (especially young men)
- people with mental health problems
- people who have attempted suicide
- people affected by the aftermath of suicidal behaviour or completed suicide
- people who abuse substances
- people in prison.

Local action plans

Each area of Scotland has developed its own local action plan which involves local stakeholders. The local plans focus on the following (Choose Life, 2006b):

- preventing suicide within communities
- improving the capacity of local communities to educate and raise awareness of suicide
- delivering prevention and intervention activities
- providing practical support to those affected by suicide
- involving a range of partners in preventing suicide.

For each area there is a nominated Choose Life coordinator who plays a key role in implementing their local plan. By working at the level of the community there is a greater opportunity to involve members of the community in understanding, recognizing and tackling people who are feeling suicidal. The delivery of suitable training programmes to health and caring professionals, self-help groups and volunteers will, it is hoped, make inroads into the high rate of suicide in Scotland when compared to England and also other parts of Europe. The Choose Life Third National Summit Report (Choose Life, 2006c) highlighted how the summit meeting of key stakeholders focused on sharing good practice, showcasing, networking and relationship-building.

Choose Life case study: Argyll and Bute

It is worth taking one example and looking at it in more depth. Argyll and Bute is a large and varied area covering more than 2700 square miles. It accounts for about 10 per cent of the land mass of Scotland. It includes 25 inhabited islands and has a population of about 91,000.

In Argyll and Bute there was an increase in deaths by intentional self-harm, suicide or undetermined intent from 17 in 2003 to 21 in 2004. When adjusted, this figure becomes equivalent to 23 deaths per 100,000 population. In particular, 86 per cent of the people who died were male.

The Argyll and Bute Choose Life (2005) public document provides background to the local action plan, local information about the population, economy, health, transport, deprivation, local rates of suicide; development and review of the local Choose Life Action Plan. The priorities for development include awareness raising, information, coordination and networking, training, general mental health awareness training, applied suicide intervention skills training (ASIST), dealing with self-harm, supporting the local voluntary, community and self-help groups, policy/protocol review and development.

The information distributed in the community includes leaflets on the *Suicide – the Myths versus the Facts* and *Self-harm – the Myths versus the Facts*. Self-help pilot projects are being set up in some areas of Argyll and Bute to tackle depression. General mental health awareness training will use the *Promoting Mental Health – Raising Awareness* training packs, which were developed by NHS Health Scotland. The objectives of this training are as follows (Argyll and Bute Choose Life, 2005):

- to raise awareness and understanding of the concept of mental health promotion and its role in keeping people well
- to improve knowledge of mental health promotion issues
- to provide information about initiatives which are effective in promoting mental health and well-being
- to provide a range of practical activities to develop the mental health promotion role
- to suggest ways in which mental health promotion activities can be monitored and evaluated.

In addition Argyll and Bute Choose Life (2005) developed a *Dealing with Self-harm* training pack. The objectives are: to identify what is meant by self-harm; to understand the causes of self-harm; and to learn practical skills and strategies for responding to self-harm.

The *applied suicide intervention skills training* with the appropriately named acronym, ASIST, is a two-day intensive course to help participants recognize risk and learn how to intervene to prevent the immediate risk of suicide. The premise is that suicide can be prevented through the actions of prepared individuals and the training helps participants to become more willing to help people at risk.

The Argyll and Bute Choose Life group have a website dedicated to all the different aspects of the suicide prevention strategy, literally a one-stop shop of information covering training, support and links with photos of the coordinator and project workers (see http://www.chooselifeinargyllandbute.org.uk/).

Three key areas were identified where policies or protocols needed to be in place and shared appropriately, across statutory, voluntary, community and private sectors. These were:

- a clear referral route in to mental health and other relevant support services – to ensure an integrated approach and reduce the risk of people falling between two stools
- a discharge protocol that ensures appropriate follow-up for people being discharged from hospital (general as well as psychiatric), care, prison etc.
- an integrated procedure for recording incidents of self-harm or suicidal behaviour and feeding any relevant information into local planning processes.

A local Choose Life group took this project forward.

It is too early to assess whether or not the Choose Life national strategy and action plan to prevent suicide in Scotland is having an impact upon the rates of suicide or more specifically intentional self-harm or undetermined intent. However, the trends will become apparent over a relatively short period.

Other issues related to suicide

No-harm contracts in therapy

Psychological therapists agreeing 'no-harm' contracts with clients may significantly reduce the risk of certain unwanted behaviours (Mothersole, 1997). However, in New Zealand, due to the intervention by the press and Members of Parliament, no-harm contracts have been dropped and replaced by management plans by some therapists. Some therapists go beyond a relatively simple contract and refuse to work with a suicidal client without the involvement or knowledge of the client's general practitioner. Worrall (1997) argues that a therapist exhibiting this high level of directiveness would be denying the client the right to control his or her own life. This would be philosophically untenable for therapists practising within the person-centred approach. In fact, the Ancient Greeks allowed older citizens the option of assisted death if they could put forward a persuasive argument (O'Connell et al., 2004).

The *APA Practice Guidelines for the Assessment and Treatment of Patients with Suicidal Behaviors* are very thorough in relation to the approach that needs to be taken (American Psychiatric Association (APA), 2003). Although developed for psychiatrists, the guidelines may be applicable to other health professionals working in similar settings and fields. It recommends that no-harm contracts or suicide prevention contracts should not be considered 'as a substitute for careful clinical assessment' (Simon and Hales, 2006, p. 592). Such contracts are not recommended for patients who are psychotic, impulsive, agitated, or under the influence of an intoxicating substance. Also the need for an established physician–patient relationship is raised as an important aspect of their use.

Health and caring professionals' concerns

Primary health care and other caring professionals such as counsellors, psychotherapists and psychologists have always been concerned to varying degrees about clients committing or attempting suicide. In particular, it is a topic which can trigger much anxiety and interest with both neophyte and experienced therapists. Since the mid-1990s there has been a steady growth in individual membership of counselling and psychotherapeutic professional bodies with more therapists becoming accredited and/or registered as qualified practitioners. Thus there has been additional pressure on therapists to adhere to professional codes of practice and ethics. To take the correct action and to be seen to take the correct action within client–therapist relationships is paramount. It could be argued that this has always been the case. However, therapists not working within a professional framework may have had less incentive to act in what would be considered a professional manner yet a very proactive approach is recommended when seeing clients with suicidal ideation (Palmer, 1995). Currently, in the UK anybody can title themselves as a psychologist, counsellor, hypnotherapist or psychotherapist and go into practice without any qualifications or experience. In these cases, inaction can sometimes prove fatal so it is incumbent upon the therapist to support and help the client through the difficult period (Curwen, 1997). The UK government is backing formal registration of all practising psychologists, counsellors and psychotherapists. When this finally occurs, these practitioners will have to work within accepted guidelines or risk being disciplined or struck off the register.

UK legal cases

While therapists ponder on what is the right action to take with actively suicidal clients, the British legal system has also needed to deal with difficult cases relating to a person's choice to die. In one case, a NHS Trust patient known as Ms B, a former senior social worker, had spent more than a year on a ventilator paralysed from the neck down. Her doctors had grown to like her and had refused to switch off the ventilator. On 22 March 2002, the High Court ruled that she had the right to decide to have the life support machine turned off. This was not physician-assisted suicide or euthanasia as it would be her medical condition that would kill her. The doctors had interrupted the natural course of her medical condition when they put her on life support. The ruling High Court Judge, Dame Elizabeth Butler-Sloss, said:

> Unless the gravity of the illness has affected the patient's capacity, a seriously disabled person has the same rights as a fit person to respect for personal autonomy. There is a serious danger, exemplified in this case, of a benevolent paternalism which does not embrace recognition of the personal autonomy of the severely disabled patient . . . [Ms B] valued the ventilator and her handicap as worse than death. Her decision was made against the advice offered and was not understood. Subjective values have to be taken into account. If at an earlier stage there had been an acknowledgement of a clash of values it might possibly have led to a different approach to management of the case . . . Those in charge must not allow a situation of deadlock or drift to occur. If there is no disagreement about competence but the doctors are for any reason unable to carry out the wishes of the patient, their duty is to find other doctors who will do so.

Surprisingly, the NHS Trust continued to defend a case it was destined to lose at a cost in excess of £100,000. The Trust had been guilty of trespass. Not only is the British law clear on these issues, but also precedents had been set in Canada and United States giving patients with the mental capacity to take decisions the right to refuse medical interventions.

This case was in contrast to Diane Pretty, who wanted her husband to be able to comply with her request for a mercy-killing without him facing prosecution. She described her story:

> I am only 43 years old. I desperately want a doctor to help me to die. Motor neurone disease has left my mind as sharp as ever, but it has gradually destroyed my muscles, making it hard for me to communicate with my family. It has left me in a wheelchair, catheterised and fed through a tube. I have fought against the disease for the last 2 years and had every possible medical treatment.
>
> I am fully aware of what the future holds and have decided to refuse artificial ventilation. Rather than die by choking or suffocation, I want a doctor to help me die when I am no longer able to communicate with my family and friends. I have discussed this with my husband of 25 years, Brian who has come to terms with what I want and respects my decision.

He says that losing me will be devastating for him and our two children but he would be pleased to know I had had the good death I want. I want to have a quick death without suffering, at home surrounded by my family so that I can say good-bye to them.

If I were physically able I could take my own life. That's not illegal. But because of the terrible nature of my illness I cannot take my own life – to carry out my wish I will need assistance. Should a doctor give me the assistance I need, he or she will be guilty of a crime that carries a lengthy prison sentence. As the law stands it makes no sense.

The law needs changing so that I, and people like me, can choose how and when we die and not be forced to endure untold suffering for no reason.

(Pretty, 2001)

On 18 October 2001, the High Court refused Mrs Pretty's request to be allowed assistance to end her life. On 29 November, five Law Lords turned down her appeal. On 19 March 2002, the European Court of Human Rights in Strasbourg heard her appeal but subsequently turned it down. Finally she died on 11 May 2002, having lost her battle to end her life in the way she wished.

These two legal cases highlight some of the complex issues involved in assisted suicide, euthanasia or termination of medical treatment. In the UK, there is great concern from some quarters about legalizing assisted suicide, in particular, religious groups. In 2006 the issue was debated in the House of Lords but the law remained unchanged. Yet in the Netherlands, where it has been legal for over two decades, only 3.4 per cent of all deaths are by doctor assisted suicide or euthanasia and in Oregon, USA, only 0.1 per cent of those dying use legal assisted suicide. It is difficult to predict whether a change in policy and legislation regarding assisted suicide will occur in Britain over the next decade. Certainly, it does not appear to be imminent. However, if assisted suicide became legal, it may cause ethical dilemmas for health professionals and psychotherapists (Palmer, 1997).

Conclusion

Suicide reduction and prevention can involve the statutory, voluntary, private and community sectors. The statistics for suicide for young men has shown a disturbing increase since the mid-1980s in the UK, and subsequently the government launched a suicide prevention strategy. The trends so far are promising but the jury is still out on whether or not the challenging targets will be achieved. Over the coming decade, British law may need to be modified regarding assisted suicide or death even though after much debate in 2006 the House of Lords did not come out in favour of any changes. On a one-to-one level, caring professionals such as psychologists and psychotherapists have greater expectations placed upon them by professional bodies to act in an appropriate manner yet the newer forms of therapy still may need to develop frameworks for intervening with clients who are actively suicidal (see Chapter 11).

Note

1 For more information on the analyses presented in this section, contact: Bruce.Whyte@health.scot.nhs.uk.

References

American Psychiatric Association (APA) (2003) Practice guidelines for the assessment and treatment of patients with suicidal behaviors. Part A: Assessment, treatment, and risk management recommendations. *American Journal of Psychiatry*, 160 (supplement), 1–60.

Argyll and Bute Choose Life (2005) *Choose Life: a national strategy and action plan to prevent suicide in Scotland. Background to local action plan: Argyll and Bute*. Retrieved on 4 September 2006 from http://www.chooselife.net/nmsruntime/saveasdialog.asp?lID=1371&sID=154

Choose Life (2006a) *About Choose Life*. Retrieved on 4 September 2006 from http://www.chooselife.net/web/site/AboutChooseLife/AboutChooseLife.asp

Choose Life (2006b) *Choose Life: Local action plans*. Retrieved on 4 September 2006 from http://www.chooselife.net/web/site/xLCLP/LCLP_Home.asp

Choose Life (2006c) *Choose Life Third National Summit: 2–3 February 2006. Summit Report*. Retrieved on 4 September 2006 from http://www.chooselife.net/nmsruntime/saveasdialog.asp?lID=1733&sID=1609

Curwen, B. (1997) Medical and psychiatric assessment, in S. Palmer and G. McMahon (eds) *Client Assessment*. London: Sage.

Department of Health (1999) *Saving Lives: Our healthier nation*. London: The Stationery Office.

Department of Health (2002) *National Suicide Prevention Strategy for England*. London: Department of Health (also see: www.doh.gov.uk/mentalhealth).

Gunnell, D. (1994) *The Potential for Preventing Suicide*. Bristol: Health Care Evaluation Unit, University of Bristol.

Hawton, K., Townsend, E., Deeks, J., Appleby, L., Gunnell, D., Bennewith, O. and Cooper, J. (2001) Effects of pack legislation restricting pack sizes of paracetamol and salicylates on self-poisoning in the United Kingdom: before and after study. *British Medical Journal*, 322(7296), 1203–1207.

Jennings, C., Barraclough, B.M. and Moss, J.R. (1974) Have the Samaritans lowered the suicide rate: a controlled study. *Psychological Medicine*, 8, 413–427.

Johnson, H., Brock, A., Griffiths, C. and Rooney, C. (2005) Mortality from suicide and drug-related poisoning by day of the week in England and Wales, 1993–2002. *Health Statistics Quarterly*, 27, 13–16.

Mothersole, G. (1997) Contracts and harmful behaviour, in C. Sills (ed.) *Contracts in Counselling*. London: Sage.

Nelson, F. (2002) Pastures new. *Health Development Today*, 9, 14–15.

NIMHE (2006) *National Suicide Prevention Strategy for England: Annual report on progress 2005*. Leeds: Care Services Improvement Partnership, National Institute for Mental Health in England.

Oates, K. (1994) *Suicide in the Highlands*. Inverness: Highland Health Board.

O'Connell, H., Chin, A., Cunningham, C. and Lawlor, B.A. (2004) Recent developments: suicide in older people. *British Medical Journal*, 329(7471), 895–899.

Office for National Statistics (2006) Suicide rates by country. *Health Statistics Quarterly*, 31, Autumn. Retrieved on 6 September 2006 from http://www.statistics.gov.uk/downloads/theme_health/HSQ31.pdf

Palmer, S. (1995) The stresses of running a stress management centre, in W. Dryden (ed.) *The Stresses of Counselling in Action*. London: Sage.

Palmer, S. (1997) Multimodal therapy, in C. Feltham (ed.) *Which Psychotherapy?* London: Sage.

Pretty, D. (2001) *Justice for Diane: story*. http://www.justice4diane.org.uk/story.asp

Pridemore, P. and Spivak, A. (2003) Patterns of suicide mortality in Russia. *Suicide and Life-Threatening Behavior*, 33, 132–150.

Scottish Executive (2002) *Choose Life: A national strategy and action plan to prevent suicide in Scotland*. Edinburgh: Scottish Executive.

Scottish Public Health Observatory (SPHO) (2006a) *Suicide by NHS Board. Scottish Public Health Observatory*. Retrieved on 4 September 2006 from http://www.scotpho.org.uk/web/site/home/Healthwell-beinganddisease/suicides/suicide_data/Suicide_NHSBoard.asp

SPHO (2006b) *Suicide by local authority. Scottish Public Health Observatory*. Retrieved on 4 September 2006 from http://www.scotpho.org.uk/web/site/home/Healthwell-beinganddisease/suicides/suicide_data/suicide_LA.asp

Simon, R.I. and Hales, R.E. (eds) (2006) *Textbook of Suicide Assessment and Management*. Washington, DC: American Psychiatric Publishing.

Williams, M. (2001) *Suicide and Attempted Suicide*. London: Penguin.

Worrall, M. (1997) Contracting within the person-centred approach, in C. Sills (ed.) *Contracts in Counselling*. London: Sage.

3   Suicide in rural areas

Cameron Stark

> The traditionally identified problems affecting rural areas are well known. They centre on problems of accessibility, and on less-developed infrastructure and public services. They are often associated with low income levels, lack of job opportunities and emigration of population to urban areas.
>
> (House of Lords Select Committee on the European Community, 1991)

Deprived areas in the UK, and many urban areas, have high rates of suicide. Rural areas, by contrast, are often felt to be attractive places to live with a high quality of life. To urban researchers, the finding of a high suicide rate in some rural areas can seem counterintuitive. This chapter explores the changing nature of rurality, and attempts to identify factors that may make life more challenging than it might at first seem, particularly to children and young people. When considered in the context of information on rural mental health, and UK information on rural suicide, it is possible to identify a more cohesive picture. The international literature on rural suicide is large, and information on gun ownership and suicide is useful in considering the UK experience.

Rural areas

The relation between rurality and health is not straightforward. Several studies have reported a non-linear relationship, with either a U- or J-shaped curve, with the best reported health in the rural fringe, or more accessible countryside (Bentham, 1984; Shouls et al., 1996; Barnett et al., 2001). This may reflect the heterogeneity of rural areas, and the difficulties of defining rurality. Low population density is often taken to be a defining characteristic of rural areas, but density operates in different ways. A rural area may have a low population density, but if people live in settlements, distance between individuals may be small despite low overall density (Smailes et al., 2002). Similarly, including urban areas in the calculation of the overall density of an area known as gross population density may be misleading compared to 'net' population density, which includes only non-urban areas in the calculation

(Smailes et al., 2002). (For example, in the Highland Council area in Scotland, around 60,000 people live in Inverness and Culloden from a total population of 208,000 – including or excluding this conurbation from an estimate of population density makes a substantial difference to the measure.) Irving and Davidson (1973) examined social density as the amount of person to person interaction taking place in an area in unit time, and in the future this type of measure may offer more insights for mental health-related research in rural areas.

The public image of rural areas may be at least as important as numerical descriptions. The concept of the rural idyll is very powerful. It 'presents happy, healthy and problem-free images of rural life safely nestling with both a close social community and a contiguous natural environment' (Cloke and Milbourne, 1992, p. 359, cited in van Dam et al., 2002). This is often taken to be related to a less hurried lifestyle closer to the natural rhythms, in which one can escape the hectic urban life (van Dam et al., 2002). Media depictments may interact with public expectations (Phillips et al., 2001). Often described as a creation of urban dwellers (Cloke et al., 1995), people living in rural areas may themselves believe these stereotypes (Walker, 2002), which may become contested between different groups. Svendsen (2004) describes two competing discourses in Denmark, one of agriculture and its needs, and a second of the social benefits felt to flow from small, closely knit rural communities. In Denmark at least, the second discourse was dominated by former town dwellers who wanted to preserve the aspects of the past they valued, strive against the perceived wrongs of urban life, and prevent *landsbydoden*, or the death of villages (Svendsen, 2004). Others may also use ideas of stewardship to support their view of preferred rural structures (Stewart et al., 2001), although motivations may be complex (Phillips, 2002).

Locating rural problems in relation to these stereotypes can affect how they are addressed. One UK study asked parents about their view of the rural area in which they lived as a suitable place to bring up children (Valentine, 1997). Rural areas were widely seen as preferable but, paradoxically, many parents did not feel that their children were safe. This proved to be because of the perceived intrusion of urban life in to the local area, including walkers and tourists, who were felt to offer a potential threat, as well as the more obvious joyriders. When asked to provide accounts of the potential threats, however, most of those cited were local rather than related to non-residents. Too great a preoccupation with the external may act to limit consideration of local actions and responsibilities.

Rural deprivation

Rural deprivation can be difficult to define, although there seem to be some important non-income variables that are important to capture. Shaw (1979, cited in Cloke et al., 1995) produced an influential description of rural deprivation in three categories that might 'combine in a self-sustaining spiral of disadvantage' (Cloke et al., 1995). His components included household deprivation, opportunity deprivation and mobility deprivation (Figure 3.1). These can be described as follows (Cloke et al., 1995, p. 352):

- *Household deprivation*: problems relating to criteria such as income and housing which dictate the ability of individuals to make use of those opportunities that are available in rural areas.
- *Opportunity deprivation*: problems relating to the loss of particular facets of rural life, such as jobs and services, from their previous rural location.
- *Mobility deprivation*: problems relating to the inability of some rural people to gain access to jobs, services and facilities which have moved away from village locations.

Measures of deprivation used in urban areas are not always as useful in rural areas. Social class distinctions may be denied, although the justifications are not always persuasive (Phillips, 2002). Cloke et al. (1995) point out that localized rural geographies mean that rates of poverty can vary markedly between different rural areas, perhaps explaining why mortality rates appear to be a less effective proxy for morbidity in rural areas than in urban (Barnett et al., 2002). Car ownership, often taken as an indicator of affluence in urban areas, may be a necessary financial burden in rural areas that exacerbates low pay (Gray et al., 2001; Christie and Fone, 2003). Barnett et al. (2001) argue

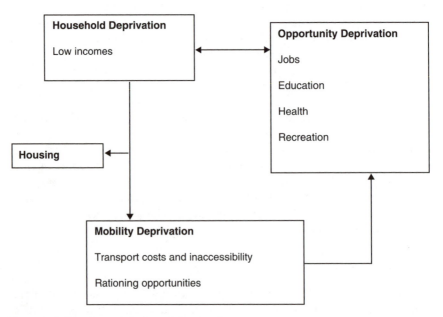

Figure 3.1 Shaw's model of rural deprivation.

Source: Shaw, 1979.

that variation within rural areas is so great that area-based measures are of limited value, and composite measures of deprivation may be unhelpful (Gilthorpe and Wilson, 2003). Residents may deny or minimize the existence of deprivation. Those living in poverty in comparatively affluent rural areas may be further isolated and disadvantaged by their 'different-ness'.

Difficult as it may be to measure, the impact of deprivation in rural areas is no less adverse than in urban areas. As Cox (1998) points out, the changes to the countryside discussed in this chapter may further isolate those who cannot afford to travel, or who have disabilities. Very rural areas may be distinct from the peri-urban fringe, as discussed further below, with higher rates of limiting long-term illness (Barnett et al., 2001).

Rural restructuring

Rural areas in developed countries have undergone many changes. These are often summarized under the rubric of 'rural restructuring'. There are critics of the term, who argue that it overstates and simplifies. However, it is useful shorthand for the following processes that are important in rural areas:

- diversification of rural activity
- diversification of farming income
- changes to population structure
- middle-class inflow in some areas (counterurbanization)
- increased environmental limits on land use
- changes to public service.

Agriculture, leisure and the countryside

The image of agriculture itself has changed (van Dam et al., 2002), with recent associations with political, environmental and health problems, including intensive farming, BSE (bovine spongiform encephalopathy), foot and mouth disease, agricultural sector subsidies and genetically modified crops. At the same time, the uses to which the countryside is put have increased with ever greater use of the countryside for leisure, commuting and conservation functions (van Dam et al., 2002). This may result in a struggle for control of the political agenda (Svendsen, 2004). Some groups have been very successful at influencing national thinking on agriculture (Reed, 2001). At local level, the demands of intensive agriculture may compete with the requirements of people who have moved to the area because of its beauty. This can contribute to hard-fought local battles over land use, such as those over wind farms and quarries. National special interest groups may also participate in such debates, at times overriding the views of local residents. This can lead to long-term rural dwellers being expected to sacrifice their short- or medium-term economic interests for the good of future urban dwellers who may wish to escape to the countryside. As one older woman in the Western Isles of Scotland put it in a conversation with a health worker, 'It may be beautiful scenery, but it's all I've got' (Emelin Collier, personal communication). The potential for divisive conflicts and loss of self-esteem of local residents is apparent.

Work

The diversification of farm activity, and an increase in off-site working, has been an important theme. Known as pluriactivity, it has sometimes been seen as a threat to farming (Kinsella et al., 2000). Variously seen as an activity forced by changes in the economic viability of farms, or as a lifestyle choice, Kinsella et al. (2000) found in Ireland that pluriactivity was important in allowing small farms to continue to function. They suggest that a reduction in pluriactivity would result in a fall in the number of farms, and therefore a reduction in services such as schools and shops (Kinsella et al., 2000).

There may be unspoken assumptions about the role of women in rural areas, with an assumption that traditional childcare roles will be followed (Little and Austin, 1996; Agg and Phillips, 1997). Despite high levels of economic activity among women in one UK study, most women also had the main responsibility for childcare. Men were often absent for most of the day, leaving women to both work and juggle informal care arrangements for much of the child's day. While this may not be a solely rural pattern, the lack of formal childcare availability in rural areas compounded the challenges (Halliday and Little, 2001).

Changing labour markets, and increased competition, may also affect work patterns. In many rural areas, primary sector employment, such as farming and fishing, has declined, while service jobs, including tourism, leisure and retail, have become more important (Lindsay et al., 2003). Long-term residents often rely on a network of contacts to identify job opportunities. In a small community, the number of such jobs may be limited, and if this is compounded with transport difficulties, access to jobs can be very restricted. New residents to the area may be more effective at competing for jobs (Stockdale et al., 2000). Lindsay et al. (2003) found that long-term unemployed people in the north of Scotland tended to be older than the national average, suggesting some migration away of younger unemployed people. Employers reported that they often relied on word of mouth and personal recommendation when recruiting staff. Male job seekers, in particular, were often unwilling to consider service sector jobs. The potential importance of these factors, both as a stressor and as a barrier for return to work in people with mental health problems, was apparent.

Migration and counterurbanization

Stockdale et al. (2000) argue that migration should be seen as in the context of rural restructuring, rather than as an individual issue. Counterurbanization, the movement of people from urban to rural areas in 'developed' countries, has been an important public discourse (Mitchell, 2004). The usual understanding of this trend is of the affluent middle classes moving in to rural areas, either to retire or to commute to urban areas. The impact is usually believed to be detrimental, with a

> focus on rising property prices and as a consequence local residents being outbid by incomers; incomers taking jobs from locals; commuters failing to use rural services leading to a decline in profitability and ultimate closure; incomer objections to rural developments and incomers 'taking over' the running of many community activities.
>
> (Stockdale et al., 2000)

This provides a way of thinking about the countryside in to which information can then be fitted, with a focus on conflict between 'locals' and 'incomers', and linking of counterurbanization with various rural problems.

The reality may be less consistent (Mitchell, 2004). Cloke suggests that counterurbanization is 'a stretched and diluted catch-all phrase' (Cloke, 1985, cited in Mitchell, 2004). It is often assumed that migration involves young people leaving, and wealthier older people moving in to rural areas. Patterns vary both between and within countries. In Scotland, migrants into rural areas tended to be younger than previous residents. They tended to increase the viability of rural schools by bringing children to the area, and often produced other benefits by generating local employment (Stockdale et al., 2000).

Decisions to move to rural areas may be related to access to jobs or education, availability of cheaper housing, perceived work–life balance, and life changes such as retirement (van Dam et al., 2002; Mitchell, 2004). People moving to rural areas are usually assumed to be more affluent than pre-existing residents. Cloke et al. (1995) reported that many of those who moved to rural areas of England in their study had lower than average incomes, although this may have been partly explained by the movement of retired people. Such migrants may, however, be seen as different and less worthy (Svendsen, 2004). Some of this movement may be explained by the availability of right-to-buy properties (previously social housing) in the UK, allowing a wider range of people to buy property in the countryside while simultaneously decreasing the availability of affordable housing for long-term local residents (Chasney and Sherwood, 2000).

At the same time as areas on the periphery of cities or population centres increase in population, very rural areas may continue to lose population. Young people may expect to move away at some stage of their life, for education or employment (Stockdale et al., 2000; Stockdale, 2002). The Norwegian term *uttynningssamfunn*, translated by Smailes et al. (2002) as 'sparsifying communities' or 'thinning communities', refers to the thinning out of populations. Aasbrenn (1998, cited in Smailes et al., 2002) suggests that this results in a more aged population; deterioration in social networks; changes in service demand' marginalized viability of service suppliers, and the decay of the physical infrastructure. It is apparent that most of the components of rural restructuring are interrelated. Part of Hoggart and Panigua's (2001) caution on the use of the term is their contention that many of these processes are not new, but rather are long-term problems rediscovered and rebadged.

Changes to public services

Cloke (1993) identified trends in services including rationalization of service provision related to economies of scale, with decisions often taken at national level, privatization of services, and the introduction of national standards for services such as education and health. As Cloke points out, charging the real cost of services in rural areas with reduced or removed cross-subsidy inevitably results in rural services that are more expensive at the point of access. Cloke also comments on the move to national standards, and suggests that the move to more competitive service environments and more demanding national standards may be of far greater benefit to urban dwellers than rural citizens, who may find themselves doubly disadvantaged.

Young people in the countryside

Factors affecting children and young people in the countryside may be a microcosm of the matters affecting the lives of all residents in rural areas. Rural areas are often marginalized, and young people in rural areas may be further marked as different (Philo, 1992; Hendry and Reid, 2000; Jones, 2002; Panelli, 2002). As with adults, children and young people are affected by both macroeconomic influences, and the social structures in small areas (Panelli, 2002).

Rather than spending time outdoors, children may have great difficulty accessing the countryside, as it has often been fenced off as private space (Davis and Ridge, 1997). Even public space may be seen as an adult domain (Matthews et al., 2000). Teenagers in particular may find country living restrictive (Davis and Ridge, 1997). Contrary to adult perceptions of rural areas, children in one UK study felt little or no sense of community (Matthews et al., 2000). As Matthews et al. (2000) comment, 'many children, especially the least affluent and teenagers, felt dislocated and detached from village life and there was a strong sense of alienation and powerlessness' (Matthews et al., 2000, p. 141).

In Australia, Gabriel (2002) comments that young people are often seen as a problem. Tasmanian newspapers saw young people as a resource to be 'kept at home' in order that communities did not fail. At the same time, Gabriel (2002) identified a prominent discourse on a brain drain, with gifted young people moving away and a skills gap being produced by those who chose to remain (or, in this discourse, who were seen as too lacking in talent to move away). Gabriel argued that these themes were both nostalgic – for an unchanging rural society – and paternalistic.

Some problems may be masked because of limited official statistics. Home-lessness has been underestimated in rural areas (Cloke et al., 2001a, 2001b). Problems in some areas of the UK have arisen from restricted housing avail-ability, resulting from rising prices, tied houses, limited private rental housing, seasonal tourism rental, problems with planning permission, and limited one and two-bedroom accommodation, of the type most wanted by young people when moving from home for the first time.

Rural areas: summary

Rural areas are not homogeneous, and are not stagnant. There have been broad social pressures in these areas, with changes in land use, changes in employment patterns, and alterations to public services. There is some evi-dence of movement in to rural areas by urban dwellers, who may also be more affluent. This may in turn alter the way the countryside is discussed, with a move to a post-productionist landscape with a focus on leisure and recreation. Deprivation exists in rural areas, and the idea of the 'rural idyll' may hide these changes and their impact. Children and young people, and perhaps all those identified as 'different' may be isolated, even within a rural community perceived by outsiders as close knit.

Mental health in rural areas in the UK

The National Morbidity Survey, conducted in 1993, is the largest UK psychia-tric morbidity survey (Paykel et al., 2000), and included both rural and urban subjects. Classification of urban and rural was dependent on a judgement by each interviewer. Unadjusted rates of neuroses (as measured by CIS-R, the Clinical Interview Schedule-Revised), alcohol dependence and drug depend-ence were highest in urban areas and lowest in rural areas, with semi-rural areas intermediate. After adjusting for a range of social variables, rural/urban differences were no longer significant for alcohol and drug dependence, and urban/rural differences for other conditions were much attenuated. As Paykel et al. (2000) point out, findings on rural/urban prevalence have been conflict-ing. Philo et al. (2003) summarize prevalence studies. It is clear that there is substantial psychological morbidity in rural areas, although the pattern in different parts of the world differs. Most of the studies cited by Philo et al. (2003) conclude that morbidity in rural areas is not dissimilar from that in urban areas. The work by Paykel et al. (2000) suggests that urban areas in the UK do have higher rates of morbidity, partly accounted for by measures of deprivation, but confirms that mental illness in rural areas is common.

Philo et al. (2003) argue that the impact of mental ill-health may be medi-ated by the characteristics of rural areas. Cloke suggests that 'a sense of belonging and cultural acceptance of their situation may well ameliorate . . . issues of the structuring of opportunities in the experience of rural people' (Cloke, 1993). In his view, the 'non-affluent, the young and the different' may not be welcomed. Rural communities may have social norms that limit behaviour (Dixon and Welch, 2000). Kane and Ennis (1996) suggested that *Gemeinschaft* characteristics of areas, the day-to-day social interactions that define and limit behaviour, may be important. Philo et al. (2003) point out that many studies assume that community support is better in rural areas. This may not, however, be the case. Parr, Philo and Burns have produced a series of working papers on the experience of being ill in the Highlands of Scotland (Parr et al., 2002a, 2002b; Philo et al., 2002). The lived experience they describe is likely to be applicable in any small town or village in the UK. Service users portray landscape in which little is private. Acts influenced by illness are noted, discussed, and remembered. Accessing services becomes even more difficult than usual, because of the high probability that such access will be noted (Parr et al., 2002a, 2002b). Some respondents described social isolation in their community stemming from knowledge of their mental health problems. Some felt that they would have greater anonymity in urban settings. At the same time, some people identified benefits associated with where they lived, including a feeling of being less hurried (Philo et al., 2002) and of having a firmer base in life. Philo et al. (2002) observe that as many people reported adverse effects of living in a rural area as found it of benefit.

Rural suicide in the UK

Selected findings of relevant studies of suicide in rural areas of the UK are shown in Table 3.1. Several other studies include data from rural areas, but are not included as they do not specifically discuss rural areas. The main points from this body of work are that some rural areas have high male suicide rates, but this is not universal; rural areas may have more adverse trends than urban areas in some age groups; firearms appear to be disproportionately important, and some rural occupations have a higher than expected proportion of deaths from suicide.

Rural suicide rates

Information on the geographical distribution of suicides in England and Wales comes from a series of articles dealing with routinely reported information from death certificates. The evidence for the association between urban deprivation and suicide is discussed elsewhere in this volume. There is evidence for a higher than average male suicide rate in some rural areas (Kelly et al., 1995). This is not homogeneous (Bunting and Kelly, 1998), and Saunderson suggested this might be related to farming patterns (Saunderson et al., 1998), with higher rates in areas where hill farming was particularly important (rural occupational associations are discussed further below).

Middleton et al. (2003) examined trends in suicide rates in England and Wales for 1981–1983, and 1991–1993. Middleton et al. (2003) reported that, in the 1980s, rates were generally higher in urban areas but that rural rates

Table 3.1 Selected work on rural suicide in the United Kingdom

Authors	Area and period	Method and findings
Crombie (1991)	Scotland	Production of standardized mortality ratios (SMRs) for areas of Scotland. Found a higher than expected SMR in men in the Highlands.
Nicholson (1992)	North Devon 1985–1989	Review of suicide and undetermined death rates from death certificates in an area reported to have a high suicide rate. Found wide variation by district in classification of deaths to 'suicide' or 'undetermined cause'. Attributed to variation between coroners. When suicide and undetermined deaths were combined, standardized mortality ratios were not found to be higher than the region average.
Pearson (1993)	North and West Devon 1988–1990	Review of information from coroner's inquest records. Some non-residents had killed themselves in the area. Compared to local residents dying by suicide, they were more likely to be male, have a history of deliberate self-harm, and to to be younger. Among local residents, violent death was over-represented, accounted for by a greater number of firearms deaths. Car exhaust deaths were also higher, although not significantly so.
Roberts et al. (1996)	North Yorkshire 1981–1990	Epidemiological review of deaths from suicide. Divided study area into 'less rural' and 'more rural'. Neither area had a significantly elevated rate, although the male rates were higher in the 'more rural' than 'less rural' area. 'Firearms and explosives' were the cause of death in 14 per cent of suicide deaths (both sexes combined) compared to 3.8 per cent in national English figures for 1985.
Saunderson and Langford (1996); Saunderson et al. (1998)	England and Wales 1989–1992	Rural areas with higher than average suicide risk in men noted. Geographical risk clusters noted in the West Country, and in North Yorkshire, the North West of England, and North and mid-Wales. Suggested to be related to areas of dairy production, and hill farming.
Inskip et al. (1996)	England and Wales 1979–1980, 1982–1990	Calculated proportional mortality ratios (PMRs) and proportional cancer mortality ratios for farmers and farmers' wives. Suicide was elevated in male farmers (156, 95 per cent CI 147–165) and female farmers (PMR 145, 95 per cent CI 103–199). Farmers' wives had a PMR of 109 (95 per cent CI 66–171). Self-employed male farmers had a higher PMR of 196 (180–213).
Malmberg et al. (1997); Hawton et al. (1998)	England and Wales 1991–1994	Psychological postmortem study in farmers, and survey of sample of farming population: 46 per cent of farmers dying by suicide had a definite mental illness, and a further 23 per cent a probable illness.

(Continued overleaf)

Table 3.1 Continued

Authors	Area and period	Method and findings
		Rates of alcohol abuse and previous deliberate self-harm were low. Financial and other occupational stresses were common, as was physical illness and relationship problems. Compared to a survey sample, more of the farmers dying by suicide lived alone, lacked close friends and had no confidant. Hanging was the commonest cause of death, but shooting was greatly over-represented.
Saunderson et al. (1998)	England and Wales 1989–1992	Examined the rate of recorded suicides, and of deaths recorded as being of undetermined causes, in rural and urban areas. Deaths by undetermined cause were low for both men and women in urban areas, and higher in more densely populated areas. Recorded male suicide rates were highest in the most rural areas.
Kelly and Bunting (1998)	England and Wales 1982–1996	Updates earlier papers by Charlton et al. (1993) and Kelly et al. (1995). Comprehensive review of information from routinely gathered data. Veterinarians, farmers, gardeners and groundsmen (sic), and forestry workers all found to have elevated proportional mortality ratios for suicide in at least part of the period. Farmers, forestry workers and vets had more deaths than expected from firearms (36 per cent actual compared to 5 per cent expected for farmers, farm managers and horticulturists).
Hawton et al. (1999)	England and Wales 1981–1993	Reviewed geographical distribution of suicide in farmers. No relationship was found between farming suicide rates and general population rates, types of farming, or density of the farming population.
Stark et al. (2002)	Highlands of Scotland 1978–1998	Male suicide rates confirmed as higher than Scottish average, after exclusion of visitors to the area. Female rates did not differ from Scotland. Male deliberate self-harm rates did not appear to be elevated. Some methods of suicide, including firearms, drowning and car exhausts, were increased. Deaths in farmers accounted for about twice the proportion expected.
Middleton et al. (2003)	England and Wales 1981–1998	Trends in suicide rates tended to be more unfavourable as population density and population potential (a measure of remoteness from highly populated areas) decreased. This was true for both men and women. Differences remained after adjusting for measures of deprivation. Choice of method did not explain the differences, other than in men aged 25–44 years where a smaller increase in car exhaust use for suicide in urban areas appeared to be important. The most adverse trends were seen in women in rural areas aged 15–24 years.

Simkin et al. (2003)	England and Wales 1982–1999	Seasonality of suicides in male farmers and non-farmers compared. Found no evidence of a seasonal effect in male farming suicides.
Stark et al. (2004)	Scotland 1981–1999	Description of epidemiology of suicide in Scotland by area. Highest rates of male suicide were in Highland, and Western Isles (rural areas) followed by Greater Glasgow (an urban area).
Levin and Leyland (2005)	Scotland 1981–1999	After adjusting for age and deprivation, there was a higher risk of suicide in men in remote rural areas in 1995–1999. Female rates tended to be lower in accessible rural areas, compared to urban areas. There had been a large increase in male rates in accessible rural areas, but there was a higher absolute rate in remote rural areas.
Stark et al. (2006a)	Scotland 1981–1999	Calculated proportional mortality ratios by occupation for men. There were higher than expected PMRs in farmers and forestry workers.
Stark et al. (2006b)	Scotland 1981–1999	Reviewed deaths of male farmers, using routinely collected death information. Deaths using firearms were over-represented (29 per cent of farming deaths compared to 3.6 per cent of all male deaths in the same age group). There was no association between male suicide rates in an area and the farming suicide rate in the same area. Areas with higher farming rates tended to be parts of Scotland in which farming was less common.

had increased and, in some cases exceeded urban rates by the 1990s. Using population potential, a measure of geographical remoteness, they found that males and females aged 15–24 years and 25–44 years in rural areas had less favourable trends than the same groups in urban areas. Rates in women in the most rural areas doubled between the two time periods. In men aged 25–44 years, rural rates (defined using the population potential measure) exceeded urban rates from the mid-1980s onwards. Controlling for measures of deprivation did not ameliorate the adverse rural trends.

In Scotland, a cross-sectional study found the highest standardized mortality ratio (SMR) for suicide in men to be in the Highland NHS Board area (Crombie, 1991). Some commentators suggested that this could be due to non-residents killing themselves in the area. Later work found that, while up to 10 per cent of the suicides and undetermined deaths in the Highland NHS Board area were deaths of non-residents, the male rate remained elevated when these deaths were removed from the figures (Stark et al., 2002). The male rate proved to be high in all age groups from 16 to 75 years of age, and to have been high for at least two decades. A Scotland-wide study found high rates in some, but not all, rural areas of Scotland (Stark et al., 2004). Levin and Leyland (2005), in an elegant study, found that male rates had increased in remote rural areas in the 1990s, after deprivation was taken in to account in the analysis.

Use of firearms

The Highland study found that a higher than expected proportion of suicide deaths involved firearms (Stark et al., 2002). This is consistent with other work. Pearson found firearms deaths to be over-represented in Devon (Pearson, 1993), as did work by Roberts in Yorkshire (Roberts et al., 1996). Kelly and Bunting (1998), updating previous work by Charlton and associates (Charlton et al., 1992; Charlton et al., 1993; Kelly et al., 1995), and Stark et al. (2006b) also found higher than expected rates of firearm use for suicide in some occupations.

Rural occupations

Research in England, Wales and Scotland has reported higher than expected proportional mortality ratios (PMRs) in some rural occupations (Kelly et al., 1995; Kelly and Bunting, 1998; Stark et al., 2006b). PMRs compare the proportion of deaths from a cause in a particular group to its proportion of deaths in the general population, taking into account age and gender. It can, therefore, represent a surfeit of deaths from a cause or a deficit of deaths from other causes, as it depends on the proportion of deaths rather than the absolute number.

Several rural occupations prove to have higher than expected PMRs. Kelly and Bunting (1998) found, in common with earlier work in England and Wales (Kelly et al., 1995), high PMRs in farmers, horticulturists and farm managers (PMR for men in 1991–1996 144, 95 per cent confidence interval (CI) 124–166). Male gardeners and groundsmen also had significantly high PMRs in the same period (PMR 117, 95 per cent CI 102–133). In the previous five-year period, forestry and farm workers also had elevated PMRs. Inskip et al. (1996) reported similar findings for both male and female farmers in England and Wales, as did Stark et al. (2006b) in Scotland.

Malmberg, Hawton and colleagues have examined farming suicides in detail in a series of Department of Health funded studies in England and Wales (Malmberg et al., 1997; Hawton et al., 1998; Hawton et al., 1999; Malmberg et al., 1999). Details of the individual studies are included in Table 3.1. This group also found higher than expected PMRs for suicide in male farmers. Their work included a review of routine data, a survey of stress in farmers, and detailed psychological postmortem studies on a group of farmers who had died by suicide.

In the period 1981–1993, they found a declining rate of suicide in male farmers in England, but not in Wales (Hawton et al., 1999). They found no association between the type of farm holding or the density of farmers and the farming suicide rate. They also reported no association between the general population male suicide rates and the local farming suicide rates in each area, a finding replicated by Stark et al. (2006b) in Scotland. This did not support Saunderson's hypothesis that types of farming might contribute to the geographical variation in rural rates (Saunderson et al., 1998). There were variations between areas, with the highest rates in Devon (the area in which Pearson (1993) reported an excess of firearm-related suicides). There was, however, no clear overall pattern to the differences found between areas, and the researchers concluded that further work was required to explore the reasons for the variations in rates identified by their study.

The psychological postmortem study conducted by these authors compared the results on eighty-four farmers to the responses to a postal survey of living farmers (Malmberg et al., 1997; Malmberg et al., 1999). Almost one-third of the dead farmers had to be excluded because they were not working in farming at the time of their death, a finding that has implications for other work on farmers that depends on data from the routine recording of deaths in the UK. In this work, pig farmers were over-represented, although this was not supported by the area findings discussed above. Farmers had experienced a variety of problems in the year before their death, including relationship, occupational, financial, and physical health problems. Mental health problems were particularly common: 46 per cent were felt to have had a definite mental illness at the time of their death, and a further 23 per cent had probable illness. Depression was particularly common, while alcohol misuse was less common than would have been expected from general population series. Other factors also appeared to be important, and compared to the farmers responding to the postal survey, more of the farmers who died by suicide lived alone (18 per cent vs. 8 per cent), lacked close friends (31 per cent vs. 5 per cent), and had no confidant (52 per cent vs. 8 per cent). Firearms were again over-represented. In keeping with these findings, Stark et al. (2006b) found in Scotland that 85 per cent of the variance in farming suicide rates between areas could be described by an inverse association with the proportion of farmers in the population. This may suggest that professional and social networks are particularly important.

Gun safety

In the light of these findings, it is helpful to consider the international literature on gun safety. Suicide attempts using guns are particularly likely to result in death. International comparisons are difficult, as gun ownership rates vary markedly in different countries. In the USA, there are over 13,000 gun deaths per year (Dresang, 2001), and almost half of US homes contain one or more firearms (Kellermann et al., 1992). Even in European countries, gun ownership can be very different from the pattern in the United Kingdom. Long guns are widely available in Finland, and it is estimated that around one-third of young men hunt with guns (Hintikka et al., 1997).

Despite this limitation, international findings provide some useful comparisons to the UK experience. Firearm suicide attempts are very likely to result in death. In a study of firearms injuries in Johnson County, North Carolina, Sadowski and Munoz (1996) found that two-thirds of all firearm injuries were non-fatal, but that in episodes designated as deliberate self-harm, only four of sixty-three were non-fatal. The media focus on violent crime in the USA can conceal the experience of firearm-related homicide. Rural areas of Washington had higher rates of gun deaths in 1980–1996 than did urban Washington (Dresang, 2001). Accidental shootings made up 3 per cent of rural gun deaths, while 70 per cent were recorded as suicide (Dresang, 2001).

In two largely urban areas of the USA, Kellermann et al. (1992) found that the ready availability of guns increased the risk of suicide in the home (adjusted odds ratio 5.8, 95 per cent CI 3.1–4.7 for handguns, and 3.0, 95 per cent CI 1.4–6.5 for long guns only). Any gun being kept loaded was associated with an adjusted odds ratio of 9.2 (CI 4.1–20.1), while unloaded guns were associated with an adjusted odds ratio of 3.3 (CI 1.7–6.1). Guns which were locked had an adjusted odds ratio of 2.4 (CI 1.0–5.7), while all guns being unlocked had an adjusted odds ratio of 5.6 (CI 3.1–10.4). According to Kellermann et al. (1992, p. 470), 'few victims acquired their guns within hours or days of their death: the vast majority had guns in the home for months or years'. There was extensive correspondence about this article, but its conclusions appeared to hold up to scrutiny.

Findings from other countries with widespread firearm ownership are similar. In Australia, firearm suicide rates in males aged 15–24 years increased fourfold in towns and cities over 4000 people, but twelvefold in towns with populations of fewer than 4000 people in the period 1964–1993 (Dudley et al., 1997). Firearms were over-represented in rural areas compared to urban figures in a study of youth suicide in Australia (Dudley et al., 1998). In Finland, in men aged 15–24, almost two-thirds of suicides were committed using guns. In 60 per cent of the Finnish firearm suicides, a licensed hunting gun stored in the victim's own home was used (Hintikka et al., 1997).

Dudley concluded that, 'beyond reasonable doubt, a causal relationship exists between gun ownership and firearm suicides and homicides' (Dudley et al., 1996, p. 370). In Australia, 'the relative availability of, and need for, firearms in small rural areas, a lack of safety in storage and usage of firearms, and dwindling populations combine to elevate rural youth firearm suicide rates' (Dudley et al. 1997, p. 258).

Given the need for farmers and others in rural occupations to have access to firearms, these findings raise obvious problems for staff. There have been several attempts in the USA to encourage health care staff to offer advice to gun owners (Christoffel, 1999; Dresang, 2001). Physical interventions can range from expensive gun cabinets, to comparatively cheap trigger locks (Dresang, 2001). Camosy (1996) suggests that, in the USA, asking about firearm safety should be as routine as asking about tobacco use. While this would not be sensible in the UK as a whole, there may be relevance to health and social care staff working with people in rural occupations in which firearm owner-ship is likely. Camosy (1996) also argues for wider publicity about firearm safety, including advocacy in schools, churches and other community groups, and with the media.

Conclusion

Rural areas are not the idyllic areas of popular imagination. They are complex areas subject to both internal and external political pressures. There have been numerous changes in areas of the UK, influenced by migration, changing land use, economic shifts away from production to the service industry, and changed public expectations. There is compelling evidence that children and young people may find rural areas particularly challenging, and this may be reflected in the trends in youth suicide identified by Middleton et al. (2003).

Mental ill-health is common in rural areas, although probably no more common that would be expected after adjusting for measures of deprivation. Compared to disadvantaged urban areas, rates of ill-health may be a little lower, but the problems of access to treatment services, including anonymity and stigma, probably mean that the overall burden of mental ill-health is comparable across the UK.

Two distinct themes arise from the literature on rural suicide in the UK. Suicide rates in some areas are higher than expected, particularly in the most rural parts of the UK. Some occupational groups have a higher than expected proportion of deaths from suicide, of which farming is the best known – and most researched – example. These have often been assumed to be reflections of the same phenomena, but this may not be the case. Hawton et al. (1999) and Stark et al. (2006b) found no association between male farming suicide rates and the local area male rate. Similarly, if the farming suicides in the Highlands of Scotland are reduced to the average Scottish male rate, the population rate remains high. This suggests that there may be two separate processes in action. First, the numerous rural problems identified in the open-ing section of this chapter may contribute to high rates of suicide. The infor-mation on young people and rurality suggests that this problem may continue to increase. Second, occupations with access to lethal means – themselves exposed to the usual rural stressors – have high suicide rates that appear to be at least partly independent of the suicide rates surrounding them.

Action will need to be on several fronts. There is considerable scope for further research. There have been no concerted efforts in the UK to promote firearm safety, perhaps because of the UK's uneasy relationship with gun ownership, and a better understanding of what safety measures would be acceptable to regular gun users would be valuable. There is very limited understanding of the factors associated with suicide in other rural occu-pational groups. It may be assumed that the same factors at play in farmers are also relevant to them, but there is little or no evidence to support this.

Intervention trials are very difficult in rural areas because of both geography and small numbers. There are, however, academic units in the UK that are developing an expertise in the conduct of trials in sparsely populated areas, and intervention trials therefore become possible. Trials with suicide reduction as the outcome measure are impractical because of the relative infrequency of suicide. Many proxy measures are available, however, and the insights from work on farmers and on staff patterns in rural areas, suggest possible ways of structuring interventions in ways that will fit with rural work patterns.

There is persuasive evidence that suicide is an important problem in rural areas of the UK. Rural areas are heterogeneous, and the impact of suicide varies. This should not dissuade services from investment in the area, nor researchers from exploration of relevant work. People in rural areas should not be doubly disadvantaged by both suicide, and by an exclusive focus on the urban experience.

References

Aasbrenn, K. (1988) *Regional Tjenesteorganisering I Uttynningsområder (Organizing Services in Marginal Areas)*, Report 5. Rena, Norway: Høgskolen I Hedmark.

Agg, J. and Phillips, M. (1997) Neglected gender dimensions of rural social restructuring, in P. Boyle and K. Halfacree (eds). *Migration into Rural Areas: Theories and issues.* Chichester: Wiley.

Barnett, S., Roderick, P., Martin, D. and Diamond, I. (2001) A multilevel analysis of the effects of rurality and social deprivation on premature limiting long term illness. *Journal of Epidemiology and Community Health*, 55(1), 44–51.

Barnett, S., Roderick, P., Martin, D., Diamond, I. and Wrigley, H. (2002) Interrelations between three proxies of health care need at the small area level: an urban/rural comparison. *Journal of Epidemiology and Community Health*, 56, 754–761.

Bentham, G. (1984) Mortality rates in the more rural areas. *Area*, 16, 219–226.

Bunting, J. and Kelly, S. (1998) Geographic variations in suicide mortality, 1982–96. *Population Trends*, 93, 7–18.

Camosy, P.A. (1996) Incorporating gun safety into clinical practice. *American Family Physician*, 54(9), 971–975.

Charlton, J., Kelly, S., Dunnell, K., Evans, B., Jenkins, R. and Wallis, R. (1992) Trends in suicide deaths in England and Wales. *Population Trends*, 69, 10–16.

Charlton, J., Kelly, S., Dunnell, K., Evans, B. and Jenkins, R. (1993) Suicide trends in England and Wales: trends in factors associated with suicide deaths. *Population Trends*, 71, 34–42.

Chasney, P. and Sherwood, K. (2000) The resale of right to buy dwellings: a case study of migration and social change in rural England. *Journal of Rural Studies*, 16, 79–94.

Christie, S.M.L. and Fone, D.L. (2003) Does car ownership reflect socio-economic disadvantage in rural areas? A cross-sectional geographical study in Wales, UK. *Public Health*, 117, 112–116.

Christoffel, K.K. (1999) Useful mnemonic for remembering the AAP's suggestions for clinical violence prevention and management. *Pediatrics*, 104 (5 pt 1), 1171.

Cloke, P. (1985) Counterurbanization: a rural perspective. *Geography*, 70, 13–23.

Cloke, P. (1993) On 'problems and solutions': the reproduction of problems for rural communities in Britain during the 1980's. *Journal of Rural Studies*, 9(2), 113–121.

Cloke, P. and Milbourne, P. (1992) Deprivation and lifestyles in rural Wales. II: Rurality and the cultural dimension. *Journal of Rural Studies*, 8, 359–371.

Cloke, P., Goodwin, P., Milbourne, C. and Thomas, C. (1995) Deprivation, poverty and maginalisation in rural lifestyles in England and Wales. *Journal of Rural Studies*, 11(4), 351–365.

Cloke, P., Milbourne, P. and Widdowfield, R. (2001a) Homelessness and rurality: exploring connection in local spaces of rural England. *Sociologica Ruralis*, 41(4), 438–453.

Cloke, P., Milbourne, P. and Widdowfield, R. (2001b) Interconnecting housing, homelessness and rurality: evidence from local authority homelessness officers in England and Wales. *Journal of Rural Studies*, 17(1), 99–111.

Cox, J. (1998) Poverty in rural areas is more hidden but no less real than in urban areas. *British Medical Journal*, 316(7133), 722–723.

Crombie, I.K. (1991) Suicide among men in the highlands of Scotland. *British Medical Journal*, 302(6779), 761–762.

Davis, J. and Ridge, T. (1997) *Same Scenery, Different Lifestyle: Rural children on low income*. London: The Children's Society.

Dixon, J. and Welch, N. (2000) Researching the rural-metropolitan health differential using the 'social determinants of health'. *Australian Journal of Rural Health*, 8, 254–260.

Dresang, L.T. (2001) Gun deaths in rural and urban settings: recommendations for prevention. *Journal of the American Board of Family Practice*, 14(2), 107–115.

Dudley, M., Cantor, C. and De Moore, G. (1996) Jumping the gun: firearms and the mental health of Australians. *Australian and New Zealand Journal of Psychiatry*, 30, 370–381.

Dudley, M., Kelk, N., Florio, T., Howard, J., Waters, B., Haski, C. and Alcock, M. (1997) Suicide among young rural Australians 1964–1993: a comparison with metropolitan trends. *Social Psychiatry and Psychiatric Epidemiology*, 32(5), 251–260.

Dudley, M., Kelk, N., Florio, T., Howard, J., Waters, B. and Taylor, D. (1998) Coroners' records of rural and non-rural cases of youth suicide in New South Wales. *Australian and New Zealand Journal of Psychiatry*, 32(2), 242–251.

Gabriel, M. (2002) Australia's regional youth exodus. *Journal of Rural Studies*, 18(2), 209–212.

Gilthorpe, M.S. and Wilson, R.C. (2003) Rural/urban differences in the association between deprivation and healthcare utilisation. *Social Science and Medicine*, 57, 2055–2063.

Gray, D., Farrington, J., Shaw, J., Martin, S. and Roberts, D. (2001) Car dependence in rural Scotland: transport policy, devolution and the impact of the fuel duty escalator. *Journal of Rural Studies*, 17(1), 113–125.

Halliday, J. and Little, J. (2001) Amongst women: exploring the reality of rural childcare. *Sociologica Ruralis*, 41(4), 423–437.

Hawton, K., Simkin, S. and Malmberg, A. (1998) *Suicide and Stress in Farmers*. London: The Stationery Office.

Hawton, K., Fagg, J., Simkin, S., Harriss, L., Malmberg, A. and Smith, D. (1999) The geographical distribution of suicides in farmers in England and Wales. *Social Psychiatry and Psychiatric Epidemiology*, 34(3), 122–127.

Hendry, L.B. and Reid, M. (2000) Social relationships and health: the meaning of social 'connectedness' and how it relates to health concerns for rural Scottish adolescents. *Journal of Adolescence*, 23, 705–719.

Hintikka, J., Lehtonen, J. and Viinamaki, H. (1997) Hunting guns in homes and suicides in 15–24-year-old males in eastern Finland. *Australian and New Zealand Journal of Psychiatry*, 31(6), 858–861.

Hoggart, A. and Paniagua, A. (2001) What rural restucturing? *Journal of Rural Studies*, 17(1), 41–62.

House of Lords Select Committee on the European Community (1991) *The Future of Rural Society*. London: HMSO.

Inskip, H., Coggon, D., Winter, P. and Pannett, B. (1996) Mortality of farmers and farmers wives in England and Wales 1979–1980, 1982–90. *Occupational and Environmental Medicine*, 53, 730–735.

Irving, H.W. and Davidson, R.N. (1973) A working note on the measurement of social interaction. *Transactions of the Barnett Society*, 9, 7–19.

Jones, J. (2002) The cultural symbolisation of disordered and deviant behaviour: young people's experiences in a Welsh rural market town. *Journal of Rural Studies*, 18(2), 213–217.

Kane, C.F. and Ennis, J.M. (1996) Healthcare reforms and rural mental health: severe mental illness. *Community Mental Health Journal*, 32, 445–462.

Kellermann, A.L., Rivara, F.P., Somes, G., Reay, D.T., Francisco, J., Banton, J.G. et al. (1992) Suicide in the home in relation to gun ownership. *New England Journal of Medicine*, 327, 467–472.

Kelly, S. and Bunting, J. (1998) Trends in suicide in England and Wales, 1982–96. *Population Trends*, 92, 29–41.

Kelly, S., Charlton, J. and Jenkins, R. (1995) Suicide deaths in England and Wales, 1982–92: the contribution of occupation and geography. *Population Trends*, 80, 16–25.

Kinsella, J., Wilson, S., De Jong, F. and Renting, H. (2000) Pluriactivity as a livelihood strategy in Irish farm households and its role in rural development. *Sociologica Ruralis*, 40(4), 481–496.

Levin K.A. and Leyland, A.H. (2005) Urban/rural inequalities in suicide in Scotland, 1981–1999. *Social Science and Medicine*, 60(12), 2877–2890.

Lindsay, C., McCracken, M. and McQuaid, R.W. (2003) Unemployment duration and employability in remote rural labour markets. *Journal of Rural Studies*, 19(2), 187–200.

Little, J. and Austin, P. (1996) Women and the rural idyll. *Journal of Rural Studies*, 12, 101–111.

Malmberg, A., Hawton, K. and Simkin, S. (1997) A study of suicide in farmers in England and Wales. *Journal of Psychosomatic Research*, 43(1), 107–111.

Malmberg, A., Simkin, S. and Hawton, K. (1999) Suicide in farmers. *British Journal of Psychiatry*, 175, 103–105.

Matthews, H., Taylor, M., Sherwood, K., Tucker, F. and Limb, M. (2000) Growing-up in the countryside: children and the rural idyll. *Journal of Rural Studies*, 16(2), 141–153.

Middleton, N., Gunnell, D., Frankel, S., Whitley, E. and Dorling, D. (2003) Urban–rural differences in suicide trends in young adults: England and Wales, 1981–1998. *Social Science and Medicine*, 57, 1183–1194.

Mitchell, C.J.A. (2004) Making sense of counterurbanization. *Journal of Rural Studies*, 20(1), 15–34.

Nicholson, S. (1992) Suicide in North Devon: epidemic or problem of classification? *Health Trends*, 24, 95–96.

Panelli, R. (2002) Young rural lives: strategies beyond diversity. *Journal of Rural Studies*, 18(2), 113–122.

Parr, H., Philo, C. and Burns, N. (2002a) *Experiences of mental health problems: social geographies of rural mental health*. Findings Paper no. 6. Department of Geography and Topographic Science, University of Glasgow.

Parr, H., Philo, C. and Burns, N. (2002b) *Visibility, gossip and intimate neighbourly knowledges: social geographies of rural mental health*. Findings Paper no. 7. Department of Geography and Topographic Science, University of Glasgow.

Paykel, E., Abbott, R., Jenkins, R., Brugha, T.S. and Meltzer, H. (2000) Urban–rural mental health differences in Great Britain: findings from the National Morbidity Survey. *Psychological Medicine*, 30(2), 269–280.

Pearson, V.A. (1993) Suicide in North and West Devon: a comparative study using coroner's inquest records. *Journal of Public Health Medicine*, 15(4), 320–326.

Phillips, M. (2002) Distant bodies? Rural studies, political-economy and poststructuralism. *Sociologica Ruralis*, 42(2), 81–105.

Phillips, M., Fish, R. and Agg, J. (2001) Putting together ruralities: towards a symbolic analysis of rurality in the British mass media. *Journal of Rural Studies*, 17, 1–27.

Philo, C. (1992) Neglected rural geographies: a review. *Journal of Rural Studies*, 8, 193–207.

Philo, C., Parr, H. and Burns, N. (2002) *Remoteness, rurality and mental health problems: social geographies of rural mental health*. Findings Paper no. 5. Department of Geography and Topographic Science, University of Glasgow.

Philo, C., Parr, H. and Burns, N. (2003) Rural madness: a geographical reading and critique of the rural mental health literature. *Journal of Rural Studies*, 19, 259–281.

Reed, M. (2001) Fight the future! How the contemporary campaigns of the UK organic movement have arisen from their composting of the past. *Sociologica Ruralis*, 41(1), 131–145.

Roberts, A.P., Simpson, C.J. and Wilkinson, J.R. (1996) A retrospective study of suicides in a rural health district over ten years. *Medicine, Science and the Law*, 36(3), 259–262.

Sadowski, L.S. and Munoz, S.R. (1996) Nonfatal and fatal firearm injuries in a rural county. *Journal of the American Medical Association*, 275(22), 1762–1764.

Saunderson, T.R. and Langford, I.H. (1996) A study of the geographical distribution of suicide rates in England and Wales 1989–92 using empirical Bayes estimates. *Social Science and Medicine*, 43(4), 489–502.

Saunderson, T., Haynes, R. and Langford, I.H. (1998) Urban–rural variations in suicides and undetermined deaths in England and Wales. *Journal of Public Health Medicine*, 20(3), 261–267.

Shaw, J.M. (1979) *Rural Deprivation and Planning*. Norwich: Geobooks.

Shouls, S., Congdon, P. and Curtis, S. (1996) Modelling inequality in reported long term illness in the UK: combining individual and area characteristics. *Journal of Epidemiology and Community Health*, 50, 366–376.

Simkin, S., Hawton, K., Yip, P.S.F. and Yam, C.H.K. (2003) Seasonality of suicide: a study of farming suicides in England and Wales. *Crisis*, 24(3), 93–97.

Smailes, P.J., Argent, N. and Griffin, T.L.C. (2002) Rural population density: its impact on social and demographic aspects of rural communities. *Journal of Rural Studies*, 18(4), 385–404.

Stark, C., Matthewson, F., O'Neill, N., Oates, K. and Hay, A. (2002) Suicide in the Highlands of Scotland. *Health Bulletin*, 60(1), 27–32.

Stark, C., Hopkins, P., Gibbs, D., Rapson, T., Belbin, A. and Hay, A. (2004) Trends in suicide in Scotland 1981–1999: age, method and geography. *BMC Public Health*, 4, 49.

Stark, C., Belbin, A., Hopkins, P., Gibbs, D., Hay, A. and Gunnell, D. (2006a) Male suicide and occupation in Scotland. *Health Statistics Quarterly*, 29, 26–29.

Stark, C., Gibbs, D., Hopkins, P., Belbin, A., Hay, A. and Selvaraj, S. (2006b) Suicide in farmers in Scotland. *Rural and Remote Health* 6 (online), 6(1), 509.

Stewart, R., Bechofer, F., McCrone, D. and Kiely, R. (2001) Keepers of the land: ideology and the identities of the Scottish rural elite. *Identities*, 8(3), 381–409.

Stockdale, A. (2002) Out-migration from rural Scotland: the importance of family and social networks. *Sociologica Ruralis*, 42(1), 41–64.

Stockdale, A., Findlay, A. and Short, D. (2000) The repopulation of rural Scotland: opportunity and threat. *Journal of Rural Studies*, 16(2), 243–257.

Svendsen, G.L.H. (2004) The right to development: construction of a non-agriculturalist discourse of rurality in Denmark. *Journal of Rural Studies*, 20(1), 79–94.

Valentine, G. (1997) A safe place to grow up? Parenting, perceptions of children's safety, and the rural idyll. *Journal of Rural Studies*, 13(2), 137–148.

Van Dam, F., Heins, S. and Elbersen, B.S. (2002) Lay discourses of the rural and stated and revealed preferences for rural living: some evidence of the existence of a rural idyll in the Netherlands. *Journal of Rural Studies*, 18(4), 461–476.

Walker, G. (2002) Contemporary clerical constructions of a rural idyll. *Sociologica Ruralis*, 42(2), 131–142.

4 Cognitive style and suicidal behaviour

Noel Sheehy and Rory C. O'Connor

Cognitive style has long been implicated as a risk factor for depression and suicidal behaviour. The concept refers to the way people search for, acquire, interpret, categorize, remember and retrieve information in making decisions and solving problems. The significance of understanding how information is processed and evaluated is perhaps best captured by Jung's (1923) theory of psychological types. Jung suggests that people are either 'sensing' or 'intuitive'. Sensing individuals prefer to gather information from their environment, focus on immediate experience and demonstrate acute powers of observation and memory for detail. Intuitive people prefer to focus on possibilities, meanings, and relationships by way of insight and deductive thinking. They tend to engage in more abstract thinking with a bias towards future orientation. Thus, people are either 'thinking' or 'feeling' oriented. 'Thinking individuals' rely on principles of cause and effect and they make decisions analytically. This is somewhat analogous to Lazarus and Folkman's (1984) problem-focused coping style. 'Feeling individuals' prefer to weigh the relative merits of an issue and to rely on an understanding of personal and group values in their decision-making. They prefer to rely on affect over cognition and tend to use logic to support feelings. This is analogous to emotion-focused coping. Clues to a person's cognitive style can be communicated in different ways. Some people may talk about how they spend a lot of time ruminating on what they should or should not have done or said. Others may indicate their agitation when people seem to jump from topic to topic in a conversation. Myers (1962) extended Jung's theory by proposing a further distinction between a preference for information-processing and information evaluation. According to Myers (1962), perceptive individuals prefer to collect rather than evaluate information, to remain flexible and to keep their options open. Evaluators prefer to assess and judge information and demonstrate a preference for order and control.

While cognitive style is a well-established theoretical construct there is considerable ambiguity in the way it has been used. Many authors have treated cognitive style and learning style as synonyms, suggesting that a negative cognitive style incorporates a way of learning that has itself been learned. Most definitions of cognitive and learning style refer to variations in individual information-processing. Thus, cognitive style has been described as a predictable pattern of behaviour within a range of individual variability (Cornett, 1983); a way of responding to and using stimuli in a learning environment (Claxton and Ralston, 1978); a preference for processing information and learning (Dunn and Dunn, 1978); the way individuals organize experiences (Kolb, 1984); and an expression of psychological differentiation within characteristic modes of information-processing (Witkin and Goodenough, 1981).

Despite the ambiguities, there is consensus that cognitive style is concerned with an unconscious strength of preference for processing information and as such is different from cognitive skill. People may choose to acquire cognitive skills that are not necessarily consonant with their preferences. They can resist or override their preferences and choose to act in ways that may appear to be inconsistent with their cognitive style. Thus, there is no suggestion that some cognitive dispositions prime people for suicide. Treating cognitive style as a psychological millstone would imply a commitment to a 'bad apple' theory of suicide: if only the 'bad apples', those who are 'suicide primed', could be detected early by identifying the telltale 'cognitive style' they could be treated appropriately at an early stage (see O'Connor and Sheehy, 2000, 2001). There is no evidence that 'thinking' and 'feeling' individuals, for instance, are differentially susceptible to suicide. The link between cognitive style and suicide is more subtle. It is based on two hypotheses. First, that suicide is associated with a constriction in cognitive style rather than with style per se. Thus, to use Jung's distinction, both sensing and intuitive styles can become constricted. Second, that suicide is correlated with an increase in negative affect.

Although we are not suggesting that particular cognitive styles lead people to become 'suicide primed' per se, the relationship between the constriction of cognitive style and suicide is usefully conceptualized within the broader diathesis-stress literature (see Ingram and Price, 2002; Ingram, 2003). Specifically, there is a growing body of work to suggest that some vulnerability (or otherwise) may be associated with relatively stable individual differences factors (like cognitive style) with the caveat that the impact of these factors may only become activated in the presence of stress. In the case of suicidal behaviour, increased risk is the result of a complex interaction between vulnerability factors (e.g. cognitive style), buffering factors (e.g. social support) and stress (Schotte and Clum, 1987; Joiner and Rudd, 1995; O'Connor et al., 2004). In a sense, the diathesis-stress hypothesis draws from both the 'bad apple' and 'rotten barrels' (i.e. social forces impact on your likelihood of engaging in suicidal behaviour) explanations of suicide. This perspective underlines the importance of the biopsychosocial framework and suggests giving due consideration to the separate and concomitant effects of biological, psychological and social factors in the suicidal process. The vulnerabilities associated with constricted cognitive style are elaborated on in the remainder of this chapter.

Suicide and impairments to cognitive style

Impaired problem-solving is a well-established suicide risk factor (see Pollock and Williams, 1998). Those at high risk tend to endure impairments in their social and interpersonal problem-solving abilities. This is often most noticeable in difficulties experienced when conceptualizing, identifying and formulating appropriate solutions to familiar social problems. For example, studies using the Means-End Problem-Solving Scale (MEPS) (Platt et al., 1975), in which respondents are invited to generate solutions to a number of social dilemmas, have shown that suicidal people generate fewer solutions and often their solutions are less relevant (Pollock and Williams, 1998; NiÉidhin et al., 2002). Other studies have shown that suicidal and depressed individuals tend to generate overly general autobiographical memories (i.e. summaries of experiences) and take longer to recall positive memories than matched controls (Williams and Broadbent, 1986; Williams, 1997). Williams explains this in terms of a 'mnemonic interlock' – the suicidal person is fixed at an intermediate level of memory recall and is able to access general but not specific memories. These memory biases have been attributed to changes in problem-solving proficiency (Evans et al., 1992). Solving personal and interpersonal problems entails recalling similar dilemmas with satisfactory solutions. Difficulties accessing specific events from long-term memory are likely to diminish one's problem-solving capacity. In effect, suicidal individuals engage in efforts to solve interpersonal dilemmas burdened by a significant information-processing handicap. In other domains of psychology it is often the case that previous behaviour is the best predictor of future behaviour but the problem-solving history of the suicidal person is often not fully available to inform the formulation of solutions to current crises. General solutions cannot provide the level of detail required to address the details in particular problems and so the suicidal person has to work harder and longer to generate a number of potential solutions and to recall positive memories that might assist them.

The suicidal person tends to endure a pessimistic view of the future, their general environment and themselves and they tend to manifest a depressogenic attributional style. Traditionally measured along three dimensions (internal–external, stable–unstable, global–specific), depressed and suicidal individuals tend to attribute negative life events to internal, stable and global causes (Peterson et al., 1982). This pattern of thinking can be particularly potent when applied to negative interpersonal experiences, such as the break-up of a long-term relationship, rather than negative achievement-related events, such as failure to pass an examination. To assess the suicidal risk of a particular negative life event on, say, a young person, it is crucial that one distinguishes between severity and impact: a relationship crisis may not appear to be *severe* (low severity from a loved one's point of view) but it can have considerable *impact* on the young person (high impact).

Consider another example: an adolescent bereaved through the suicide of a parent may believe that they played a contributory role (an internal cause) either by their own actions or their failure to notice signs of their parent's troubled mind. They may perceive their role in the suicide as an expression of some intractable (stable) personal characteristic and find evidence for this in selective memories of other relationships in which they rejected, or were rejected by, others (a global characteristic). This pattern of thinking can be associated with an extended phase of negative affect and cognition, leading to decrements in problem-solving and an increased sense of hopelessness which in turn elevates their suicide risk. Indeed their constricted problem-solving may lead them to conclude that their own suicide would be a logically appropriate way of permanently removing the gap between themselves and their deceased parent.

Future thinking and suicidal behaviour

The relationship between positive future thinking and hopelessness provides a crucial insight into the suicidal mind (e.g. MacLeod et al., 2005). Moreover, the fact that one can experience a decrement in positive future thinking independently of depression points to a complex relationship between cognitive style and hopelessness. The proceeding paragraphs describe this relationship in parasuicide patients.[1] O'Connor et al. (2000a) assessed a sample of parasuicidal patients and matched hospital controls the day following admission to hospital on measures of cognitive style, depression, anxiety, future-oriented thinking and hopelessness. They measured cognitive style using the Cognitive Style Questionnaire (see Abramson et al., 1998) which, in addition to assessing the traditional attributional dimensions, includes measures of consequences and self-worth. They found that people in their parasuicide sample differed from hospital controls on measures of depression, future positive expectations and negative cognitive style in the predicted directions and that these three measures explained 70.5 per cent of the variation in hopelessness. They also found that positive future thinking was not correlated with depression or negative cognitive style. Their findings suggest that a negative cognitive style, as distinct from depression, is not related to impaired positive thinking.

What is more, this outcome is a partial replication of MacLeod and colleagues' original work on prospective cognitions. They investigated whether the cognitive style of suicidal individuals was similarly characterized by the presence of negative future expectations or the lack of positive future positive cognitions (MacLeod et al., 1993, 1997) and whether this pattern differed from the non-suicidal-depressed and matched controls. Their evidence demonstrated that parasuicides did not differ from the depressed group in terms of the number of negative future cognitions but were significantly impaired in their ability to generate positive future cognitions. This is a key study as it demonstrated for the first time that positive and negative prospective cognitions are not functionally equivalent. A characteristic of those who engage in parasuicidal acts is the paucity of their positive future cognitions, what sets parasuicides apart from the rest is their lack of positive future cognitions. More recently, Hunter and O'Connor (2003) investigated another sample of general hospital parasuicides as well as two control groups (hospital and community controls). Once again there was evidence for this future thinking effect. There was no difference between the groups in terms of negative thoughts, but the parasuicides reported significantly fewer positive future thoughts than the community controls but not the hospital controls. Although this effect was not as strong as MacLeod et al. (1993, 1997), a discriminant function analysis (to determine which factors were statistically important to distinguish the parasuicides from the controls) revealed that positive future thinking, when considered alongside the traditional mood variables (depression, anxiety and hopelessness), was important in predicting group membership. As noted at the outset of this section, this dearth cannot be attributed to depression because, as O'Connor, MacLeod and colleagues (MacLeod et al., 1993, 1997; O'Connor et al., 2000a; Hunter and O'Connor, 2003) have shown impairment in future positive cognitions can occur independently of depression and also of negative cognitive style. This has prompted further speculation about the correlates of diminished positive prospective cognitions.

One possible correlate is that of perfectionistic tendencies. It is conceivable that higher levels of perfectionism are associated with apprehension for future events because each event represents a potential occasion for failure. To this end, perfectionism has been implicated in psychopathology for some time (Pacht, 1984), in particular in eating disorders, arguably another type of self-harming (Vohs et al., 1999). Consequently, its association with suicidal behaviour should not be surprising. Dean and Range (1999) using the Multidimensional Perfectionism Scale (MPS: Hewitt and Flett, 1991) assessed 132 clinical outpatients on measures of life events, multidimensional perfectionism, depression, hopelessness, reasons for living, and suicide ideation. The MPS consists of three subscales: socially prescribed perfectionism, self-oriented perfectionism and other-oriented perfectionism. Socially prescribed perfectionism taps beliefs about the excessive expectations we perceive significant others have of us and self-oriented perfectionism focuses on the standards we set for ourselves. Other-oriented perfectionism is the extent to which we possess high expectations and standards for other people's behaviour. The evidence in the research literature suggests that two components of the MPS may be especially pernicious in precipitating suicide risk: socially prescribed perfectionism and self-oriented perfectionism (Hewitt and Flett, 1991)[2]. Socially prescribed perfectionism is consistently associated with suicidality (for a review see Shafran and Mansell, 2001) although, the story is less clear for self-oriented perfectionism (see O'Connor and O'Connor, 2003). Dean and Range's (1999) finding with social perfectionism is typical of that found in the literature: They identified a significant pathway from socially prescribed perfectionism to depression, from depression to hopelessness, and from hopelessness to suicidal thinking and impoverished reasons for living. In another study in Scotland, Hunter and O'Connor (2003) found a negative correlation between socially prescribed perfectionism and positive future thoughts but the converse for self-oriented perfectionism. The latter was positively correlated with positive future thinking. Contrary to their predictions, these data suggested that self-oriented perfectionism may not precipitate risk, rather it may buffer against hopelessness. The authors speculated that in some instances self-oriented perfectionism may be beneficial if it is tapping issues around gaining control over daily hassles. Such an interpretation also fits with two additional studies with university students where O'Connor and colleagues found that the impact of self-oriented perfectionism on well-being was moderated by other factors, sometimes leading to decreased distress (O'Connor et al., 2004), other times associated with elevated distress (O'Connor and O'Connor, 2003). Taken together, these relationships are tentative and have yet to be demonstrated within prospective study designs.

Escape, entrapment and the cry of pain

Many different models of suicidal behaviour have been postulated, some have included cognitive risk factors, others have not. Those like Blumenthal's overlap model of youth suicidal behaviour (Blumenthal and Kupfer, 1990) or Maris' notion of a suicidal career (Maris, 1994) have served as useful heuristics but lacked predictive utility. More recently, Williams (1997, 2001) incorporated his conceptualization of self-harm as a cry of pain into an escape theory of suicide (Baumeister, 1990). To our thinking, this model makes intuitive, theoretical and clinical sense. However, before describing Williams' model and illustrating how it fits with the cognitive style perspective, it is useful to summarize escape theory. In an attempt to extend the theoretical perspectives on suicide, Baumeister (1990) critiqued current research in social and personality theory and explored how it related to suicidal behaviour. Thereafter, he concluded that the central action of suicide was to escape from the painful self-awareness of certain symbolic interpretations or implications about the self. From this viewpoint, suicide is seen as the final step in a series of causally related events that begins with a severe experience (or series of experiences) that is appraised as a personal failure and for which you blame yourself. This leads to negative affect which you wish to escape from, cognitive deconstuction and numbness. The resultant numbness culminates in disinhibition which, in turn, increases suicidal risk. Although escape theory is a useful model, it requires further definition, to determine more clearly the conditions which are most insidious. Hence, Williams drew from animal research, in particular from work on 'arrested flight' (entrapment),[3] and from examples of this conceptualization applied to the explanation of human depression (Gilbert and Allan, 1998).

Specifically, Williams argues (Williams, 2001; Williams and Pollock, 2001) that suicidal behaviour is a 'cry' or a response to a stressful situation that has three components (see Figure 4.1). First, the situation causes feelings of defeat or rejection. Second, the individual wishes to escape from this situation and hence evaluates their escapability and concludes that there is no escape. Third, they conclude that there are no rescue factors (e.g. social support) to alleviate the crisis. This triumvirate is then thought to activate a psycho-biological 'helplessness script' (similar to the learned helplessness paradigm in animals) that facilitates the impulse to escape by suicidal actions. Whether or not suicidal solutions are preferred is determined by other factors includ-ing modelling effects and the availability of means. Hence, an individual's judgements as to (first) how stressful, (second) how escapable the situation is, and (third) how much support is available are affected by memory and atten-tional biases, as outlined above. According to this view suicidal behaviour is not inherently abnormal, the product of abnormal psychological processes, rather it is the expression of normal psychological processes and this affords opportunities to explore new avenues to suicide prevention.

Indeed, in a case-control study, O'Connor (2003) compared a sample of parasuicides with matched controls on the cry of pain measures and yielded clear evidence to support Williams' cry of pain model. Not only did the measures of defeat/rejection, escape and rescue (i.e. perceived social support) independently discriminate between the parasuicides and the hospital controls but also the relationship between escape potential and the probability of being suicidal was attenuated by social support. What is more, in a multivariate

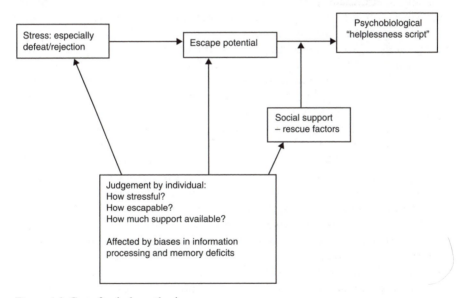

Figure 4.1 Cry of pain hypothesis.

Source: Williams, J.M.G. and Pollock, L.R. (2001) 'Psychological aspects of the suicidal pro-cess', in K. van Heeringen (ed.) *Understanding Suicidal Behaviour*. Chichester: Wiley. Copyright © 2001 John Wiley and Sons Limited. Reproduced with permission.

logistic regression analysis (when all the variables are included in one analysis to determine the relative importance of each variable), where the cry of pain variables and measures of affect were included together to predict status (i.e., parasuicide or control), the cry of pain variables were the most important factors. In summary, this model affords a meaningful representation of the suicidal process but requires further elucidation.

Family cognitive styles?

Just as individuals appear to have cognitive preferences, ongoing intact groups such as families may also have stable cognitive preferences which have developed over time and remain relatively consistent across situations. We may better understand decision-making processes within families by viewing them as 'group dispositions' that develop over time and remain relatively consistent across settings. After all, the family context provides a significant environment for children to acquire attributional styles (Nolen-Hoeksema et al., 1986). Moreover, decision-making and problem-solving often involve information-processing and evaluation by a group of family members rather than by an isolated individual. Even when individuals seek to solve problems entirely on their own the imagined reactions from, and impact on, family members will often be taken into account. Thus, it is reasonable to propose that a group-level variable, family cognitive style, may be implicated in suicide. The evidence for this is, at present, largely indirect. For example, maladaptive attributions have been found to predict the level of family distress and have proved useful in ranking abusive families in terms of prognosis for rehabilitation (Silvester et al., 1995). More specifically, a history of psychopathology is a well-established risk factor for suicide (O'Connor and Sheehy, 2000) and more recent research has identified other familial risk factors that may be implicated in suicide risk, including poor family communication and problem-solving skills, a tendency to scapegoating, the perceived or actual loss of a significant attachment figure and marital dysfunction (Bongar et al., 2000).

Suicide is known to affect the interpersonal dynamics of bereavement (Thornton et al., 1989). Suicide bereaved children generally come from families with a history of psychopathology and substantial family disruption (Cerel et al., 2000). Families of suicidal young people are often described as disorganized, unstable and rigid (Pfeffer, 1989; Davidson and Linnoila, 1990), characteristics that we also associate with the suicidal person. It is well established that suicide within the family can cause disturbances to family dynamics, although the possibility of a reciprocal interaction has not been studied in any detail (Fergusson et al., 2000). It may be, for example, that the occurrence of suicide within a family increases the likelihood that other family members will incorporate this into their repertoire of problem-solving behaviours. There is some evidence, albeit of a preliminary nature, that there may be an intergenerational cycle of adverse childhood attachment experiences implicated in childhood suicide (Séguin et al., 1995; Maris et al., 2000).

Implications for therapy and counselling

If cognitive, affective and psychological traits are relatively stable stylistic indicators of how people perceive and interact with others, changes in style may index increased risk for suicide. These may be more easily noticed when the changes are abrupt but more difficult to detect when the changes are gradual and cumulative. However, one implication for prevention is that therapeutic interventions can beneficially track transformations in problem-solving and autobiographical memories and use these as one indicator of change in suicide risk. A second is that working with the person to remove these impairments in problem-solving can have positive consequences which can promote self-esteem and reduce hopelessness. Of course, to help a suicidal person become a better problem-solver is not a trivial task, especially if the client has severe problem-solving deficits and has not consistently adapted well to their environment for some time. A suicidal person may have spent years using maladaptive problem-solving styles that served some psychological function for them. Half a dozen sessions targeted on enriching their problem-solving skills will not make much of a difference with a chronically poor problem-solver (Heppner, 1990). Moreover, gains achieved with the support of a therapist may be difficult to sustain beyond the therapeutic setting. Nonetheless, a meta-analysis has pointed to the effectiveness of brief problem-solving therapy for deliberate self-harm patients (Townsend et al., 2001).

Interventions should also be developed further to address the tendency towards social perfectionism. To this end, some treatments have already been developed to modify perfectionism itself (e.g. Antony and Swinson, 1998). Changes to perfectionism may also have a knock-on effect on positive future thinking. Hunter and O'Connor (2003) speculated that social perfectionism may act on future cognitions by reducing the likelihood that an individual encodes or retrieves positive future events. Such an interpretation fits with the conceptualization of social perfectionism as being driven by the fear of failure or the avoidance of punishment (e.g. Deci and Ryan, 1985).

MacLeod et al. (1998) attempted to help their clients improve positive future thinking (and thereby reduce the risk of repetitive parasuicide) through a brief, manual-assisted cognitive behavioural therapeutic intervention (MACT: Evans et al., 1999). Their clients were offered a series of six cognitive-orientated, problem-focused therapeutic sessions. At follow-up, six months later, those who received the MACT intervention showed a significant improvement in positive future thinking compared with a group of parasuicidal people who had treatment as usual. This finding was complicated by the fact that the non-hospital control group also showed an improvement in positive future thinking. More convincing evidence has been reported with people who had suffered from depression (Williams, 2000). Recovered depressed people were randomly allocated to mindfulness-based cognitive therapy or treatment as usual. Those who received the cognitive therapy showed a significant reduction in the recall of generic memories, compared to the control group. These findings have yet to be replicated with a parasuicide population.

Sidley et al. (1999) attempted to improve the specificity of risk assessment for parasuicide repetition by supplementing established socio-demographic predictors (Kreitman and Foster, 1991) with two psychological variables: personal future fluency or prospective cognitions (MacLeod et al., 1997) and autobiographical memory (Williams and Broadbent, 1986). They assessed a high-risk group of people as soon as practicable after their parasuicide episode and followed them for a year. They found that scores on the Beck Hopelessness Scale were the best predictors of future self-harm at six months follow-up, and that history of previous parasuicides was the strongest predictor one year later. However, neither personal future fluency nor specificity of autobiographical memory increased risk assessment.

Although the majority of research has focused on modifying the 'process' predictors of hopelessness and suicidality per se (e.g. future thinking, problem-solving), it may also be useful to develop frameworks of intervention to modify the cry of pain 'outcome' variables directly given that they were developed to understand suicidal behaviour itself. At the very least, they could be used as 'at-risk' markers during therapy or treatment.

At this point we wish to introduce a caveat concerning the putative primacy of cognition in therapy and counselling. Clark (1995) has pointed out that cognition is often given implicit primacy in the therapeutic process for pragmatic considerations; it is often easier to structure work with and through cognitive issues and processes. There is a danger of overemphasizing the influence of cognition on emotion and bodily states and underestimating the effect of emotions and bodily states on cognitive processes. If cognition, emotion and sensation are actually integrated, a therapeutic change can occur either through modification of beliefs or alteration of emotional and somatic feelings. Damasio (1999) has suggested that a number of brain circuits are implicated in the links between cognition, emotion and bodily sensations. These neural circuits allow awareness of a feeling to start when mental images connect in specific brain circuits to the perception of bodily states. The brain is constantly monitoring these circuits and mental scenarios can be 'marked' by memories of positive or negative bodily states. This process of somatic marking is of particular importance when making rational choices. Damasio (1999) cites clinical evidence for this claim in cases of individuals suffering brain lesions which cause them to lose the ability to experience emotions while retaining a capacity for rational thought. The absence of emotional experience means that these individuals are not capable of making rational choices in their everyday lives. He attributes this to an absence of 'emotional-somatic marking'. If emotions are absent, then it is not possible to make appropriate evaluations of the consequences of an action. This, in turn, leads to an inability to reduce the nearly infinite set of possible future scenarios to a limited number of options. The opposite can also happen:

mental scenarios can be 'marked' by memories of negative bodily states – the kinds of debilitating states that Williams refers to in his cry of pain model.

Conclusion

A cognitive learning style is a relatively stable preference for perceiving and organizing information and of responding to stimulation. Enriching cognitive styles through the development of thinking skills in therapeutic settings is supported by theories of cognition that see people as active creators of their knowledge. Clients are viewed as creating new ways to solve personal and interpersonal problems by learning to search out meanings and impose structures. This implies that therapy occasions will have a degree of open-endedness and uncertainty in order to provide opportunities to explore ways to impose meaning, to make judgements or to produce multiple solutions. Clients need the time and opportunity to talk about their thinking processes, to make their own thought processes more explicit, to reflect on their problem-solving strategies and thereby gain a greater sense of being in control of their own thinking. Thus, acquiring and using meta-cognitive skills has emerged as a powerful idea for promoting enriched thinking in a therapeutic context.

New knowledge and alternative strategies for thinking are socially constructed not only through informed therapist guidance but also through practical dialogue, reflection and discussion. Enriching one's cognitive style may have as much to do with creating a disposition to be a good thinker as it has to do with acquiring specific skills and strategies to address particular interpersonal problems. Therapy sessions to enrich cognitive styles are likely to be characterized by open-minded attitudes about the nature of knowledge and thinking and an atmosphere where talking about thinking – questioning, predicting, contradicting, doubting – is actively pursued. Thus, enriching cognitive styles, developing problem-solving skills, and modifying their expectations for the future has implications not only for clients' thinking but also for inspiring therapists' ways of thinking too, as well as for the ethos of the therapy session as a learning collaboration.

Notes

1 Parasuicide is defined as 'an act with non-fatal outcome, in which an individual deliberately initiates a non-habitual behaviour that, without intervention from others, will cause self-harm, or deliberately ingests a substance in excess of the prescribed or generally recognised therapeutic dosage, and which the subject desired via the actual or expected physical consequences' (Platt et al., 1992, p. 98; see also O'Connor et al., 2000b).

2 Indeed there is some evidence to suggest that other-oriented perfectionism buffers against suicide risk by directing the individual away from focus on self to others (see Musson and Alloy, 1988; O'Connor and O'Connor, 2003).

3 Arrested flight describes a situation where an animal, say a bird, is defeated but cannot escape (see Gilbert and Allan, 1998).

References

Abramson, L.Y., Alloy, L.B., Hogan, M.E., Whitehouse, W.G., Cornette, M., Akhavan, S. and Chiara, A. (1998) Suicidality and cognitive vulnerability to depression among college students: a prospective study. *Journal of Adolescence*, 21, 473–487.

Antony, M.M. and Swinson, R.P. (1998) *When Perfect isn't Good Enough: Strategies for coping with perfectionism*. Oakland, CA: New Harbinger.

Baumeister, R.F. (1990) Suicide as escape from self. *Psychological Review*, 97, 90–113.

Blumenthal, S. and Kupfer, D.J. (eds) (1990) *Suicide across the Life Cycle: Risk factors, assessment, and treatment of suicidal patients*. Washington, DC: American Psychiatric Press.

Bongar, B., Goldberg, L., Cleary, K. and Brown, K. (2000) Marriage, family, family therapy, and suicide, in R.W. Maris, A.L. Berman and M. Silverman (eds) *Comprehensive Textbook of Suicidology*. New York: Guilford.

Cerel, J., Fristad, M.A., Weller, E.B. and Weller, R.A. (2000) Suicide-bereaved children and adolescents: II. Parental and family functioning. *Journal of the American Academy of Child and Adolescent Psychiatry*, 39, 437–444.

Clark, D.A. (1995) Perceived limitations of standard cognitive therapy: a consideration of efforts to revise Beck's theory and therapy. *Journal of Cognitive Psychotherapy*, 9, 153–172.

Claxton, C.S. and Ralston, Y. (1978) *Learning Styles: Their impact on teaching and administration. ASHE-ERIC/Higher Education Research Report, No. 10*. Washington, DC: Association for the Study of Higher Education.

Cornett, C.E. (1983) *What You Should Know about Learning Styles*. Bloomington, IN: Phi Delta Kappa.

Damasio, A.R. (1999) *The Feeling of What Happens: Body and emotion in the making of consciousness*. New York: Harcourt Brace.

Davidson, L. and Linnoila, M. (1990) *Risk Factors for Youth Suicide*. New York: Hemisphere.

Dean, P.J. and Range, L.M. (1999) Testing the escape theory of suicide in an outpatient clinical population. *Cognitive Therapy and Research*, 23, 561–572.

Deci, E.L. and Ryan, R.M. (1985) *Intrinsic Motivation and Self-determination in Human Behaviour*. New York: Plenum.

Dunn, R. and Dunn, K. (1978) *Teaching Students through their Learning Styles*. Englewood Cliffs, NJ: Prentice Hall.

Evans, K., Tyrer, P., Catalan, J., Schmidt, U., Davidson, K., Dent, J. et al. (1992) Autobiographical memory and problem-solving strategies in parasuicide patients. *Psychological Medicine*, 22, 399–405.

Evans, K., Tyrer, P., Catalan, J., Schmidt, U., Davidson, K., Dent, J. et al. (1999) Manual-assisted cognitive-behaviour theory (MACT): a randomized controlled trial of a brief intervention with bibliotherapy in the treatment of recurrent deliberate self-harm. *Psychological Medicine*, 29, 19–25.

Fergusson, D.M., Woodward, L.J. and Horwood, L.J. (2000) Risk factors and life processes associated with the onset of suicidal behaviour during adolescence and early adulthood. *Psychological Medicine*, 30, 23–39.

Gilbert, P. and Allan, S. (1998) The role of defeat and entrapment (arrested flight) in depression: an exploration of an evolutionary view. *Psychological Medicine*, 28, 585–598.

Heppner, P.P. (1990) Future directions for problem-solving training for adults. *Journal of Cognitive Psychotherapy*, 4, 3.

Hewitt, P.L. and Flett, G.L. (1991) Perfectionism in the self and social contexts: conceptualisation, assessment and association with psychopathology. *Journal of Personality and Social Psychology*, 60, 456–470.

Hunter, E.C. and O'Connor, R.C. (2003) Hopelessness and future thinking in para-suicide: the role of perfectionism. *British Journal of Clinical Psychology*, 42, 1–11.

Ingram, R.E. (2003) Origins of cognitive vulnerability to depression. *Cognitive Therapy and Research*, 27, 77–88.

Ingram, R.E. and Price, J.M. (2002) *Vulnerability to Psychopathology: Risk across the lifespan*. New York: Guilford.

Joiner, T.E. and Rudd, M.D. (1995) Negative attributional style for interpersonal events and the occurrence of severe interpersonal disruption as predictors of self-reported ideation. *Suicide and Life-threatening Behavior*, 25, 297–304.

Jung, C. (1923) *Psychological Types*. London: Routledge & Kegan Paul.

Kolb, D.A. (1984) *Experiential Learning: Experience as the source of learning and development*. Englewood Cliffs, NJ: Prentice Hall.

Kreitman, N. and Foster, J. (1991) The construction and selection of predictive scales with particular reference to parasuicide. *British Journal of Psychiatry*, 159, 185–192.

Lazarus, R.S. and Folkman, S. (1984) *Stress, Appraisal and Coping*. New York: Springer.

MacLeod, A.K., Rose, G.S. and Williams, J.M.G. (1993) Components of hopelessness and the future in parasuicide. *Cognitive Therapy and Research*, 17, 441–455.

MacLeod, A.K., Pankhania, B., Lee, M. and Mitchell, D. (1997) Parasuicide, depression and the anticipation of positive and negative future experiences. *Psychological Medicine*, 27, 973–977.

MacLeod, A.K., Tata, P., Evans, K., Tyrer, P., Schmidt, U., Davidson, K. et al. (1998) Recovery of positive future thinking within a high-risk parasuicide group: results from a pilot randomized controlled trial. *British Journal of Clinical Psychology*, 37, 371–379.

MacLeod, A.K., Tata, P., Tyrer, P., Schmidt, U., Davidson, K. and Thompson, S. (2005) Hopelessness and positive and negative future thinking in parasuicide. *British Journal of Clinical Psychology*, 44(4), 495–504.

Maris, R.W. (1994) The prediction of suicide, in M.J. Kelleher (ed.) *Divergent Perspectives on Suicidal Behaviour*. Cork: O'Leary.

Maris, R.W., Berman, A.L. and Silverman, M.M. (2000) *Comprehensive Textbook of Suicidology*. New York: Guilford.

Musson, R.F. and Alloy, L.B. (1988) Depression and self-focused attention, in L.B. Alloy (ed.) *Cognitive Processes in Depression*. New York: Guilford.

Myers, I. (1962) *The Myers-Briggs Type Indicator*. Palo Alto, CA: Consulting Psychologists Press.

NiÉidhin, M., Sheehy, N., O'Sullivan, M. and McLeavey, B. (2002) Perceptions of the environment, suicidal ideation and problem-solving deficits in an offender population. *British Journal of Legal and Criminological Psychology*, 17, 187–201.

Nolen-Hoeksema, S., Girgus, J. and Seligman, M.E.P. (1986) Learned helplessness in children: a longitudinal study of depression, achievement, and explanatory style. *Journal of Personality and Social Psychology*, 51, 435–442.

O'Connor, R.C. (2003) Suicidal behavior as a cry of pain: test of a psychological model. *Archives of Suicide Research*, 7, 297–308.

O'Connor, R.C. and O'Connor, D.B. (2003) Predicting hopelessness and psychological distress: the role of perfectionism and coping. *Journal of Counseling Psychology*, 50, 362–372.

O'Connor, R.C. and Sheehy, N.P. (2000) *Understanding Suicidal Behaviour*. Leicester: BPS Blackwell.

O'Connor, R.C. and Sheehy, N.P. (2001) State of the art: suicidal behaviour. *The Psychologist*, 14, 20–24.

O'Connor, R.C., Connery, H. and Cheyne, W. (2000a) Hopelessness: the role of depression, future directed thinking and cognitive vulnerability. *Psychology, Health and Medicine*, 5(2), 155–161.

O'Connor, R.C., Sheehy, N.P. and O'Connor, D.B. (2000b) Fifty cases of general hospital parasuicide. *British Journal of Health Psychology*, 5, 83–95.

O'Connor, R.C., O'Connor, D.B., O'Connor, S.M., Smallwood, J.M. and Miles, J.M. (2004) Hopelessness, stress and perfectionism: the moderating effects of future thinking. *Cognition and Emotion*, 18(8), 1099–1120.

Pacht, A.R. (1984) Reflections on perfection. *American Psychologist*, 39, 386–390.

Peterson, C., Semmel, A., von Baeyer, C., Abramson, L., Metalksy, G. and Seligman, M. (1982) The attributional style questionnaire. *Cognitive Therapy and Research*, 6, 287–299.

Pfeffer, C.R. (1989) *Suicide among Youth*. Washington, DC: American Psychiatric Press.

Platt, J.J., Spivack, G. and Bloom, W. (1975) *Manual for the Means-End Problem-solving Procedure (MEPS): A measure of interpersonal problem-solving skill*. Philadephia, PA: Hahnemann Medical College and Hospital, Department of Mental Health Sciences, Hahnemann Community MH/MR Center.

Platt, S., Bille-Brahe, U., Kerkhof, A., Schmidke, A., Bjerke, T., Crepet, P., et al. (1992) Parasuicide in Europe: the WHO/EURO Multicentre Study on Parasuicide I. Introduction and preliminary analysis for 1989. *Acta Psychiatrica Scandinavica*, 85, 97–104.

Pollock, L.R. and Williams, J.M.G. (1998) Problem-solving and suicidal behavior. *Suicide and Life-Threatening Behavior*, 28, 375–387.

Schotte, D. and Clum, G. (1987) Problem-solving skills in suicidal psychiatric patients. *Journal of Consulting and Clinical Psychology*, 55, 49–54.

Séguin, M., Lesage, A.D. and Kiely, M. (1995) History of early loss among a group of suicide survivors. *Crisis*, 16, 121–125.

Shafran, R. and Mansell, W. (2001) Perfectionism and psychopathology: a review of research and treatment. *Clinical Psychology Review*, 21, 879–906.

Sidley, G.L., Calam, R., Wells, A., Hughes, T. and Whitaker, K. (1999) The prediction of parasuicide repetition in a high-risk group. *British Journal of Clinical Psychology*, 38, 375–386.

Silvester, J., Bentovim, A., Stratton, P. and Hanks, H.G.I. (1995) Using spoken attributions to classify abusive families. *Child Abuse and Neglect*, 19, 1221–1232.

Thornton, G., Whittemore, K.D. and Robertson, D.U. (1989) Evaluation of people bereaved by suicide. *Death Studies*, 13, 119–126.

Townsend, E., Hawton, K., Altman, D.G., Arensman, E., Gunnell, D., Hazell, P. et al. (2001) The efficacy of problem-solving treatments after deliberate self-harm: meta-analysis of randomized controlled trials with respect to depression, hopelessness and improvement in problems. *Psychological Medicine*, 31(6), 979–988.

Vohs, K.D., Bardone, A.M., Joiner, T.E. and Abramson, L.Y. (1999) Perfectionism, perceived weight status, and self-esteem interact to predict bulimic symptoms: a model of bulimic symptom development. *Journal of Abnormal Psychology*, 108, 695–700.

Williams, J.M.G. (1997) *Cry of Pain*. London: Penguin.

Williams, J.M.G. (2000) Mindfulness-based cognitive therapy reduces overgeneral autobiographical memory in formerly depressed patients. *Journal of Abnormal Psychology*, 109, 150–155.

Williams, J.M.G. (2001) *Suicide and Attempted Suicide*. London: Penguin.

Williams, J.M.G. and Broadbent, K. (1986) Autobiographical memory in attempted suicide patients. *Journal of Abnormal Psychology*, 95, 144–149.

Williams, J.M.G. and Pollock, L.R. (2001) Psychological aspects of the suicidal process, in K. van Heeringen (ed.) *Understanding Suicidal Behaviour*. Chichester: Wiley.

Witkin, H.A. and Goodenough, D.R. (1981) *Cognitive Styles: Essence and origins*. New York: International Universities Press.

5 Understanding suicidal ideation and assessing for risk

Peter Ruddell and Berni Curwen

This chapter will mainly focus on the assessment of individuals who may be experiencing suicidal ideation and assessing the risks of such thought processes leading to suicidal behaviour. We will consider what suicidal ideation is and how it can be explored with a client to ascertain likely risks for an individual. We will proceed by considering which particular groups of individuals are at greatest risk of attempting suicide. Even while working with an individual, it is important for workers to have a broad understanding of suicide and to appreciate some of the moves to reduce suicide at a national level and be aware of some of the major initiatives (many of which are at a government level) to reduce the number of suicides. It is here we will begin.

The wider picture

It is not precisely known how many suicides take place in the UK because a number of suicides go unrecorded. In England and Wales coroners decide suicide verdicts. Two types of evidence are required for a verdict of suicide to be recorded. First, the act must be self-inflicted. Second, the death must be intended, for example a suicide note. Given the difficulty of producing evidence, official suicide statistics therefore underestimate the true suicide rate.

'Accidental death' or 'undetermined cause' will be recorded by the coroner. Most undetermined deaths are suicides (Williams and Morgan, 1994; Department of Health, 2001, p. 12). Recognizing the necessity for a strategic approach to suicide reduction, the UK government published a health strategy, *The Health of the Nation*, which included a target for reducing the population suicide rates by 15 per cent over an eight-year period (Department of Health, 1992). This thrust has been carried forward in subsequent work embodied in the ninth standard of the *National Service Framework for Mental Health* (Department of Health,1999), *Safety First: Five Year Report of the National Confidential Inquiry into Suicide and Homicide by People with Mental Illness* (Department of Health, 2001) and *National Suicide Prevention Strategy for England* (Department of Health, 2002). This strategic work aims to reduce suicide by focusing on preventative measures at levels beyond the individual (see Chapter 1 for more details). The evidence so far is that it is having a positive impact upon the reduction of suicide rates (see NIMHE, 2006).

At an individual level the detection of suicidal ideation and the accurate assessment of those who may be at risk of suicide is crucial to enable appropriate interventions to take place (see Simon and Hales, 2006). Any person who wants to end his or her own life may find a way to do so. For example, Professor Keith Hawton, at the public inquiry into the high-profile death of Dr David Kelly, noted that a lay person would certainly not have predicted his death (www.the-hutton-inquiry.org.uk, 135: 4–7). It is most important for the clinician to approach any potential suicide with the conviction that it is possible to prevent at least some suicides.

Common myths surrounding suicide

Many myths are associated with suicide, and are often culturally endorsed. However, many of these (like many of the thought distortions discussed in Chapter 9) are factually incorrect. It is important for the practitioner to confront these myths or misconceptions so as not to unwittingly collaborate with an individual's distorted visions of reality at the time she or he experiences suicidal ideation. We have incorporated some of these into this text, e.g. that talking about suicide will make it more likely to happen. For a fuller discussion of themes identified through research to be misconceptions see Fujimura et al. (1985) and Shneidman et al. (1976). Other misconceptions deserving attention and related to childhood suicide have been identified by Greene (1994). Given in Table 5.1 is a list provided by Fujimura et al. (1985) outlining the most common misconceptions or myths that they identify together with those of Greene (1994) relating to children, accompanied by their factual challenges.

Understanding suicidal ideation

A cognitive behavioural perspective recognizes that thoughts (or ideas) are always associated with feelings and behaviour (or action). Consequently, anyone who is in any way moving towards suicide will experience suicidal thoughts or ideation (Rudd et al., 2001). The cognitive behavioural perspective will be more fully explored in Chapter 9. The expression of these thoughts should always be taken seriously. The thoughts may not always be expressed openly but may be demonstrated in various ways such as in behaviour, writing, pictures or verbally. Occasional suicidal thoughts are not uncommon in 'normal' individuals. Exploring suicidal ideation with an individual does not make suicidal behaviour more likely. The contrary is true provided your approach is sensitive and embodies the principles outlined below in the following section. Ambivalence has commonly been detected in the suicidal person and even the person with the strongest death-wish is confused and invariably grasping for life (Shneidman et al., 1976, p. 128).

Table 5.1 Myths associated with suicide

---

1 *Discussing suicide will cause the client to move toward doing it.* The opposite is generally true. Discussing it with an empathic person will more likely provide the client with a sense of relief and a desire to buy time to regain control.
2 *Clients who threaten suicide don't do it.* A large percentage of people who kill themselves have previously threatened it or disclosed their intent to others.
3 *Suicide is an irrational act.* Nearly all suicides and suicide attempts make perfect sense when viewed from the perspective of the persons doing them.
4 *Persons who commit suicide are insane.* Only a small percentage of persons attempting or committing suicide are psychotic or crazy. Most of them appear to be normal people who are severely depressed, lonely, hopeless, helpless, newly aggrieved, shocked, deeply disappointed, jilted, or otherwise overcome by some emotionally charged situation.
5 *Suicide runs in families – it is an inherited tendency.* Suicidal tendency is not inherited. It is either learned or situational.
6 *Once suicidal, always suicidal.* A large proportion of people contemplate suicide at some time during their existence. Most of these individuals recover from the immediate threat, learn appropriate responses and controls, and live long, productive lives, free from the threat of self-inflicted harm.
7 *When a person has attempted suicide and pulls out of it, the danger is over.* Probably the greatest period of danger is during the upswing period, when the suicidal person becomes energized following a period of severe depression. One danger signal is a period of euphoria following a depressed or suicidal episode.
8 *A suicidal person who begins to show generosity and share personal possessions is showing signs of renewal and recovery.* Many suicidal persons begin to dispose of their prized possessions once they experience enough upswing in energy to make a definite plan. Such disposal of personal effects is sometimes tantamount to acting out the last will and testament.
9 *Suicide is always an impulsive act.* There are several types of suicide. Some involve impulsive actions; some are very deliberately planned and carried out.

Five childhood myths

10 *Children under the age of 6 do not commit suicide.* On the contrary, too frequently, children in the age range 5–14 have completed suicide.
11 *Suicide in the latency years is extremely rare.* Since the mid-1990s, the child and adolescent suicide rate has increased.
12 *Psychodynamically and developmentally, true depression is not possible in childhood.* This outmoded myth has been proved untrue by recent findings in developmental psychology.
13 *A child cannot understand the finality of death.* The issue is not whether this myth is true or false; the fact is that children do attempt and complete suicide.
14 *Children are cognitively and physically incapable of implementing a suicide plan successfully.* The increasing number of childhood suicides is prima facie evidence of the error of this myth.

Sources: Fujimara et al., 1985; Greene, 1994.

This ambivalence can be helpful in working with suicidal ideation as open discussion and frankness will enable the client to feel understood and less alienated.

In their problem-solving strategies it will assist a person to adopt solutions other than suicide. It is important to note that as soon as assessment begins with a client, an intervention has also begun. The skilled practitioner will recognize 'the immense value of reaching out and listening to resolve a suicidal crisis, no matter how complex and apparently insoluble the individual's problems may seem' (Williams and Morgan, 1994, p. 16). It is important to assess whether a client is entertaining suicidal ideas at the present time. Open questions are used, such as, 'How do you feel about the future?' The client's response may be verbal and indirect, for example, 'I wish I could go to sleep and never wake up', or more direct, 'I wish I was dead'. Suicidal intentions are often expressed indirectly through non-verbal indications such as giving away personal possessions, or tidying up personal affairs. Paradoxically, the suicidal person's most serious attempt may occur as their mental state starts to improve. Now they have more energy and capability rather than when they were in the depths of depression (Gilliland and James, 1997; Joiner et al., 1999). Other non-verbal indications of suicide are the cessation of eating or drinking. Any expressions of hopelessness, helplessness or pessimism about the client's situation or the chances of recovery are important indicators of suicidal ideation.

A cognitive behavioural therapy perspective recognizes suicide as consistent with a person's thought processes (even though these might contain 'thinking errors' and may require elicitation). This contrasts with the generalized view that suicide is a senseless act. Suicide has its own coherence to the person who takes his or her own life. Although each suicide, like the person who commits it, is unique, it is a great help if the practitioner can make sense of a potential suicide from the client's point of view. This empathic understanding of the individual's suicidal framework of meaning is crucial for the practitioner to be able to help the individual take a step towards accepting life and its sometimes considerable difficulties. Developing cultural competence is also important (see Wendler and Matthews, 2006).

Ruddell and Curwen (2002) have tabulated some common characteristics proposed by Shneidman (1985, 1987) to help the practitioner to begin to understand this difficult process (see Table 5.2).

Assessing for risk of suicide

We have noted that the expression of suicidal ideation should always be taken seriously. It is important to view any individual who presents with suicidal symptomatology as posing a potential risk of suicide (Joiner et al., 1999, p. 448). When faced with an individual expressing suicidal tendencies, it is important to assess the content and degree of their current state (or to refer on to a suitable practitioner for such an assessment). An understanding of the factors helping to identify those at most risk of suicide is essential (Cooper and Kapur, 2004). We shall consider such risk factors first and then proceed to examine individual assessment.

For those who are at risk of suicide, well-established risk factors exist.

Table 5.2 Characteristics of suicide

Characteristic	Aspects of suicide	
Situational	Stimulus *'unendurable psychological pain'*	Stressor *'frustrated psychological needs'*
Conative	Purpose *'to seek solution'*	Goal *'cessation of consciousness'*
Affective	Emotion *'hopelessness/helplessness'*	Internal attitude *'ambivalence'*
Cognitive	Cognitive state *'constriction'* *(narrowing/blocking of ideas)*	
Relational	Interpersonal act *'communication of intention'*	Action *'egression' (departing)*
Serial	Consistency *'lifelong coping patterns'*	

Source: adapted from Shneidman, 1985.

These are shown in Table 5.3 and have been drawn from a range of sources (Bernard and Bernard, 1985; Gilliland, 1985; Hersh, 1985; Battle, 1991; Battle et al., 1993; Hazell and Lewin, 1993; Williams and Morgan, 1994; Department of Health, 2001; Cassells et al., 2005).

The risk factors are helpful in a number of ways. First, they may alert the practitioner to the potential for suicide of a person who appears to present no overt or explicit risk. Second, Gilliland and James (1997) suggest that the individual should be treated as high risk if four to five or more of the factors shown with an asterisk are manifested. Third, it is noteworthy that in 85 per cent of completed suicides, the individual had been regarded as being of low risk or no risk of suicide at their last contact with health professionals (Department of Health, 2001, p. 35).

Suicide is less common under the age of 14 (Shaffer, 1974) but an alarming increase in suicides of 75 per cent in the male 15–24 age group from 1982 has been recorded (Williams and Morgan, 1994) and there was a sharp peak in the male 25–34 age group (Department of Health, 2001, p. 17). Since the early 1980s, suicide rates have fallen in older men and women. The majority of suicides now occur in young adult males; in men under 35, suicide is the most common cause of death (Department of Health, 2002, p. 7).

Suicide is more common in men than women by a ratio of approximately three to one, increasing to five to one in adolescents (Department of Health, 2001, p. 17). Approximately one in four of the people committing suicide had been in contact with mental health services in the year before death (Department of Health, 2001, p. 3; see also Isometsa, 2000) and mental health teams in England and Wales regarded 22 per cent of suicides by people under mental health services as preventable (Department of Health, 2001,

Table 5.3 Factors associated with increased risk of suicide

Male

Single

Widowed

Divorced/separated

Elderly

Psychiatric illness (in decreasing order of risk)

- Depression*
- Schizophrenia
- Alcoholism*
- Drug addiction*
- Organic cerebral disorder (e.g. epilepsy, brain injury, mild dementia)
- Personality disorder (especially sociopathy, impulsivity, aggression, lability of mood)
- Anxiety disorders

Psychosis*

Hopelessness / helplessness*

Previous suicide attempt(s) / self-harm (parasuicide)*

Social isolation*/ rejection by others

Physical illness (life threatening / chronic / debilitating)*

Unemployed / retired

Family history of affective disorder, alcoholism or suicide*

Bereavement / loss (recent); preoccupation with anniversary of traumatic loss*

Childhood bereavement

Social classes I and V (i.e. the wealthiest and the poorest)

Family destabilization due to loss, personal abuse, violence, sexual abuse*

Recent trauma (physical / psychological)*

Specific suicide plan formulated*

Giving away prized possessions / putting personal affairs in order*

Radical changes in characteristic behaviours or moods*

Exhibits one or more uncharacteristic intense negative emotions*

Preoccupation with earlier abuse*

Note: As suggested by Gilliland and James (1997), an individual should be treated as high risk if four to five or more of the factors shown with an asterisk are manifested.

p. 3). The *National Suicide Prevention Strategy for England* (Department of Health, 2002) seeks to redress this situation by implementing the *Twelve Points to a Safer Service* (developed from the work of the National Confidential Inquiry: Appleby et al., 2001).

Over 90 per cent of people who commit suicide have been judged to have some form of psychiatric illness (Barraclough et al., 1974; Rich et al., 1986), with depression, schizophrenia, drug addiction and alcohol addiction as the main diagnoses found among suicide victims. Other risk factors for suicide include social problems, personality disorders, physical illness and life events. Research into life events, stress and illness shows that problems occur in both mental and physical health (Heikkinen et al., 1994). In the USA, people with AIDS have sixty-six times higher suicide rates than the general population (Marzuk et al., 1988). Prior to committing suicide a vast majority of people have made their intentions known to at least one other person (Robins et al., 1959). Between 23 per cent and 30 per cent of people discharged from psychiatric inpatient care in Great Britain successfully committed suicide within three months, with a peak within the first two weeks (Department of Health, 2001).

Roy (1982, 1992) has researched genetic and biological risk factors for suicide in depressive disorders. The tendency to suicidal behaviour may be familially transmitted by a mechanism distinct from the familial transmission of other psychiatric conditions (Brent et al., 1996). This is consistent with research distinguishing the familial aggregation of suicide from affective illness (Egeland and Sussex, 1985) and from endogenous psychosis (Mitterauer, 1990). However, the genetics of suicide is a complex area of research (Baldessarini and Hennen, 2004).

While suicidal risk often extends over a long period of time before suicide finally occurs, most individuals who recover from the immediate threat 'learn appropriate responses and controls, and live long, productive lives free of the threat of self-inflicted harm' (Gilliland and James, 1997, p. 194.) Although no two potential suicides are identical, the risk factors coupled with clinical observation can alert us to common patterns.

Methods used for suicide

Individuals who commit suicide use many different methods. Drug overdoses account for about two-thirds of suicides among women and one-third in men. The drugs commonly used are analgesics and antidepressants. In the UK from September 1998, the maximum pack size for over-the-counter sales of paracetamol and aspirin was reduced to thirty-two for pharmacies and sixteen for other outlets. This appears to have led to an initial fall in overdose deaths using these substances (Hawton et al., 2001). The most common methods used by males for suicide are hanging and car exhaust poisoning. The introduction of catalytic converters in motor vehicles for environmental reasons has led to a reduction in the number of suicides by this method (Amos et al., 2001). Men tend to use acts of violence more than women. Shooting is another form of suicide used by males but is much more common in the United States, where firearms are readily available. The remaining deaths in England and Wales are by a variety of physical means: jumping from high places, falling in front of moving vehicles or trains, drowning, cutting or stabbing, suffocation and electrocution (Symonds, 1985;

Department of Health, 2001, pp. 16–17). We have included these details because it is sometimes possible to remove the means of suicide either permanently (such as the removal of points in psychiatric hospitals from which patients can hang themselves) or temporarily until risk is diminished (such as limiting prescribed medication to only two weeks' supply: Department of Health, 2001, p. 10).

Suicide, like all other issues for which psychological help may be sought, is influenced by cultural differences. For example, some countries have a higher incidence of successful suicides than others, Japan being among the highest. Suicide is culturally prominent in Japan (Retterstol, 1993). For counsellors, psychotherapists, psychologists and other health professionals, cultural competence, i.e. the ability to work successfully in a multicultural and multiethnic society, is important and in particular, this applies to working with suicidal clients and patients. According to Wendler and Matthews (2006, p. 160), the practitioner needs to be

- sensitive to the operation of culture in human behaviour, including suicidal behaviour
- willing to get cultural consultation when necessary
- empathic to the emotional issues posed by cultural factors
- willing to view the clinician–patient interaction in a cultural context
- willing to use cultural factors in developing treatment plans and approaches.

Exploring suicidal ideation: the warning signs

The usual principles of good counselling and psychotherapy practice are especially important to enable a therapeutic bond and effective and efficient practice to take place: appropriate physical setting with low risk of interruption, unhurried pace, and conveying empathy using language appropriate to the client and sensitivity to cultural variations. The use of non-directive open questions will allow the client to ventilate issues and feelings that are important. Empathy is aided by using language that is appropriate for the client: this includes both the words chosen and the way they are spoken. Rapidly developing rapport and avoiding a brusque, challenging and judgemental approach are essential skills in this challenging work. Often, the client will repetitively discuss issues and themes pertinent to the suicidal process and this is best not discouraged. An inappropriate interview technique such as an aggressive questioning style may place individuals at risk. This is particularly so with impulsive personality-disordered individuals or those who are severely depressed and morbidly guilt-ridden (Goh et al., 1989).

Information gathering is very important in assessing a client for suicidality. Information may be available from a number of sources (Duffy and Ryan, 2004). While information gathered from the client, now, is the primary source, a number of other sources may be important too. If other agencies are involved, and your client consents, it may be helpful to obtain information from these, usually in the form of assessments or reports. Examples are the general practitioner, community mental health worker, social worker, counsellor, psychologist or psychiatric specialist. Where previous medical notes are available, then study the mental state examination. This will reveal whether a client has told someone before that they were thinking of hurting themselves or of suicide. If clients have made an attempt on their life previously, whether dangerous or token, this is an important predictor that suicide may be contemplated in the future. Prior to 1950, suicide and parasuicide were regarded as a single problem. Stengel (1952) then distinguished between the two forms of behaviour. He developed this distinction further a few years later (Stengel and Cook, 1958).

It is helpful to consider information from the client (whether obtained directly or from the sources referred to above) in the context of the risk factors outlined earlier. Three important factors to consider are as follows.

First, a person with a history of substance misuse may be particularly vulnerable because drugs and alcohol can prevent a person thinking logically and lead to impulsive suicidal behaviour. Second, a family history of suicide may model suicidal behaviour as a problem-solving technique. Third, cognitions of hopelessness have been shown to be one of the best predictors of suicidal ideation (Beck et al., 1974b). If a client strongly believes that living is an endless cycle of emotional pain and distress, suicide may be viewed as a more viable option than living. Once a practitioner has entered into discussion and dialogue about suicidal ideation, detailed notes should be made for later reference.

When suicidal ideation has been exposed or is suspected, open questioning is best continued to gently enquire whether a suicide plan exists, what methods have been considered and the degree to which there is a firm intention to act upon these thoughts. 'Tell me about any thoughts you've had of wanting to harm yourself?' is a simple question that may reveal the client has no plans of suicide: 'I've never really thought about it'. The question may reveal that a specific method has been considered: 'I've thought about just throwing myself off the bridge'. Discover when the client last had these thoughts of harming himself and how often they occur. Continue to explore such themes to establish the intensity of self-harming thoughts and whether they interfere with the individual's life. Before an act of suicide, a client may become more comfortable with the thought of dying and communicate no fear; she may communicate that death is seen as a happy release from suffering or as an opportunity for reunion with a dead parent or spouse. For example, Professor Hawton commented that Dr David Kelly's 'perfectly normal' behaviour just prior to his death was

> consistent with the notion that he had made a decision before that to end
> his life . . . and certainly it is not an unusual experience in people who
> have died by suicide, for people who knew them, or came into contact

with them shortly beforehand to say that they seemed actually better than they had been shortly before suicide . . . it is having decided on how to deal with the problem that leads to a sort of sense of peace and calm.

(www.the-hutton-inquiry.org.uk, 122: 5–14)

A person with a definite, clear and lethal plan to commit suicide in the next 24–48 hours is a severe risk. A place of safety or hospitalization is usually indicated. Supervision is required to prevent a suicide attempt by high-risk clients through close monitoring. This level of supervision may depend upon the setting in which the practitioner works. Some may be able to arrange for a psychiatric assessment immediately from within their own agency. Others may themselves need to take the client to their own general practitioner, or to the local accident and emergency unit for an assessment by a psychiatric doctor. Occasionally individuals may live with reliable and willing relatives or friends who understand the responsibilities and are able to fulfil them. This is a grave responsibility and a safe environment is vital. The practitioner's responsibility is to assess: individuals with an immediate, lethal and precise suicide plan will require a safe environment or hospitalization. It may be necessary to go outside the realms of the confidential relationship to prevent suicidal ideation becoming a reality.

While such a plan for suicide constitutes a high risk, suicide may also be an impulsive act. Williams and Morgan (1994, p. 21) note that 'it is likely that the easy availability of an effective method of self-destruction can be crucial at a time when hope fails and despair worsens'. They point out that as despair is often a transient state, lasting minutes or hours, 'the technique of playing for time, and devising ways of defusing such crises, and identifying life-lines, can be of great importance in reducing the acute risk of suicide'. Goal 3 of the *National Suicide Prevention Strategy for England* aims to reduce the availability and lethality of suicide methods such as the identification of additional steps that can be taken to promote safer prescribing of antidepressants and analgesics and helping local services identify their suicide 'hotspots' such as railways and bridges and take steps to improve safety at these (Department of Health, 2002).

While suicidal risk often extends over a long period of time before suicide finally occurs, most individuals who recover from the immediate threat 'learn appropriate responses and controls, and live long, productive lives free of the threat of self-inflicted harm' (Gilliland and James, 1997, p. 194). Although no two potential suicides are identical, the risk factors coupled with clinical observation can alert us to common patterns.

Assessment forms and questionnaires

Assessment forms and questionnaires may be very useful as tools to be used in conjunction with other clinical methods to assess the suicidal potential of the individual and to evaluate progress throughout therapy. The advantages of such forms are that they can enhance the effectiveness of the assessment (Bloom and Fischer, 1982). However, there are important caveats: 'suicide risk in any individual can only be assessed effectively by full clinical evaluation consisting of a thorough review of the history and present illness, assessment of mental state and then a diagnostic formulation' (Williams and Morgan, 1994, p. 19); the potential for suicide is too complex to be measured by a single score or sign (Eyman and Eyman, 1991); and effective intervention and prevention activities require a comprehensive assessment for suicidality (Schwartz and Rogers, 2004). Regardless of the assessment and tools used, the prediction of suicide still remains difficult (see Amsel and Mann, 2001).

Questionnaires can assist the practitioner to make a rapid and efficient assessment, and are generally easy to administer. The forms are readily available (to suitably qualified professionals) and provide access to information about the client that may be hard to observe overtly. By using questionnaires, comparisons can be made with some established norms and a client's progress measured. Scores are best regarded as provisional and should not be accepted uncritically. Individual components (or questions) within an assessment form can also be used as starting points for ongoing therapeutic work.

Some useful questionnaires relating to suicide are as follows:

- Reasons for Living Scale (Linehan, 1985) to measure adaptive characteristics in suicide
- Scale for Suicide Ideation (Beck et al., 1971)
- Hopelessness Scale / Beck Hopelessness Scale (Beck et al., 1974b; Beck, 1993) to assess degree of suicide risk
- Prediction of Suicide Scale (Beck et al., 1974a)
- Los Angeles Suicide Prevention Scale (Los Angeles Center for Suicide Prevention, 1973)
- Beck Depression Inventory – II (Beck et al., 1961; Beck, 1978; Beck and Steer, 1987; Beck et al., 1996)
- Scale for Assessment of Suicidal Potentiality (Battle, 1985)
- PATHOS Screening questionnaire (following adolescent deliberate self-harm) (Kingsbury, 1993)
- The SAD PERSONS Scale (Patterson et al., 1983): an acronym for assessing Sex, Age, Depression, Previous attempt, Ethanol (or other substance abuse), Rational thinking loss, Social supports lacking, Organized plan, No spouse and Sickness (chronic, severe or debilitating medical/psychiatric illness)
- Minnesota Multiphasic Personality Inventory – Two suicide items (MMPI–2) (Butcher et al., 1989)
- Suicide Probability Scale (Cull and Gill, 1982)
- Suicide Assessment Checklist (Rogers et al., 1994)
- Thematic Guide for Suicide Prediction (TGSP) (see Leenaars, 2004).

It is worth reading Reinecke and Franklin-Scott (2005) if the intention is to use Beck's scales for assessing mood and suicidailty, and Range and Knott (1997) for an evaluation of twenty suicide assessment instruments. The use of some tests such as the Rorschach Inkblot Test has been overtaken by more sophisticated tools such as the MMPI–2 (see Sullivan and Bongar, 2006).

Conclusion

Any person who wishes to end their life may find a way to do so. It is hoped that the initiatives referred to by governments and others in *the wider picture* will reduce the numbers of completed suicides. At an individual level, the use of the information in this chapter alongside the principles and practice of the models in which practitioners are trained can help to reduce such actions too (Rudd et al., 2001). It is important to remain aware of the factors that have been identified for those most at risk of suicide and to be fully aware of the challenges to the common myths associated with suicide that we have outlined above. The majority of people who commit suicide have made their intentions known to at least one other person and it is therefore important to take all messages about suicide seriously. A previous attempt at suicide is an important predictor that suicide may be contemplated in the future. Exploring suicidal ideation with a client does not make suicidal behaviour more likely. The opposite is true and it is important to approach with the conviction that it is possible to prevent at least some suicides and to reach out with the potential suicidal client to find different solutions to their problems. It is particularly important to ensure that appropriate clinical supervision is utilized, and where appropriate a multidisciplinary team be involved alongside the client in any decision-making process. Questionnaires are helpful in assessing the suicidal potential of individuals when used in conjunction with other assessment methods. Clients with an immediate, lethal and precise suicide plan will require a safe environment or hospitalization. Knowledge of methods used for suicides may enable the practitioner to be aware of the potential dangers for a particular individual. Practitioners may benefit by continuing to develop their knowledge and understanding of suicide from this book and from other sources and training. A good starting point can be found in *Safety First: Five Year Report of the National Confidential Enquiry into Suicide and Homicide by People with Mental Illness* (Department of Health, 2001), which is freely available on the internet, or for an advanced book, the *Textbook of Suicide Assessment and Management* (Simon and Hales, 2006).

References

Amos, T., Appleby, L. and Kieran, K. (2001) Changes in rate of suicide by car exhaust asphyxiation in England and Wales. *Psychological Medicine*, 31, 935–939.
Amsel, L. and Mann, J.J. (2001) Suicide risk assessment and the suicidal process

approach, in K. van Heeringen (ed.) *Understanding Suicidal Behaviour: The suicidal process approach to research, treatment and prevention.* Chichester: Wiley.

Appleby, L., Shaw, J., Sherratt, J., Amos, T., Robinson, J., McDonnell, R. et al. (2001) *Safety First: National Confidential Inquiry into Suicide and Homicide by People with Mental Illness.* London: Department of Health.

Baldessarini, R.J. and Hennen, J. (2004) Genetics of suicide: an overview. *Harvard Review of Psychiatry*, 12(1), 1–13.

Barraclough, B.M., Bunch, J., Nelson, B. and Sainsbury, P. (1974) A hundred cases of suicide: clinical aspects. *British Journal of Psychiatry*, 125, 355–373.

Battle, A.O. (1985) *Outpatient management of the suicidal adolescent* (paper, presentation, and assessment instrument). Symposium on Suicide in Teenagers and Young Adults, University of Tennessee, College of Medicine, Department of Psychiatry, Memphis, TN, USA.

Battle, A.O. (1991) *Factors in assessing suicidal lethality.* Paper presented at Crisis Center Preservice Volunteer Training, University of Tennessee, College of Medicine, Department of Psychiatry, Memphis, TN, USA.

Battle, A.O., Battle, M.V. and Tolley, E.A. (1993) Potential for suicide and aggression in delinquents at juvenile court in a southern city. *Suicide and Life-Threatening Behavior*, 23(3), 230–243.

Beck, A.T. (1978) *Depression Inventory.* Philadelphia, PA: Center for Cognitive Therapy.

Beck, A.T. (1993) *Beck Hopelessness Scale.* San Antonio, TX: The Psychological Corporation.

Beck, A.T. and Steer, R.A. (1987) *Manual for the Revised Beck Depression Inventory.* San Antonio, TX: The Psychological Corporation.

Beck, A.T., Ward, C.H., Mendelson, M., Mock, J.E. and Erbaugh, J.K. (1961) An inventory for measuring depression. *Archives of General Psychiatry*, 4, 451–471.

Beck, A.T., Kovacs, M. and Weissman, A. (1971) Assessment of suicidal ideation: the scale for suicidal ideation. *Journal of Consulting and Clinical Psychology*, 47, 343–352.

Beck, A.T., Schuyler, D. and Herman, I. (1974a) Development of suicidal intent scales, in A.T. Beck, H.L.P. Resnik and D.J. Lettieri (eds) *The Prediction of Suicide.* Bowie, MD: Charles Press.

Beck, A.T., Weissman, A., Lester, D. and Trexter, L. (1974b) The measurement of pessimism: the hopelessness scale. *Journal of Consulting and Clinical Psychology*, 42, 861–865.

Beck, A.T., Steer, R.A. and Brown, G.K. (1996) *Depression Inventory – II* San Antonio, TX: The Psychological Corporation.

Bernard, J.L. and Bernard, M.L. (1985) Suicide on campus: response to the problem, in E.S. Zinner (ed.) *Coping with Death on Campus.* San Francisco, CA: Jossey-Bass.

Bloom, M. and Fischer, J. (1982) *Evaluating Practice: Guidelines for the accountable professional.* Englewood Cliffs, NJ: Prentice Hall.

Brent, D.A., Bridge, J., Johnson, B.A. and Connolly, J. (1996) Suicidal behavior runs in families: a controlled family study of adolescent suicide victims. *Archives of General Psychiatry*, 53, 1145–1152.

Butcher, J.N., Dahlstrom, W.G., Graham, J.R., Tellegen, A.M. and Kaemmer, B. (1989) *MMPI–2 Manual for Administration and Scoring.* Minneapolis, MN: University of Minneapolis Press.

Cassells, C., Paterson, B., Dawding, D. and Morrison, R. (2005) Long- and short-term risk factors in the prediction of inpatient suicide: a review of the literature. *Crisis*, 26(2), 53–63.

Cooper, J. and Kapur, N. (2004) Assessing suicide risk, in D. Duffy and T. Ryan (eds) *New Approaches to Preventing Suicide: A manual for practitioners*. London: Jessica Kingsley Publishers.

Cull, J.G. and Gill, W.S. (1982) *Suicide Probability Scale Manual*. Los Angeles, CA: Western Psychological Services.

Department of Health (1992) *The Health of the Nation: A strategy for health in England*. London: HMSO.

Department of Health (1999) *National Service Framework for Mental Health: Modern standards and service models*. London: HMSO.

Department of Health (2001) *Safety First: Five year report of the National Confidential Enquiry into Suicide and Homicide by People with Mental Illness*. London: HMSO.

Department of Health (2002) *National Suicide Prevention Strategy for England*. London. Department of Health Publications.

Duffy, D. and Ryan, T. (eds) (2004) *New Approaches to Preventing Suicide: A manual for practitioners*. London: Jessica Kingsley Publishers.

Egeland, J.A. and Sussex, J.N. (1985) Suicide and family loading for affective disorders. *Journal of the American Medical Association*, 254, 915–918.

Eyman, J.R. and Eyman, S.K. (1991) Personality assessment in suicide prediction. *Suicide and Life-Threatening Behavior*, 21, 37–55.

Fujimura, L.E., Weis, D.M. and Cochran, J.R. (1985) Suicide: dynamics and implications for counselling. *Journal of Counseling and Development*, 63, 612–615.

Gilliland, B.E. (1985) *Surviving college: teaching college students to cope* (paper and presentation). Symposium on Suicide in Teenagers and Young Adults, University of Tennessee, College of Medicine, Department of Psychiatry, Memphis, TN, USA.

Gilliland, B.E. and James, R.K. (1997) *Crisis Intervention Strategies*. New York: Brooks Cole.

Goh, S.E., Salmons, P.H. and Whittington, R.M. (1989) Suicide in psychiatric hospitals. *British Journal of Psychiatry*, 154, 247–250.

Greene, D.B. (1994) Childhood suicide and myths surrounding it. *Social Work*, 39, 230–233.

Hawton, K., Townsend, E., Deeks, J., Appleby, L., Gunnell, D., Bennewith, O. and Cooper, J. (2001) Effects of pack legislation restricting pack sizes of paracetamol and salicylates on self-poisoning in the United Kingdom: before and after study. *British Medical Journal*, 322(7296), 1203–1207.

Hazell, P. and Lewin, T. (1993) An evaluation of postvention following adolescent suicide. *Suicide and Life Threatening Behavior*, 23(2), 101–109.

Heikkinen, M., Aro, H. and Lonnquist, J. (1994) Recent life events, social support and suicide. *Acta Psychiatrica Scandinavica*, 377, 65–72.

Hersh, J.B. (1985) Interviewing college students in crisis. *Journal of Counseling and Development*, 63, 286–289.

Hutton Inquiry (2003) www.the-hutton-inquiry.org.uk

Isometsa, E.T. (2000) Suicide. *Current Opinion in Psychiatry*, 13, 143–147.

Joiner, T., Walker, R., Rudd, M. and Jobes, D (1999) Scientising and routinising the assessment of suicidality in outpatient practice. *Professional Psychology: Research and Practice*, 30(5), 447–453.

Kingsbury, S. (1993) Parasuicide in adolescence: a message in a bottle. *Association for Child Psychology and Psychiatry Review and Newsletter*, 15, 253–259.

Leenaars, A.A. (2004) *Psychotherapy with suicidal people: a person-centred approach.* Chichester: Wiley.

Linehan, M.M. (1985) The reasons for living scale, in P.A. Keller and L.G. Ritts (eds) *Innovations in Clinical Practice: A source book*, Volume 4. Sarasota, FL: Professional Resource Exchange.

Los Angeles Center for Suicide Prevention (LACSP) (1973) *Los Angeles Suicide Prevention Scale.* Los Angeles, CA: LACSP.

Marzuk, P., Tierney, H., Tardiff, K., Gross, E., Morgan, E., Hsu, M.A. and Mann, J. (1988) Increased risk of suicide in persons with AIDS. *Journal of the American Medical Association*, 259(9), 1333–1337.

Mitterauer, B. (1990) A contribution to the discussion of the role of the genetic factor in suicide, based on five studies in an epidemiologically defined area (Province of Salzburg, Austria). *Comprehensive Psychiatry*, 31, 557–565.

NIMHE (2006) *National Suicide Prevention Strategy for England. Annual report on progress 2005.* Leeds: Care Services Improvement Partnership, National Institute for Mental Health in England.

Patterson, W.M., Dohn, H.H., Bird, J. and Patterson, G.A. (1983) Evaluation of suicidal patients: the SAD PERSONS Scale. *Psychosomatics*, 24(4), 343–345, 348–349.

Range, L.M. and Knott, E.C. (1997) Twenty suicide assessment instruments: evaluation and recommendations. *Death Studies*, 21, 25–58.

Reinecke, M.A. and Franklin-Scott, R.L. (2005) Assessment of suicide: Beck's scales for assessing mood and suicidality, in R.I.Yufit and D. Lester (eds) *Assessment, Treatment, and Prevention of Suicidal Behavior.* New York: Wiley.

Retterstol, N. (1993) *Suicide: A European perspective.* Cambridge: Cambridge University Press.

Rich, C.L., Young, D. and Fowler, R.C. (1986) San Diego suicide study I: young vs old subjects. *Archives of General Psychiatry*, 43, 577–582.

Robins, E., Gassner, S., Kayes, J., Wilkinson, R.H. and Murphy, G.E. (1959) The communication of suicidal intent: a study of 134 successful (completed) suicides. *American Journal of Psychiatry*, 115, 724–733.

Rogers, J.R., Alexander, R.A. and Subich, L.M. (1994) Development and psychometric analysis of the suicide assessment checklist. *Journal of Mental Health Counselling*, 16, 352–368.

Roy, A. (1982) Risk factors for suicide in psychiatric patients. *Archives of General Psychiatry*, 39, 1089–1095.

Roy, A. (1992) Marked reductions in indexes of dopamine metabolism among patients with depression who attempted suicide. *Archives of General Psychiatry*, 49, 447–450.

Rudd, M.D., Joiner, T. and Rajab, M.H. (2001) *Treating Suicidal Behavior: An effective, time-limited approach.* New York: Guilford.

Ruddell, P. and Curwen, B. (2002) Understanding suicidal ideation and assessing for risk. *British Journal of Guidance and Counselling*, 30(4), 363–372.

Schwartz, R.C. and Rogers, J.R. (2004) Suicide assessment and evaluation strategies: a primer for counselling psychologists. *Counselling Psychology Quarterly*, 17(1), 89–97.

Shneidman, E.S. (1985) *Definition of Suicide.* New York: Wiley.

Shneidman, E.S. (1987) At the point of no return: suicidal thinking follows a predictable path. *Psychology Today*, March, 54–58.

Shneidman, E.S., Farberow, N.L. and Litman, R.E. (1976) *The Psychology of Suicide*. New York: Aronson.

Shaffer, D. (1974) Suicide in childhood and early adolescence. *Journal of Child Psychology and Psychiatry*, 15, 275–291.

Simon, R.I. and Hales, R.E. (2006) *Textbook of Suicide Assessment and Management*. Washington, DC: American Psychiatric Publishing.

Stengel, E. (1952) Enquiries into attempted suicide. *Proceedings of the Royal Society of Medicine*, 45, 613–620.

Stengel, E. and Cook, N.G. (1958) *Attempted Suicide: Its social significance and effects*. Maudsley Monograph no. 4. London: Chapman and Hall.

Sullivan, G.R. and Bongar, B. (2006) Psychological testing in suicide risk management, in R.I. Simon and R.E. Hales (eds) *Textbook of Suicide Assessment and Management*. Washington, DC: American Psychiatric Publishing.

Symonds, R.L. (1985) Psychiatric aspects of railway fatalities. *Psychological Medicine*, 15, 609–621.

Wendler, S. and Matthews, D. (2006) Cultural competence in suicide risk assessment, in R.I. Simon and R.E. Hales (eds) *Textbook of Suicide Assessment and Management*. Washington, DC: American Psychiatric Publishing.

Williams, R. and Morgan, H.G. (eds) (1994) *Suicide Prevention: The challenge confronted*. London: HMSO.

Part II

Personal experience of suicide

6 It's a funny thing about suicide

Susan Walen

In contrast to discussions about suicide from medical, psychiatric, psychological and other objectivist perspectives, this chapter focuses vividly on its personal, subjective aspects. The complex role of suicidal rumination in the *course of a chronic and intermittently exacerbated depression* is discussed, as are the importance of cognitive schema, interpersonal *perturbations*, and failed diagnosis. A key feature of this chapter is the central heuristic of a therapist disclosing and examining her own suicidality.

The woman behind me tapped me on the shoulder and, smiling at my face, wanted to know if I'd been into the wine too much. On my right, my husband whispered to me, 'It isn't *that* funny, is it?' I was laughing too loudly, or too much, I suppose. I was in a good mood, but I'm beginning to fear that I can't trust those any more. They've become thinner and thinner, like an opaque glass floor being abraded until it's crazed. Like me. Until it's so thin that I can see where I'm going to fall. I know that place; it's my depression.

'My' depression. I sort of smile as I write that, as if it's a 'thing', a thing which I claim, almost with a sense of pride. I've largely stopped being ashamed of it, although each time I 'come out', on the ledge where you find me now, it's always a little scary. I've studied this 'thing' for decades, I've held my patients as they fight it, I've loved people who suffer it, I've observed its terrible tidal force in my own life, but dare I try to tell you about it?

My depression is so enormous, so engulfing, so ephemeral, so personal. How can I find words to speak of it, when the organ I need to use can get twisted by its own pain that-is-not-pain. It's so tricky. Sometimes it's a fog with no edges, no clear boundaries, so that I can't tell it's beginning to swirl around me until I'm deeply lost in it or until it lifts and I can look back on it from a happier place. Other times, like now, it's as if I've fallen through one of those cracks in my glass floor. My leg is caught but I know that soon, if I'm calm and methodical, I'll be able to hoist myself up again.

When I'm very sick, I yearn for death. I dream of it, I fantasize about it, it feels as though it would be as sweet as yielding to anaesthesia. It's an ace in the hole. It's my safety net. Thinking about it gives me the only relief I can find, sometimes. Strangely, suicide gives me hope. Very few people understand this, especially my family. They have a hard time grasping that depression, when I'm in it, makes me numb. I know they love me, but I can't feel it, just as I love them, but cannot transmit it. When I'm really sick, I say to myself that I can't remember why I'm supposed to stay alive.

Would it surprise you to learn that I also love my depression? It's been with me all my life. I grew up in its lap, learning to be silly to make my sad mother smile for a moment. She trained us all to be clowns: my father, my sister, and me. From the stories, I think my Russian grandmother had it too. She was said to be quite lovely but also melancholic, sitting by the window for endless hours, hand-stitching and singing the same mournful love song over and over. I know that song. It's been passed down as a bittersweet legacy to my daughter, along with the illness.

I like the rhythm that depression gives to my life, although the beats are getting stronger and the tempo seems to be picking up as I age. In some ways, I prefer its sharp rhythm; it comes like seasons in a year or cycles in the moon. The tides of these waves have defined the eras of my life. Now I understand why my childhood memories are so draped by our mulberry tree. It was small, like me then, and I spent great caches of time alone, feeling protected under its drooping branches, only occasionally finding the pleasure of the perfectly ripened berry. I realized only later why I was the thinnest girl in our Bat Mitzvah group in my thirteenth year. I realize now why love has always hit me so hard, especially when it's nurturing, or again, when it's over. Before I knew its name, I would describe myself as a passionate person, but depression has a much grander and more elongated sweep than passion.

Depression has been my teacher and I've been its excited student, not looking forward to the next lesson, but inevitably stretched and enlightened by the encounter. It's humbled me, tumbled me, but always taught me something. I can sense its presence around me, I can see it in the eyes of others, I can tell when I'm sitting with someone who's felt it themselves. We are kinfolk, and there are so many of us. I'll often recognize you before you do.

The essay above, written during a writing programme in the summer of 1997, was the last piece I wrote on depression. This past fall, I received an email from Dr Stephen Palmer, who wrote:

Some years ago I read a very moving chapter of yours while undertaking my Rational Emotive Behaviour Therapy (REBT) training and I wondered whether you would consider writing an article for the symposium on: 'Suicidal despair: a personal perspective'. I hope you do not mind me writing to you about this personal issue.

Mind? I was delighted that the work had been read, remembered, and most importantly, had moved someone. What better lemonade could one make from the lemon of depression?

The piece to which Dr Palmer referred was entitled 'Depression and RET: perspectives from wounded healers' (Walen and Rader, 1991). It too was solicited by an editor, Michael Bernard, who invited 'seasoned practitioners' of rational emotive therapy (the previous name for REBT) to write about how their practice had evolved and improved in the years since our training. I agreed to write on the treatment of depression, but warned Michael that my topic would include when *not* to do RET, and even when RET can have 'dire iatrogenic consequences' (Walen and Rader, 1991, pp. 248–252).

In the same spirit of contrariness, I suppose, you may note that I have changed Dr Palmer's suggested title of 'Suicidal despair' to 'It's a funny thing about suicide'. I would like to give you the perspective of one 'wounded healer's' experience of suicidality.

First: on self-disclosure

It is never easy. Not only is there a very real stigma associated with 'mental illness', but also it is worse when the patient is a mental health practitioner. In an anonymously published account of his depression, one British psychiatrist described his plight as follows: 'God, how I longed then that my depression be magically changed into a decent, straightforward physical ailment! The psychiatric hospital is intolerant of weakness in its staff. Compassion is for patients; for "them" not "us" ' (Rippere and Williams, 1985, p. 15).

If coming out of the closet with depression as a chronic, recurrent illness runs the risk of stigmatization, how much greater the feeling of vulnerability to describe a lifelong fascination with and flirtation with death. This has been a secret affair, my private experience, difficult to share with even (or especially) my closest friends. Death, to most people, seems to be such a fearsome and terrible thing, it seems a kindness not to discuss it.

It is also difficult to describe what Jamison (1999) has so beautifully named the 'moods of death' because, in some way, I cannot truly re-experience them. Perhaps it is like childbirth: most women remember the experience cognitively, but affectively or somatically, they dissociate from it. I can remember the experience of deep depression, but without the full affective loading, which may be a naturally protective repression process. Or perhaps it is merely that memory is state-dependent; affective pain may not be encoded for memory retrieval in a non-depressed state. Another part of me is perhaps also afraid that I *will* be affected by writing about depression and suicide.[1] Nonetheless, I will try to re-create some of the phenomenology, largely by weaving together bits and pieces of previously silent and private journal entries.

A bit of personal background

I remember thinking about death as early as I can remember thinking. Mostly, those were times of night terrors as a very small child, worrying about dying. I can picture myself running to my parents' bedroom, crying and not having the words to describe my fears, and I can see their faces, confused and irritated. One such episode stands out in my memory quite vividly. That night I finally was able to say my fear aloud: 'I am afraid of dying!' And I remember what my mother taught me that night. She said dying was like childbirth. When you are pregnant, she said, you're afraid of the birth, of the pain ... but as the baby grows and the mother gets more uncomfortable, she actually looks forward to the birth, as a relief. It's the same with death, she assured me; when you get very old and it's time to die, you no longer are afraid of it, but you look forward to it. Strangely, I remember being comforted by those words.

Affective disorders clearly run down the maternal line of my family. It was probably depression along with the grinding toll of poverty that kept my grandmother from adequately nurturing her youngest and most anxious child, my mother, who, instead, was largely tended by the oldest daughter, 13 years of age. That anxious maternal bond was broken when I was 2; my grandmother was hit by a car and killed while on her way to English class one rainy night. I do not remember her, but I remember the endless reliving of that death and the ones that followed it. Illness, accident and death seemed to lurk in the corners of the house and were greatly to be feared. In fact, we were not allowed to have pets as children, because they could die.

'Now I lay me down to sleep. I pray my Lord my soul to keep. If I should die before I wake, I pray my Lord my soul to take.' That was the nightly prayer for my sister and me, which took on a particularly potent quality when we were ill, for our childhood illnesses clearly distressed my mother. Typically, she would sleep in our room when we were sick, curled at the foot of the bed to ward off the named danger.

I have a sense of being alone a great deal as a child, out of which came repeated requests for a sibling to play with, although my mother's ability to tolerate children seemed to be already sorely taxed by me, whom she usually referred to as 'a handful'. The arrival of my sister did not improve things, however, as my mother sank into what I later realized was a severe post-partum depression. I can recall a 'lady in white' who walked with strangely quiet shoes in and out of the darkened bedroom, reminding me to be quiet so mother could rest. Sadly, I discovered that the new baby could not play, and I was not allowed to touch her for fear that I would hurt her. I spent many hours reading.

As a consequence, words have always interested me, and I remember, as a child, finding one word that seemed particularly delicious: euthanasia. The look of it, the sound of it, and the meaning of it captivated me. I think I wrote my first term paper on it in the fifth grade.

For many years, I held a deep conviction that I would 'die young', by which I meant some time before age 25. In some peculiar way, a part of me was disappointed each year when that never came about.

Somewhere in young adulthood I read of the Scottish right-to-die society, and sent off a letter of inquiry addressed just that way, to Scotland. Many, many months later I actually received a reply, referring me to several fledgling organizations in the United States. Years later, I attended the first meeting of the Hemlock Society, became a charter member of the state division, and donated some of my savings to become a lifetime member. My library of newsletters, pamphlets, and books on death, suicide and aid in dying is quite extensive.

I'll close this section of the chapter by telling you the exact moment when I lost my fear of death. It occurred in my kitchen, in a small town in Germany, just after I put my 2-year-old son down for his afternoon nap. Looking out over the potato field that was our back yard, I was suddenly suffused with a profound sense of peace, settling over me like a warm cape on my shoulders. I recall asking myself what that could be, and it came to me that – although I could not have enumerated my life goals had I been asked – I had done all that I would have wanted to do. I had married, attained my PhD, had a child, and seen a bit of the world. The rest was gravy. If the 'grim reaper' came for me, I might not go happily, but I would not feel I had been cheated of any important life experience. I felt very lucky, indeed.

Depressive despair and suicidal relief

I want to register a complaint about the word 'depression.' . . . Melancholia, as opposed to depression, would appear to be a far more apt and evocative word for the blacker forms of the disorder, but it was usurped by a term with such a bland tonality that it lacks any magisterial presence, used indifferently to describe an economic decline or a rut in the ground, a true wimp of a word for such a major illness . . . for 75 years the word has slithered innocuously through the language like a slug, leaving little trace of its intrinsic malevolence and preventing, by its very insipidity, a general awareness of the horrible intensity of the disease when out of control. As one who has suffered from the malady in extremis, yet returned to tell the tale, I would lobby for a truly arresting designation. 'Brainstorm', for instance, has unfortunately been preempted to describe, somewhat jocularly, intellectual inspiration. But something along these lines is needed. Told that someone's mood disorder had evolved into a storm – a veritable howling tempest in the brain – which is indeed what clinical depression resembles like nothing else – even the uninformed layman might display sympathy rather than the standard reaction that depression evokes, something akin to 'So what?' or 'You'll pull out of it' or 'We all have a bad day.'

(Styron, 1989)

It is very difficult to describe and to delineate what we mean by depression, for most people use the word loosely, sometimes to describe a downward turn in mood (more properly, sadness, a *symptom*). Sometimes the mood is accompanied by certain cognitive and behavioural changes (separate *clinical signs*), but most precisely, we speak of biologically based and clinically variant forms of major affective disorders (or *syndromal illnesses*). Let me try to recapture some of the experience I had when I was quite ill by referring to my journals, which often served merely as nursing notes. The personal writings from my journals are set in italics.

I felt sick

I'm shaky and racing inside, comforted only when I carry the doll clutched to my chest like a madwoman. I just want to stay in bed. My muscles feel achy. I'm more and more draggy as the day wears on. I could feel my blood pressure was up, experienced as swells. My rod (night) vision seemed to deteriorate. I was very tense in my muscles, and my teeth were almost constantly clenched. I had a sense of frenzy, crankiness, and illness.

My internal thermometer seems to be broken. I was alternately shaking with chills or feeling hot. I kept taking my temperature, but it was always normal. Nevertheless, the cold was felt very keenly in my extremities, especially in my hands and feet.

Sleep was often unavailable. *Woke before the children's alarms; vivid dreams, twice, about being robbed. Didn't sleep last night till after 4:30. Night before last, I went to sleep at 10 and was awake at 10:45! Yesterday, I was so groggy I could barely work or drive.* So, both quality and quantity of sleep were disturbed; I woke many times in a night, had early morning awakening, and always awoke with a startle reaction.

I literally could not eat. Food looked nauseating to me. *Tried to eat, but later had terrible stomach distress and explosive bowel movement. Stomach sour . . . lots of gas . . . making so much noise!* I felt like my digestive system had shut down.

My brain felt sick

My thoughts are very obsessional. I'm going over and over the same stuff . . . different angles, but same stuff. At one point, my teenaged son tearfully told me I was frightening him because I kept asking him the same questions repeatedly (e.g. 'Do you think I made a mistake?'). Even when I could check my verbalizations, the ruminative thinking went on, unchecked and uncheckable.

My concentration was sorely taxed. *I'm feeling spacey . . . having trouble concentrating. My thoughts drift off into reveries, fantasies, longings, etc. My head feels as if it's stuffed with toilet paper. Wooly headed and shaky. Somewhat hard to read and concentrate.* I had a mild, chronic headache or sense of pressure, and a 'buzzing' sensation in my head. My thinking felt fuzzy. I experienced a dullness of my intellect. My memory, especially in retrieval, was significantly impaired.

My mood was barely malleable

This doesn't feel quite the same as the trapped despair I felt when I was unhappily married the first time, although I sure was sad then. Nor like the intense sadness and longing when R. and I parted, although I certainly sobbed plenty then. This feels sick! This sadness had a unique feel to it, and a depth that was difficult to describe, often mixed with a welter of other emotions. *Very very sad again. Distracted and guilty and anxious. I'm getting scared.* More to the point, I was unable to shift my mood, no matter what techniques I used, for more than a few moments at a time. *My conversation is filled with depressing talk, and it's like I can't stop it . . .* and, *I cannot sustain my positive mood with cognitive therapy.*

Even crying was strange. *Wept for about an hour today. I can talk aloud to myself and dry up my tears, but within a minute, they're back again.* The crying I did was unlike crying spells I'd ever had. I had always cried quietly and privately. Now, when I cried, I was racked with sobs. I would frequently cry through the course of a day. Often, at midday, I would have an unexplained crying spell, not tied to any environmental happening. At those times, I would weep for hours. My emotional lability was astonishing to me.

I felt so alone. *There is a huge gulf between me and all others; I have a sense of being a speck in the void. I can't feel connected!* Aloneness was particularly striking and was probably the most painful part of the depression for me. There was a terrifying sense of being totally alone in the universe and existentially isolated from all of humanity. I was unconnected with my children, my parents, friends, and even from my psychiatrist. No one was in the same plane of existence as I. I was totally in a vacuum and left floating in the universe, horribly alone.

I was in pain

I have had patients say that the pain of depression is worse than any physical pain they'd experienced, and now I can truly understand what they meant. Living, in periods of depression, were the most painful times in my life. The suffering seemed worse than any prior suffering. It is difficult to express how intense an experience it was. Even William Styron, Pulitzer Prize winning author, found his descriptive powers challenged. He states: 'depression's exquisite torment can never really be communicated . . . my days were pervaded by a gray drizzle of unrelenting horror. This horror is virtually indescribable, since it bears no relation to normal experience' (Styron, 1989, p. 214).

Only two things comforted me: keeping nursing notes on myself (which I did at least every 15 minutes or so when very ill) and fantasizing about death.

Coping by dreaming of suicide

One of the funny things about death thoughts, as I reflect on them, is that in the midst of the pain of a deep depressive episode, there is little ability to plan, little energy to do, little pleasure to be had from the fantasy of dying. My death thoughts at those times were more like images or little scenes (of hanging, jumping, shooting, for example), but contained no plan and few details. I have never held a gun nor learned to tie a decent knot. Yet the thoughts would bubble up into my head throughout the day, and I would drift with them unless I was otherwise occupied. Although the lethality of these thoughts was high, my intent (or my ability to intend) was low. I also knew that I had to wrap up my affairs before I could die; I did not want to leave a mess or a messy estate for my loved ones, and I was in no shape to do all that planning and decision-making. But in fantasy, I have died many hundreds of times.

At the other extreme, perhaps, are the very passive death thoughts: e.g., I don't care if I wake up tomorrow. I don't care if the plane I'm on crashes. Or, at the end of the year, writing what others might mail out as their Christmas letter, I wrote as my private summary: *It's been a very rich, full year of family, friends, travels and accomplishments, but I really don't care if I have another one.* Year after year, my journal ends on that note, even though I would have denied depression, and the world would not have seen me as depressed for much of that time. To me, that note is not sad; it just 'is'.

So, although I feel that my death has been just behind my left shoulder most of my life, there was only one time that I turned to meet it, head on, and that will be my last story.

Thinking about dying can make living beautiful

In my young fifties, I married for the second time, after a long and torturous courtship and despite serious last-minute doubts (which my married friends helped me reconcile as normal wedding jitters!). To effect this match, I left my home, my city, my tenured academic job, my friends, and my clinical practice, and began anew as the part-time stepmother of three and wife of a wealthy, prominent and very solitary man. In the clarity of retrospective vision, it was hardly likely to be a good match for my depression and schema-driven issues.[2] In fact, both began to fester, and I found it harder and harder to feel content with my life, and as my mood foundered, so did my problem-solving. I worked hard to accept my situation and not 'awfulize' about it, I tried delicately (and indelicately) to create relationship changes, I tried avoidance by throwing myself into other activities to feel fulfilled and appreciated, and I even took in two lively puppies to love and be sources of kisses. Yet the path of my mood continued downward. I was able to convince my husband to do some couples therapy, a year with one therapist, somewhat less with a second, adding medications for my growing depression along the way, none of which helped. The home became more tense, its population more bifurcated into them and me, and I drifted further into a hopeless despair. I could no longer leave and go back to my old life; that was gone. I could not envision leaving this marriage and striding out on my own financially, professionally, socially in this new town now in my mid-fifties and depressed. I felt trapped in a cold, golden cage. But one night I decided it was time to exit, and everything changed:

> I recommitted to it this morning. I don't plan to tell anyone, but I'll do it in a month. That gives me time to get my affairs in some kind of order. I'll have had a chance to visit with my kids and my sister, to write my will very carefully, to write letters to everyone, to shred and dispose properly of old patient records, to box up things I want to be sure go to certain people and move them over to a storage place with keys just for my kids. My timing will be when my husband takes his children on a vacation out of town. I'll put the animals in the vet's care. Cancel the newspapers. Cancel the mail. Cancel the maids. Change my phone message. Write letters to notify my patients and suggest further care for them. I'll give myself plenty of time alone.
>
> I feel competent and quieted to be planning this. I don't like my life with [husband], and I can't foresee anything except increased hardship when I leave him. I've spent over a half-century here . . . that's enough. I've done all the things I really want to do, and it's time to move on. [later that night]
>
> I know that death will be like it is when I'm under anaesthesia or as it was before I was born. I do yearn for that. I always liked 'going under'. And now will be so much better than when I'm older, more alone, more ill. Now feels like a very good time. I'm still enjoying things. My days have some pleasure and joy. Little difficulties seem to be staying little. I made a countdown today. I've got more than a month to get ready. [two days later]
>
> How strange it feels throughout the day to be aware of the brevity of time left! I'm not scared or sad. Instead, I feel lightened. I'm unburdening myself, literally and figuratively. I threw out lots of clothing today, keeping only what really fits and I like and may wear in the next month. I'll do more of that each day. Today, for example, I wore heels and hose to the university . . . thinking of it as one of the last times I'll have to do that . . . and threw away the heels when I got home!
>
> I lectured on depression today; I have so much to teach on the topic. And I talked to them of the morbidity of the diagnosis, the 15 per cent 'completed' suicides, higher among female mental health care professionals . . . and thought, the whole time . . . if they only knew . . . they'd find it so hard to square this up with the vivacious, lively woman who's forcefully (and if I must say so myself, quite brilliantly) lecturing to them.
>
> I think of death as I say loving things to people, and it's made me want to be more loving.

When my husband says or does disappointing things, it really doesn't bother me as much because I realize how temporary it is. It no longer really matters. I can eat what I want; it doesn't matter any more, so I got the GIANT box of Frosted Flakes!

I decided to donate my books to the school. I will make a list of friends and family and specify what I will give to each. I will plan my cremation. So the days go by and I feel consistently good about my decision.
[from later days]

I find myself being directed by my plan in so many ways. I'm not so irritated by [husband, stepchildren], I'm kinder to people, doing a little more for others and reaching out to them more. Each day(s) seems precious because they are fewer. I feel happy and excited about this. And every time I have a problem, even an annoying one like my back 'going out' and my muscles 'locking' in pain, I say to myself, 'Well, soon this'll be over'.

The dogs are a daily delight. They get ever sweeter and more loving.
[later still]

Still enjoying my project. Here's what I accomplished today: (1) Re-read several books on Rational Suicide. (2) Decided to write a letter in the manner of Jo Roman (1980). (3) Got some papers together for the will. (4) Got the sleeping pills and can get more if needed. (5) Had my 'roots' done for the last time, and treated myself to the whole kebab, snoozing happily through the blow-dry. (6) Arranged for another therapist to pick up one difficult family case.

Every day feels precious, and almost every mess seems trivial. I've wanted to do this for a very long time. I've yearned for peace. I've yearned to be done. I've longed for death as a sweet.
[further along]

God, I'm glad I'm going. I can't wait. Actually it occupies most of my time and my attention. It pervades every hour I'm awake. I begrudge every minute I have to spend doing other things. And there's so much to do.

I want to re-read Jo Roman's book.

I want to write about what it feels like to want to die so badly you can taste it.
****

My disconnection from everyone and everything is so great now. Except for moments when I stare into the eyes of one of those puppies. They are the only source of gladness right now. I look at older people and I don't want to be one. I look at young people and I don't want to be one of those either.

I only hope I don't screw it up. If I do, somehow, I'll find another way.
****

It would be awfully wonderful to be able to talk to someone about this who would understand . . . and even help me if I get stuck or screw it up

in my sleep. (My biggest fear is that I'll be semiconscious and pull the bag off. I would like not to have to do something messy like opening my veins . . . but I may choose to do so.) I'd love to talk to a Hemlock person, but don't know if anyone there is safe either. I emailed the 'deathnet' group this morning on the internet to ask for information.
****

This morning I practised with my Exit Bag. If the pills are sufficient, this should indeed be easy and calm. I'm not at all anxious. Just eager.

All I can think about is why do people live? Why do it? To see one more spring? Eat one more egg? See one more movie? One more building? Why? The whole thing seems so silly to me. I've lived as well as I could. The rest is redundant. I'm almost ready to do it. Almost. But not quite. Wouldn't it be bizarre if I died tonight?
****

From Jo Roman's book: 'Bringing one's life to a responsible good end is NOT the same as killing oneself.' 'I'd had enough . . . The relief I felt was energizing.' She too discarded possessions and wrote notes and noticed how beautiful things were and wanted to tell people of her good feelings for them. She writes: 'When someone commits suicide, the more rational it is, the more likely it is to be artfully concealed.'

Suicide has been a theme throughout my life. I do wish I could just check into a place like the one described in one of Kurt Vonnegut's novels, where I could get my hair done, my nails done, and then go into a massage room where, after a mere needle stick, I could drift off to sleep with some nice nurse rubbing my feet. It would be so much easier.

Determining the moment of my own death is my right. I've come to a time when I'm ready to die and would like to do so. My death will endanger no one.
****

Life is beautiful and the world is full of beauty, yet I have no need to cling to it. I've had enough. I'm not a quitter. Nor evil. Nor deranged. Nor depressed. Nor a coward. Just a woman making a quiet choice.

The aftermath

Shortly before my death, I went away for five days with my sister; we laughed and bonded and I was able to tell her many positive things I had been wanting to say. We got so close, in fact, that on our last day together, I trusted her with my secret. Of course, she called my husband, which annoyed me, even though I knew it meant she loved me. Predictably, his emotional response was to be very angry at me for all the inconvenience and disruption I would cause to him. He was terminally unsupportive, if you'll pardon the pun.

That day, someone, either my sister or my husband, also called my old psychiatrist, who called me back immediately. He gently asked how I was doing, told me to come in the next day to see him, and then said: 'I'm your doctor. *I never should have let you go!*' Once in a while, a sentence can change a life. The love and caring embedded in *that* one melted me – and still brings me to tears as I write it. I was welcomed back the next day, and bathed in his mini-tirade at the other doctors who had not taken good enough care of 'his' patient. So, I was loved, given new medication, and supported through the ugly process of separation and divorce. How was I loved? My doctor was angry on my behalf; that's love. He took me in eagerly and quickly (to what I'm sure was an already overcrowded schedule); that's love. He was going to help me though this; that's love. He wasn't angry at *me*; that's love. He put the onus on the outside people and forces, and now he and I were reunited and together we would fix this . . . and we did . . . and that was love. And feeling loved, I stopped yearning to die.

The unhappy marriage was resolved by divorce, itself a protracted and punishing procedure, as is often the case. But now I have my own little house, have been happily engaged in a new and very loving relationship, am professionally stable and my practice is growing, have taken up the fiddle and other new hobbies, and frequently tell people that this is the happiest era of my life. I still think of death almost daily.

So what's my point?

Over the years of my unhappy slide into a state of suicidal hopelessness, I was seen by several therapists, marriage therapists and excellent psychopharmacologists. How is it that no one knew I was suicidal? One part of the answer is very simple: no one asked. In truth, even if they had, I never felt I had enough of a relationship with any one of them to have discussed something as personal and potentially shameful as my suicidality. Besides, they might have recommended hospitalization, which I knew I did not want to do. But surely each of these therapists saw me as deeply unhappy and often crying; you may wonder why they did not think of investigating depression and despair and suicide.

Unfortunately, in most instances of marital therapy, the focus is on saving the relationship; the relationship is the client. I think it is rare for a marriage therapist to ask one of the parties in a meaningful way, 'Do you want to continue this marriage? Are you happy with this person as your partner? Do you think this is a good relationship for you to stay in?'

What about the psychopharmacologists? Let me give an example: one evening, after a particularly toxic encounter with my husband, I went to my scheduled 'med-check' with my biological psychiatrist, a physician whom I liked and respected. I was so agitated by the trouble at home, that as soon as I sat down, I started sobbing and trying to tell him what had happened. I saw him look anxiously at his clock; I only 'owned' about 20 minutes of his time. Soon he stopped me and empathically offered that it *did* sound like things were quite bad at home, but it was clear that I was also deeply depressed, and couldn't evaluate the marriage against the depression as a backdrop. It was his job to smooth out the background, treat the depression, so that I could better decide how to deal with the marriage. Quite reasonable, I thought, but what of the impact of a bad marriage on depression?[3]

When I was in graduate school, a professor taught us that one should never ask too directly nor explicitly discuss suicidality. One must be careful not to put the idea into the client's head, we were told, or the patient may act on it. May I ask you, the reader, whether you are feeling suicidal as a result of our discussion?

There is an enormous difference between thought and deed. Please do not be afraid to ask your clients about their death thoughts. I assure you they have had them; most people have.[4]

Please do not assume that suicidal thinking means you need to hospitalize your client. In fact, your client may not share that – and other symptoms – for fear of such an automatic response. Empathize first, and ask how the suicidal thoughts affected them (e.g. did those thoughts frighten you? Or were they calming in any way?). Ask for the details: how often do these thoughts occur? What is the nature of the thoughts? How detailed are they? How lethal are they? How pressing do they feel? How does it feel to talk about these thoughts? Why would they *not* act on these thoughts? Teach. Discuss. Understand and help the client to appreciate that suicidal thinking is a symptom, not for all depressed clients, but for most. In some cases, such as mine, it is a primary symptom, even an early warning sign.

Keep asking, so that your client knows you care, you're willing to hear about this symptom without overreacting to it, and you're not afraid of it. You might remind them that the decision to die is such an important one, such a final choice, that we want to be sure it is being made wisely and well. It is not a decision to be made impulsively, or in an altered state (such as under the influence of alcohol), or when one's brain is ill.

Do not ever assume that your clients can volunteer information on the suicidal impulses; they are in a closed system. Alvarez (1972), a self-described failed suicide, describes this closed world: 'Once a man decides to take his own life he enters a shut-off, impregnable but wholly convincing world where every detail fits and every incident reinforces his decision.' In her memoir of depression, Jamison (1995) writes:

> I simply wanted to die and be done with it. I resolved to kill myself. I was cold-bloodedly determined not to give any indication of my plans or the state of my mind. I was successful. The only note made by my psychiatrist on the day before I attempted suicide was: *Severely depressed. Very quiet.*
>
> (Jamison, 1995, p. 113)

Remember that the purpose of suicide is to seek a solution, and its goal is cessation of consciousness. Shneidman (1998) describes it well:

To a suicidal individual, to be unconscious means to be in a state of tranquil quiet, a nothingness and oblivion that is total and complete. Problems are not merely taken care of; there are no problems, and, even better, there is no consciousness of the possibility of problems – or of anything else. The action of suicide is an exiting, a departure from a painful life. Even in Hell this is so. A concentration camp prisoner wrote about his thoughts while in the camp: 'I look at those hanging and am jealous of the peace that they know'.

(Shneidman, 1998, p. 157)

Being able to speak openly about wanting to die may take much of the propulsive force out of the thought. Knowing that at least your therapist will be checking on you regularly to monitor this symptom may lift what Sylvia Plath (1971) so poignantly called 'the bell jar', the impenetrable isolation of depression. Perhaps there are others in the client's life who can reach through and let the client know how important his or her presence on the planet is to them. By all means, hospitalize if that feels like the best way to keep the client safe from the impulse, but remember that many determined suicides occur in the hospital.[5]

The clinical conundrum about suicide that you face as the potential helper is this: the suicidal person is yearning for escape and peace, and the fact is that choosing to live means the continuation, at least for a time, of pain. Shneidman (1998) offers this maxim:

Never kill yourself while you are suicidal. You can, if you must, think about suicide as much as your mind wishes and let the thought of suicide – the possibility that you could do it – carry you through the dark night. Night after night. Day after day, until the thought of self-destruction runs its course, and a fresh view of your own frustrated needs comes into clearer focus in your mind and you can, at last, pursue the realistic aspects, however dire, of your natural life.

(Shneidman, 1998, p. 166)

I would add only one important piece: you and your client are team mates or colleagues in the fight against depression and despair. Your contribution at this empathic juncture requires your *active* support, your *unflagging* optimism that pain will pass, your *conviction* that problems can be managed, and your *dogged* devotion to the client. I learned that from experience.

Going out on a few conceptual limbs

mood disorders may give an advantage to both individuals and their societies. Depression, characterized as it is by a conservation of energy during times of scant resources, a reduction of activity at times of non-negotiable threat, or a slowing or cessation of sexual behavior when environmental conditions are poor, is a not surprising biological reaction during times of change or stress. Its existence in mild forms may act as an alerting mechanism to other animals to act similarly and may, as some have argued, help to maintain a stable social hierarchy as well. . . . The discontents and darkness of the depressive mind may also create – through the arts and philosophy – a useful perspective in the collective social awareness.

(Jamison, 1999, p. 179)

I have wondered whether the physiological (vegetative) symptoms of depression may have a homeostatic value. One of my journal entries suggests this:

When my appetite shut down and I could not eat, it seems to have been appropriate not to do so. My attempts to nurture myself with soup merely led to bowel distress. It was as if my guts were saying to me, 'We're too sick, so don't feed us now; we're busy doing other things and don't have a good blood supply for the stomach and its digestive work'.

The sleep disorder may also have a corrective function. In fact, some research suggests that a sleep-deprivation period may serve to elevate mood, potentiate drug effects, and reset the disturbed sleep cycle (Goodwin, 1989). A sleepless night can be used to advantage if the client can be encouraged to be sure to stay fully awake through the night and the next day, returning to bed at the normal time the following night.

The homeostasis of appetite loss and sleeplessness seem akin to Mother Nature's use of 'paradoxical intention' (prescribing the symptom) and can be used to advantage by the therapist if cognitively reframed for the client so that he or she will come to welcome these symptoms rather than be frightened by them. The reconceptualization is that the body is 'taking a break' and trying in some way to heal itself and recover physiologically.

In such a way, even suicidal thinking can be viewed as a comforting option. Depression can be such an extraordinarily painful experience, the thought that one will not have to struggle unremittingly and eternally can paradoxically provide a sense of hope. The contemplation of suicide may be an effective way of keeping oneself from committing suicide out of total hopelessness and despair. It has always been *my* ace-in-the-hole.

As a kindergartner in the world of neurophysiological knowledge, I have a kind of *Sesame Street* picture of these vegetative functions in the brain.[6] There's the 'feeding centre', which, when sick, can cause us to overeat or undereat, and the 'sleeping centre', from which we can oversleep or suffer insomnias. Even the appetite for sex, love, and connection can be disrupted. I even imagine life and death centres, the disturbance of which can affect the energy for movement and living in either direction – from anergia to mania, and from the awareness of to movement toward death. Perhaps Freud was right: there may be a little Thanatos node in our midbrain.

So, why do I continue to think about death so much? The fact that it is still with me may mean that I am still (chronically) depressed, although not according to the Beck Depression Inventory, which is not known for false negatives (see Walen and Rader, 1991). Or, perhaps the Thanatos centre in my brain just never got reset properly – like the anorexic who can keep her weight up but never really 'changes her mind' about her body image. Or, perhaps this once, my mother really did give me good advice: perhaps at the end of a long life, death really can be a welcoming door.

Postscript

Well, I suppose I'm really out of the closet now. It is comforting to know I'm in good company, although when my colleague and I began to write about our experiences in 1991, there was hardly anything published about depression in the helping professional. The best I could find was the largely anonymous collection of self-reports in the British book, *Wounded Healers* (Rippere and Williams, 1985). Today, of course, there are the marvellous autobiographical writings of experts, like Dr Kay Jamison, followed by her client, Dr Martha Manning, followed by her client, Tracy Thompson, and others. I have taken great comfort in reading these stories and I will leave you with a short list of some especially brave and poignant autobiographies, which I recommend to you.

> *An Unquiet Mind: A Memoir of Moods and Madness* by Kay Redfield Jamison (1995)
> *Undercurrents: A Life Beneath the Surface* by Martha Manning (1995)
> *The Beast: A Reckoning with Depression* by Tracy Thompson (1995)

Acknowledgements

I would like to thank Dr Stephen Palmer, not only for the invitation to write this piece, but also for his kind and patient guidance as I struggled with it. Thanks also to the publisher, for being brave enough to actually publish it.

Notes

1 An early postscript: In fact, preparation of this manuscript *was* very moving for me: I was excited about the project and enjoyed the craft, as I always have, of stringing words like beads, but I underestimated the poignancy and the emotional toll it would take on me and on several friends whom I asked for an editorial read.
2 A schema, in contemporary models of cognitive therapy, is a broad pattern of viewing the self and the world that can be laid down early in childhood in the day-to-day experiences of the family, and which can be dysfunctional to a significant degree in adulthood. When triggered by contemporary events, the result is a strong negative emotion, accompanied by cognitions that are experienced as a priori truths. While painful, these experiences are familiar, and we often recreate in adult

life those conditions that in childhood were most painful for us. More specifically, those of us who grew up with depressed mothers often bear schemas of emotional deprivation, abandonment, and defectiveness. Paradoxically, we may be drawn, unconsciously, to emotionally detached, cold, or unaffectionate partners, which somehow 'feel like home' (see Young and Klosko, 1993).

3 Jamison (1999, p. 199) reminds us that suicide, to some extent, can be protected against by 'religious beliefs, the presence of children in the household, financial security, strong social supports, or a good marriage.'

4 Suicide has tripled in the past half-century. It is now the third leading cause of death in young people, and the second for college students. One in ten had seriously considered suicide during the prior year, and most had drawn up a plan (Jamison, 1999, p. 21). Every seventeen minutes in America, someone commits suicide (Jamison, 1999, p. 309).

5 Between 5 and 10 per cent of all suicides take place in mental hospitals. More than 40 per cent of those who committed suicide had been on fifteen-minute checks at the time they killed themselves (Jamison, 1999, pp. 149–153).

6 For a much more sophisticated view of the biology of suicide, read Jamison (1999, Chapters 6 and 7).

References

Alvarez, A. (1972) *The Savage God: A study of suicide*. New York: Random House.

Goodwin, F.K. (1989) Mood disorders: diagnosis and treatment. Paper presented at the Mood Disorders Symposium, Spring Grove Hospital Center, Catonsville, MD.

Jamison, K.R. (1995) *An Unquiet Mind: A memoir of moods and madness*. New York: Alfred A. Knopf.

Jamison, K.R. (1999) *Night Falls Fast: Understanding suicide*. New York: Vintage.

Manning, M. (1995) *Undercurrents: A Life beneath the surface*. San Francisco, CA: HarperCollins.

Plath, S. (1971) *The Bell Jar*. New York: Bantam.

Rippere, V. and Williams, R. (eds) (1985) *Wounded Healers: Mental health workers' experiences of depression*. Chichester: Wiley.

Roman, J. (1980) *Exit House*. New York: Seaview.

Shneidman, E.S. (1998) *The Suicidal Mind*. New York: Oxford University Press.

Styron, W. (1989) Darkness Visible. *Vanity Fair*, December.

Thompson, T. (1995) *The Beast: A reckoning with depression*. New York: G.P. Putnam.

Walen, S.R. and Rader, M. (1991) Depression and RET: perspectives from wounded healers, in M. Bernard (ed.) *Using Rational-Emotive Therapy Effectively*. New York: Plenum.

Young, J. and Klosko, J. (1993) *Reinventing your Life*. New York: Plume.

7   A friend's view of suicide

David Cooke

My friend Daniel moved into the house next door when I was 10 years old, he would have been 8 at the time. I can clearly remember our first conversation, a heated debate over whose garden we should play football in. Eventually we compromised and decided to use the school playing field just behind our homes.

The pair of us spent countless days playing sports or riding bikes on that field over the next year or so. Soon however we both made new friends at secondary school and saw considerably less of each other over the next three years. We did, however, remain good friends and once the pair of us had both finished school we became close again.

Once Daniel had finished school he spent a long period of time without work, much to the annoyance of his mother and stepfather. This frustration was fuelled by the fact that, rather than working, Daniel spent a lot of his time smoking cannabis. I can recall many times having to encourage Daniel to find work; occasionally he would help out at the restaurant where I worked for some extra cash. Eventually he started work as an apprentice at a local motor garage and seemed much happier with life in general.

By this time Daniel would have been 17 years old. He had a good-looking girlfriend and was extremely well liked by the local youngsters in the small town where we lived. At this time I was preparing to leave home for university. I can remember spending a lot of time with my friends during the last week of the summer, and I can remember saying goodbye to Daniel just moments before I left for university.

When I came home for Christmas from university I met up with most of my friends, including Daniel, and nothing really seemed different or strange. The same could be said for the Easter holiday when we spent most of our free time, as we always did, drinking pints and smoking the odd crafty joint. On the last night of my break from university Daniel had to escort (or pretty much carry) me home. I wish more than many things that I could better remember our conversation that evening.

The day of Daniel's death: 2 June 2004

I arrived back from university in Carlisle for my summer holiday on the evening of Wednesday 2 June. My mother and sister had come to collect me from the train station where I greeted them with my usual complaints about the non-smoking policy on Virgin trains. I knew something was wrong when my mum told me to have a cigarette in the car so we could get home quickly. About halfway home one of my closest friends called me. I can clearly recall his words, mumbled behind tears but painfully clear: '. . . it's Dan, he . . . he killed himself, he's dead.'

My mother and sister knew what had been said. They could hear me sobbing in the back seat of the car just as clearly as they could hear Daniel's mother scream when she discovered his body hanging in the garage upon her return from work at 5.30 p.m.

When I got home there were police cars parked at the front of the house. I tried to start unpacking my things from the car but I was not able to. I went into the back garden, sat on the ground and cried. It was no use to stop crying because when I did I could hear his mother, still close to hysterics nearly three hours after finding her son.

My friend who had called me to tell me of the news arrived at my house about an hour later. The pair of us, good friends since school, had not seen each other in two months but we did not say a word. We stopped by the off-licence on the way to his house where we drank beer while he filled me in on the events leading up to Daniel's death.

The nub of the story is this: Daniel and his girlfriend had an argument. He went out for a drink and saw his girlfriend's ex-boyfriend's car. Still feeling bad he kicked the sides of the car in and carried on home. The following day he had an upsetting altercation with a local person. After work he went into his garage and hung himself from a wooden beam with a blue rope, like the type used for clotheslines.

How I felt

Over the next few days I felt a mixture of different emotions. Daniel's girlfriend is also a close friend of mine and she called me on the evening of his death. Obviously upset, she wanted to meet up with me the next day. When I was talking to her she was concerned that people would hold her responsible for his actions. In contrast to the guilt she felt about the situation, I felt very angry about the whole situation. Angry with Daniel for what he had done and also angry with the person who physically threatened him.

I found my moods over the next few days changed frequently; anger, confusion and a deep sadness that a part of my life would never be the same again. I had experienced the death of friends before, but never when they had taken their own life. It felt very strange to be grieving for a person whom you also felt a great anger towards. I spent a lot of time with my friends, mainly in the pub. During this time I can remember that we spent most of the time sat in silence, everyone fearful that the slightest word out of place would upset others.

Personally I had nothing to say. I had spent the first few days after Daniel's death arranging the pallbearers for his funeral, which was to be held ten days later in the church only a few hundred yards away from both of our homes. His mother had asked me to act as a pallbearer along with five others. I met with his girlfriend and some others close to him to discuss whom we should ask to carry his coffin and the depressing nature of this task had caused me much distress. I guess because the situation seemed like one that should never happen, let alone be caused by a friend.

In the days leading up to the funeral I visited the chapel of rest parlour where Daniel's body lay. The first time was with his girlfriend. I went inside to see him on my own first because she was too frightened. Once inside I looked down on my friend, lying pale and cold in a coffin, but I could see no person. Only a body, lifeless and empty. I could look at the body for only a few seconds at a time; I was weak at the knees and weeping uncontrollably. After a few minutes I attempted to say goodbye but there was a lump in my throat. I couldn't bring myself to leave but I felt I had to go. I think this is probably the moment where I fully realized that I would never see my friend again.

The aftermath

Daniel's funeral was held at 10 a.m. on a sunny Saturday morning in June. The five other pallbearers and myself met at my house 30 minutes before where we all had some whiskey to help us through the ordeal. We waited for the hearse outside the church and watched people on their way into the church. The six of us were dressed in surf shorts and T-shirts, as a small kind of tribute to our friend.

Soon the coffin was being taken from the back of the hearse and we proceeded towards the church. At this point I was shaking uncontrollably, as were the others. Every footstep seemed to take an age as we walked into the packed church. I can remember looking through my tears into the eyes of the many people who I knew, hoping to find some comfort, but soon realizing that everyone was crying.

During the funeral I stared out of the window, trying desperately not to hear or see anything in the church. I didn't want to be in there and felt angry that I was. When we took our seats at the front of the church I snapped at the lady who was handing out the order of service because I did not have one. Once I was given the programme I tossed it on to the floor. Throughout the funeral I felt very resentful towards the vicar. I don't really know why, because his words were very kind and gentle but I kind of felt like he was calling time on Daniel's life.

After we had put the coffin back in the hearse the family went to the crematorium and we went to the pub. I drank very heavily; I had no appetite and was a bit of a mess by the mid afternoon. I can't really remember much of that day other than it was the first time I had ever drank to avoid reality.

A few months after Daniel's death I no longer felt the same anger. I must have thought about him every day throughout that summer. I felt sad for him; how must he have been feeling at the time? What were his last few moments of life like? Was he crying and shaking when he did it?

Many times that summer I sat in his house with his mother, talking about the times we had spent together. She found it comforting to be told how we took her car to the beach while she was on holiday, or how we stole beer from her garage. She was obviously very upset about his death and the fact that it was her who discovered his body. She told me once how he was when she found him; his tongue like a 'squash ball', his neck '2 feet long', just 18 years old.

At the end of the summer I returned to university and thought about Daniel a little less. I think it helped me to talk about his death with my friends there who did not know him or anyone else involved. At this point I felt disappointed at Daniel. I couldn't understand why he didn't speak to any of his friends or face up to reality.

It is now just over two years since Daniel's death. I still think of him often, not really of his death but of the times we spent together. When I am at home I still miss him, sometimes expecting him to jump over the wall for a sly joint, but at the same time wondering if that could have been a factor; did drugs affect his state of mind? Not according to the coroner's report, which said his body was free from alcohol or drugs.

That is about the only question that I have which will ever be answered about his death. I will never truly know why he did it or if I could have helped him. I guess I like to fool myself into thinking that he didn't mean to do it, that he still really wanted to be alive.

This chapter is dedicated to the memory of Daniel.

8 Client suicide and its effect on the therapist

Anopama Kapoor

The death of a loved one is difficult to deal with, but when that person's death occurs due to suicide, grieving processes can be complex. There is evidence that survivors of suicidal deaths have a unique and very difficult time handling their grief. An example of this could be overwhelming feelings at the time of the loss, which may cause the person to delay the grieving process (Worden, 1991).

The average professional psychologist in their career has a greater than 20 per cent chance of losing their patient to suicide (Bersoff, 1999). However, while training courses and books cover the risk of suicide, very little is on therapists' reactions and coping styles when it actually happens. However, there are notable exceptions which attempt to inform how to support staff and patients after a suicide (e.g. Duffy and Ryan, 2004; Pallin, 2004). Reactions and coping styles are important topics to discuss, as therapists work closely with suicidal clients on a regular basis, and there is evidence that the death of a client does affect the therapist. This also can apply to other health professionals in a similar line of work such as psychiatrists (see Gitlin, 2006).

Following my own experience, I decided to research and write about it. The material that I found helpful to read is discussed in this chapter. The literature on the effect of a client's suicide on the therapist, the effect on the trainee and what has been suggested to counteract these effects and the implications for training and practice, is examined. My own personal experience follows.

Personal experience

My experience of a client's suicide occurred while I was training. My initial reaction was shock. I remember shaking for a few hours afterwards and unable to cope with my other clients. I felt hurt, and my confidence was shattered. One of my first thoughts was, 'Did I help her enough?' It was helpful talking to others but no one could ease my feelings of self-recrimination and doubting my professional knowledge. Although I shed tears and found everyone very helpful, I ruminated about my client and her last words to me.

My client had been recently discharged from hospital. I last saw her at the hospital, and at the end of the session, she asked me to 'not leave her', and stated that she felt that she could only speak to me. When I heard about her death, I wanted to go back to that day, and spend more time with her, so that I could reach out and 'rescue' her. I knew it was not possible, but I wanted to change her mind, I wanted to turn back time.

I was left with a number of dilemmas, one being what Peter Lomas speaks about in Dryden (1985), the dilemma of 'who am I to teach morals'. If my client wanted to escape from her 'madness' then who was I to say what was right or wrong? But I did want to say, I felt angry with her and I wondered why. I could not understand why she had done it. But my feelings conflicted; I also understood why she had done it because I knew how distressed and how desperate she felt. These were difficult feelings to deal with, as I wondered why as a professional, I was having these thoughts and feelings.

I wished my training institution had done something to prepare me for this. I felt that a large part of my training was missing and did not feel able to speak to my peers openly about my feelings. I felt embarrassed by these feelings. I know I was grieving but I continuously thought, why did this happen so early on in my career; I felt marked by the experience. I felt scared and alone, especially when there was an internal inquiry up coming. I had to swallow my pride, to ask for help and support during this time. My supervisor was extremely helpful and understanding. I was not open about all my feelings as I felt I had to get through this by myself.

Upon reflection

For a long time I was haunted by the question, 'Could I have done something to prevent it?' Although I knew there was nothing I could have done, I could not stop questioning myself.

In the long term, this experience has left me more anxious, cautious and lacking in confidence, especially when I work with suicidal clients. Initially I have feelings of panic, and then I run through all the procedures in my mind. I have realized that when clients who are extremely distressed do not attend sessions, I worry slightly and think to myself, 'Are they all right? I hope something has not happened?' I feel that this is due to my awareness of the effect a client's suicide can have on a therapist, personally and professionally, and my feelings of anxiety about it happening again. The memory is as clear in my mind as though it happened yesterday. I think this is because the experience had a great impact on me, and it was a time when I struggled with separating my personal feelings from work.

However, I feel that the negative feelings do disappear. I how feel a lot better about the experience, and believe that I have learnt a lot from it. Not only about myself but also from my research, I learnt about therapists' reactions to various situations, and different coping styles. I have become more reflective, and think more deeply about the issues that affect therapists in their everyday work. A recent experience has also made me think about how therapists deal with the loss of a loved one through suicide, and about the effect of a therapist's personal life on their work.

It did take me a long time to overcome the feelings that result from a client's suicide but time healed. The experience left me with more questions than I had answers to. I changed as a person and I learnt a lot about myself as a therapist. I feel the above experience has benefited me, in that I have gained a greater awareness, and do not feel scared of what could happen in my work, as I was in the beginning of my training. I realize that my reactions were part of my mourning process and when I wrote about my experience, I was able to deal with most of my feelings. Reading the literature on this subject helped me to realize that my feelings were similar to others and were natural. I know that sometimes my work will affect me personally and it is important to work through these feelings, using the available support. Literature on this area will be discussed next.

The reactions of therapists to a client's suicide

Therapists work with suicidal clients almost every day of their lives. However, when one of these clients commits suicide, how is the therapist affected?

Litman (1965) notes that psychotherapists tend to be philosophical about death and have tranquil attitudes and yet the same person might describe a quite different emotional experience after a direct encounter with death as an actual event. He reported observations from interviews with more than 200 therapists. His first observation was how hard it was to elicit therapists' attitudes and reactions to the death of their client through suicide: therapists were either philosophical, casual and flippant or introduced ethics as reasons for not speaking about it. Litman (1965) states that

> according to my observations therapists react to the death of a patient, personally, as human beings, in much the same way as do other people. They react, secondly, in accordance with their special role in society. Their theoretical, philosophical, and scientific attitudes serve as a defensive and reparative function, being used to overcome the pain which they feel as human beings and as therapists.
>
> (Litman, 1965, p. 572)

In addition Litman (1965) states that personal reactions depend on a variety of factors such as how the therapists viewed the client, how long and how close as well as the degree of professional commitment. However, therapists have described their first experience as the worst, where lack of confidence, intense sadness and shock are experienced. He likened the guilt experienced by therapists as an exact replica of guilt experienced by relatives of person who committed suicide as well as feelings such as anger and pain. Litman (1965), from his observations, suggests that the psychological mechanisms that are universal in relatives and therapists were denial and repression. He notes that therapists' reactions (as therapists) emphasized fears concerning blame, responsibility and inadequacy and were sometimes marked and exposed. Therapists also described high anxiety when working with suicidal clients after they experienced the death of a client and a number reported that they no longer worked with suicidal clients.

Litman (1965) suggests that a supportive environment, presentation of cases and a feeling of shared responsibility tend to help therapists work through their grief. However, he does not observe any change in general attitudes towards suicide but found that therapists said they tried to use their experience to broaden their horizon, become a person who is more sensitive and with improved professional judgements and actions. Litman (1965) endorses this view and cautions therapists to be aware that if part of the pain is repressed, it does return later. He encourages therapists to work through the traumatic incident so that a personal change and a professional broadening can be manifested.

Similarly, Levinson (1972) describes the necessity and difficulty in mourning the loss of a client through suicide, and notes how aggression towards the deceased can interfere in the satisfactory working through of the loss. Alexander (1977) reiterates this theme. He describes his own experiences and states that aggression in the pre-loss relationship to the client, if not recognized, can complicate the therapist's mourning for the patient.

In contrast, Kolodny et al. (1979), in their article on the working through of patients' suicides by four therapists, extensively explore the reactions and thoughts of each therapist. During the spring of 1976, four trainees experienced the death of a client through suicide. They then met as a group and discussed their experiences. One therapist stated that when they found out, they felt a wave of panic, anger at the reactions of other therapists and then feeling alone. Upon reflection the therapists began to doubt their therapeutic decisions and wondered what they could have done differently. The therapist described that they felt alarmed at how much support they needed and how easily they could seek it. They describe needing to seek support for reassurance, comfort and to learn from their experience. After presenting the case at a conference, they were amazed at the empathy and interest that they received but also were able to come to terms with their loss. The therapist then describes thinking about things on a deeper level, thinking of the client for months afterwards, grieving, sadness and hospitalizing clients more accompanied with increased anxiety.

Similarly, the second therapist in this article describes their initial reaction as disbelief, and need for support. They then felt shame and embarrassment, followed by questioning their interventions, feeling responsible and anger at the advice they received from their supervisor and at themselves for listening to the advice. After presenting the case at a conference, they became aware of feelings of loss, feelings that continued for months afterwards accompanied by over-cautiousness with regard to any suicide risk.

The third therapist describes similar feelings after finding out about the death of their client. Again initial reactions were disbelief, shame and guilt as well as doubting their work and attempting to discuss with supervisors what went wrong. These feelings were followed by a need for privacy and a sense of shame, not wanting anyone to know. They then describe a feeling of 'why me?', anger, a feeling of loss, continued reflection about their work with the client and worry over other clients. These feelings continued for two months afterwards, followed by feelings of loneliness and sadness as well as dreams about the client. It was not until ten weeks after the suicide that this therapist was able to share the experience.

The fourth therapist again describes disbelief as an initial reaction, then questioning of their methods and a need for support. They then recognized feelings of guilt and wanting punishment, followed by anger and grief. Through the discussion groups, the therapists were able to work through their feelings and attempt to understand what had happened to each of them. Processes of intellectual and affective mastery followed this phase. The group concluded that they each went through a process of mourning over a long period of time. They state, 'we are convinced that no support system or understanding on the part of colleagues or supervisors can entirely alleviate the pain and self-examination one must go through in the wake of a patient' suicide' (Kolodny et al., 1979, p. 44). However, they emphasize the need for support, open discussion in supervision and a respect for the therapist's mourning, after the death of a client.

In comparison, Gorkin (1985) describes the psychological difficulties experienced by therapists when their client commits suicide. He states that suicide is a traumatic occurrence and loss that must be worked through. Using case material as an example, he describes his initial reaction of shock. Then follows a need to work through, slowly and often painfully, any feelings of failure or narcissistic injury, along with an acceptance that some patients do commit suicide and there is a possibility that the therapist's errors and failings play a role in a patient's decision to commit suicide.

Gorkin (1985) states that two factors affect the therapist's ability to work through the loss and accept the ambiguity that remains: first, the degree of omnipotence in the therapist's therapeutic strivings, and second, the nature of the therapist's relationship to the client. Gorkin (1985) points out that the more omnipotence the therapist has, the more difficulty he or she may have in accepting feelings of failure engendered by suicide. This in itself can manifest in denial of guilt and narcissistic injury or a sense of worthlessness. Gorkin (1985) also points out that the extent to which the relationship is coloured by hostility, can make it more difficult for the therapist to work through the loss. Gorkin (1985) states that an awareness of any aggression can increase the therapist's ability to work through the loss.

Gorkin (1985) notes that the therapist can experience pathological guilt, which can impact on their future work. He states that when feelings of guilt, worthlessness, depression and expectation of recrimination are profound and long lasting then this can indicate the presence of pathological mourning. He also points out that when narcissistic manifestations are exaggerated and unremitting, it is a signal of the therapist's pathological mourning. Pathological mourning can influence behaviour towards other clients, acceptance of referrals and leave the therapist with high anxiety.

In comparison, Horn (1994), in his literature review, states that bereavement following suicide is atypical. It leaves the bereaved with overwhelming feelings of stigma, guilt, anger and confusion. However, mental health professionals experience a client's suicide in two ways: first, as people who have lost a significant other, and second, as professionals experiencing a critical event in their professional development. This results in a complex situation. Horn (1994) reports that without some sort of model to help professionals through a client suicide, understanding and intervening become an insurmountable challenge.

He describes similar reactions as those described above, these being first shock, then anger, shame and guilt, sometimes depression and feelings of incompetence or self-doubt and lastly the final stages involve acceptance and resolution. Horn (1994) describes cognitive responses as thoughts of self-doubt about clinical judgements and beliefs as well as fantasies of silent accusations and criticisms by colleagues and supervisors. He then describes the therapist as having intrusive thoughts about the suicide and concerns relating to malpractice or legal issues. In the later stages, the cognitive reactions are characterized by hypervigilance, depressive ruminations and cognitive dissonance. Finally, when the therapist reaches the final stages, he/she develops an appreciation for how little control they have over another individual's life, without becoming discouraged about the process of psychotherapy.

Horn (1994) states that behaviourally, therapists might neglect work and other clients and avoid treating clients who are depressed. Horn (1994) also found that reactions of grief by therapists are related to life events. He states that trainees and therapists who spend more time doing therapy experience high stress levels; the greater the experience and the more years worked in the field result in lower stress levels. The type of client and treatment setting also affected stress levels. Outpatient therapists reported feelings of loneliness and isolation whereas inpatient therapists immediately prepared their explanation. Horn (1994) concludes that further research is needed in this area; he promotes positive responses and states that discussing this experience helps to normalize therapists' reactions.

Similarly, Valente (1994) examined the reactions of psychotherapists to the suicide of a patient and found similar conclusions to those described above. She states that psychotherapists are often unprepared for a patient's suicide and that, 'perhaps influenced by a culture that denies death, or seduced by the notion that a "good enough" therapist should effectively prevent suicide, psychotherapists have reported being traumatised by a patient's suicide' (Valente, 1994, p. 614). Valente (1994) concludes that therapists do mourn a patient's suicide and unless support groups are in place, grief can be long term and typically characterized by increased questioning and self-recrimination.

Each person's experience is unique, and how therapists experience the death of a client depends on a number of factors. Grad et al. (1997) conducted a study on gender differences in bereavement reactions of therapists. They state that the most frequently reported reactions by therapists were increased caution and an increased conferring with colleagues. Their sample consisted of sixty-three therapists, who completed a questionnaire probing the emotional reactions and behaviour after a patient's suicide. They had more women (57 per cent) than men (43 per cent) and more psychiatrists than psychologists; theoretical orientation and age varied across the sample.

Grad et al. (1997) found that respondents became more cautious (93.6 per cent) and had talked to their colleagues after the event (90.5 per cent). Close to two-thirds of the respondents reported that they had felt guilty (68.3 per cent), had spoken to their partner (63.5 per cent) and had continued working as usual (60.3 per cent). Gender differences did emerge. Women felt more shame, experienced more guilt, needed more consolation and professed more doubts about their professional knowledge. In addition, fewer women reported working as usual after the patient's death. From open-ended questions, both sexes reported first grief and second anguish, guilt, uneasiness, feeling hurt and horror. Third, men reported uneasiness and women reported guilt. With regard to feelings, men reported helplessness and uneasiness while women's responses were anguish and sleeplessness. Men were more helped by work (30 per cent) and talking (30 per cent), with a few helped by the passage of time. Women (75 per cent) reported that talking helped them the most. No significant differences were found with age and experience.

Grad et al. (1997) put forward two explanations for the gender differences. First, they say it could be due to the fact that more men are 'leaders' in this field and so cannot afford to show emotions. Their second explanation is that women tend to recognize and talk easily about their insights. They say that this could be due to stereotypical socializing effects of upbringing. They also recognize the importance of support and the role of the supervisor, to help the therapists work through the grief and state that the above gender difference should be taken into consideration.

In comparison, Gurrister and Kane (1978) found that therapists who had experienced a suicidal death in their career significantly differed in their theoretical formulations than those who had not. The purpose of the study was to ask therapists about their different theoretical formulations regarding suicide and their therapeutic preferences in working with suicidal clients. Twenty-seven therapists in a large mental health centre were interviewed. The interviews centred on the therapists' view of suicidal individuals, their therapeutic preferences and their agreement or disagreement with various views on suicide discussed in the literature. Demographic details and experience were also discussed. Differences between groups and correlations between various formulations and therapeutic preferences were tested using the Fisher Exact Test.

In the study the feelings provoked by suicidal patients were anxiety, anger, frustration, protectiveness, concern and 'mixed feelings'. Those who described the suicide of a client as having the greatest impact, described feelings of predominately anxiety and those who described a lesser impact described feelings of anger and frustration, when working with suicidal clients. During the above study it became apparent that a great deal of emotional involvement on the part of the therapist is needed in order to lend strength to the patient during the time of crisis.

Therefore several studies provide evidence of the serious effects on the therapist of a client's suicide. As I was a trainee when my experience occurred, I was very interested in the effect on trainees. This is an important area to discuss because if there is a greater impact of a client's suicide on trainees, then it is likely that some trainees might not continue with their career and might become seriously distressed. Therefore we need to pinpoint the effects of a client's suicide and then employ the recommended suggestions from the literature, so that therapists and trainees feel not only supported but also prepared for the possibility that one of their clients could die through suicide. Literature covering the effect on the trainee will be examined next.

The effect on trainees

Brown (1987) notes that training experiences are deeply etched into our memories, and a patient's suicide at such a time has a strong and unforgettable impact. After a survey, he found that patient suicide is not rare among trainee mental health professionals. First, he reports that trainees usually have a small caseload of difficult patients, therefore how to do a good job tends to ride on how well these patients fare. If one of these patients commits suicide then this may impact on a trainee's motivation and self-confidence. Second, because trainees feel they know very little in the beginning they tend to bring only themselves and rely more on their personal qualities to help their clients.

Consequently, Brown (1987) states that if a patient commits suicide then the trainee feels that he or she has failed as a person. He states that, 'it takes time and supervision to work out the complex amalgam of true personal intimacy and objective professional skill which must characterise effective psychotherapeutic practice. Trainees usually have not yet had time to do this' (Brown, 1987, p. 106). Third, he reports that trainees may lack adequate skill to understand and help seriously suicidal patients, or these patients may not be able to make use of what any therapist has to offer. In either case, Brown (1987) says that the trainee is likely to feel that he or she has failed. Finally Brown (1987) notes that trainees are as yet not comfortable or familiar with reactions that occur during psychotherapeutic practice, and therefore when the opportunity to grow together is suddenly terminated, there is 'instead a sudden and shocking confrontation with loss and what often feels like failure' (Brown, 1987, p. 107).

Brown (1987) states that the earlier this experience occurs in training, the more shocking and problematic it becomes. From his interviews, Brown (1987) found that none of the trainees described their experience as affecting their development for the worse; they saw it as an opportunity to grow and accepted that this was part of life, and appreciated how little control they had over the situation which helped them later on in their career. However, he notes that the experience for trainees was deeply emotional and found that they still vividly remembered each detail of the experience including the name of the person years later.

He states that we must recognize that a patient's suicide is not rare during training and that they must not be left to cope by themselves. He puts forward that growth through this crisis will be strongly influenced by trainees' preparation and reactions, plus important sustaining relationships within the training programme. He states that to facilitate this growth every training programme should have a conscious perspective and approach to this crisis.

Similarly Kleespies et al. (1990) found that trainees with patient suicides reported a greater emotional impact and stress levels equivalent to that found in patient samples with bereavement and higher than that found with professional clinicians who had patient suicides.

In support, Valente (1994) reports that the most serious reactions to the suicide of one's client have occurred among trainee therapists. She states that many training programmes neglect the topic of suicide evaluation or prevention and thereby ignore the potential effects of suicide on the therapist.

The above studies have shown that the impact on the trainee of a client's suicide is not only as serious as those on therapists but greater. All have highlighted the importance of training programmes and support. Following on from this, the implications will be examined next.

Implications for the future

Reading the suggestions from the studies helped me to work through my experience, and made me realize the importance of support and allowing ourselves to mourn. Changes in training programmes are recommended. Pope and Tabachnick (1993) in their study found that respondents stated that their graduate training left them largely unprepared for the feelings that occurred during a therapist's work. In support, Sommers-Flanagan et al. (2000) note that there are no formalized training programmes that are designed to teach suicide assessment skills. They strongly recommend that psychology training programmes 'should devote more time and energy to teaching integrated and professional approaches to suicide assessment interviewing' (Sommers-Flanagan et al., 2000, p. 100).

Kolodny et al. (1979) recommend that training institutions should provide some forum at which difficult patients can be discussed, which would lead to an exchange of ideas and also experiences by experienced clinicians and careful considerations of the impact of therapeutic inevitabilities on the client. In conclusion, they state that we need to know much about the processes involved in therapist mourning so that when a death does occur, a supportive environment can be facilitated, an environment which recognizes that such an experience is both painful and lonely and also an opportunity for growth and mastery.

To work through the loss, Gorkin (1985) highlights the importance of supervision and support. He suggests a forum for reviewing the case, as a matter of standard procedure, aside from any administrative procedures. Gorkin (1985) states that this should be available immediately after the event and at intervals during the year.

Horn (1994) also highlights the importance of support and the role of supervisors. He states that supervisors 'play an integral part in promoting therapists' growth' (Horn, 1994, p. 194). They should create both formal and informal supports, and facilitate positive behavioural responses. As well as creating life experiences that will positively affect the therapist's schema, supervisors should assist them through the grieving process by creating support groups, holding post-suicide reviews, arranging a psychological autopsy and attending the client's funeral.

Valente (1994) also supports the need for a psychological autopsy, so that therapists can understand and learn from the experience and establish or refine procedures that can help to prevent future suicides. Not only this but also the autopsy can be a means of support for the therapists and an opportunity to express feelings about the suicide. She states: 'with peer support, therapists can resolve bereavement, continue their personal and professional growth, and experience a heightened commitment to assessing suicide risk' (Valente, 1994, p. 620).

Douglas and Brown (1989) recommend a five-phase system to be incorporated into training programmes. First, *Anticipation*, where trainers take the responsibility to teach trainees that it is likely that one of their patients will commit suicide in their career. Douglas and Brown (1989) recommend that trainees need to be prepared for this eventuality and that it might help if they were to rehearse how it might feel if a patient commits suicide. Second, *Acute Impact*, where training directors, supervisors and others should reach out to the trainee, as well as respect and support the trainee's adaptive style. Douglas and Brown (1989) state that during this phase trainees should be encouraged to meet the relatives of the deceased client but with a significant amount of support from others.

Douglas and Brown (1989) describe the third phase as *Clarification and Working Through*. During this phase preceptors and supervisors should encourage the trainee to examine the possible influences of the suicide on his/her work and participate in a psychological autopsy. Fourth, *Reorganization*, where the trainee meets with the trainee director, and assesses how the experience has affected them, as well as taking up any issues of failure and blame. Finally, there is *Preparation for Reactivation and Post-Training Practice*, where the training programme should help trainees to anticipate the transition to post-training. Douglas and Brown (1989) state that some preparation should go in to future work with suicidal patients, for those trainees who have been affected and those that have not. The value of ongoing learning, consultation, and no isolation from colleagues should be emphasized. The importance of reaching out empathetically, non-judgementally and constructively to fellow professionals in difficulty should be stressed.

In contrast, Bobele (1987) puts the responsibility on the therapist and states that therapists tend to engage in more of the same behaviour, when dealing with suicidal clients and use methods consistent with their therapeutic orientation. Bobele (1987) states that it is important that therapists have the ability to speak the client's language, to join in the client's worldview and tailor therapeutic interventions to this. They should be able to reject methods used before and attempt to work in teams to prevent them engaging in 'more of the same solutions'.

Stone (1971) presents situations in which psychotherapy can precipitate suicide. He states that the therapists can force the client into a situation where they are forcibly induced to see the reality of their situation as empty of any possible gratification and an inability to change their situation. This state of hopelessness can lead to the client committing suicide. Stone (1971) points out that therapists need to be alert and aware of the transference issues that can arise and the possibility of malignant intervention. Similarly Judd (1996) found that a degree of negative transference was associated with varying levels of suicidality. She points out that therapists must continue to monitor their countertransference carefully, particularly their unconscious countertransference reactions.

A number of recommendations are made. Most of them emphasize the need for support mechanisms and the role of training institutions. They demonstrate that there is more we can do to lessen the impact of a client's suicide on the therapist.

Conclusion

Working with clients does have an effect on the therapist. The studies discussed in this chapter have demonstrated that therapists are affected by the suicide of a client. This effect is emotional, psychological and philosophical. They extend to the therapist's personal and professional work. There are also positive effects in this experience: therapists do seem to learn a lot and use it as an opportunity to grow as professionals. Trainee therapists are affected more than therapists with years of experience.

A number of suggestions have been made. In particular, a change in training courses and support mechanisms is emphasized. Suicide is a taboo subject, we need to move beyond this so that we may examine suicide more effectively, enforce preventive measures and prevent the death of a client having a significant impact on the therapist. I believe that things are improving and have noticed that training institutions are including the topic on their courses. However, awareness needs to be not only within training institutions but also in workplaces.

Continued awareness is important, as it will help therapists to be prepared for the above feelings and the sudden shock, when or if they hear about the death of a client through suicide. Above all it is important that therapists recognize that they are human, and the feelings that do occur after the suicide of a client are natural. I would encourage open discussions about these feelings, as an essential part of the healing process.

References

Alexander, P. (1977) A psychotherapist's reaction to his patient's death. *Suicide and Life-Threatening Behavior*, 7, 203–210.

Bersoff, D.N. (1999) *Ethical Conflicts in Psychology* (2nd edn). Washington, DC: American Psychological Association.

Bobele, M. (1987) Therapeutic interventions in life threatening situations. *Journal of Marital and Family Therapy*, 13(3), 225–239.

Brown, H.N. (1987) The impact of suicide on therapists in training. *Comprehensive Psychiatry*, 28(2), 101–112.

Douglas, J. and Brown, H.N. (1989) *Suicide: Understanding and responding. Harvard Medical School Perspectives*. Madison, CT: International Universities Press.

Dryden, W. (1985) *Therapists' Dilemmas*. London: Harper & Row.

Duffy, D. and Ryan, T. (eds) (2004) *New Approaches to Preventing Suicide: A manual for practitioners*. London: Jessica Kingsley Publishers.

Gitlin, M. (2006) Psychiatrist reactions to patient suicide, in R.I. Simon and R.E. Hales (eds) *Textbook of Suicide Assessment and Management*. Washington, DC: American Psychiatric Publishing.

Gorkin, M. (1985) On the suicide of one's patient. *Bulletin of the Menninger Clinic*, 49(1), 1–9.

Grad, O.T., Zavasnik, A. and Groleger, U. (1997) Suicide of a patient: gender differences in bereavement reactions of therapists. *Suicide and Life-Threatening Behavior*, 27(4), 379–386.

Gurrister, L. and Kane, R.A. (1978) How therapists perceive and treat suicidal patients. *Community Mental Health Journal*, 14(1), 3–13.

Horn, P.J. (1994) Therapists' psychological adaptation to client suicide. *Psychotherapy*, 31(1), 190–195.

Judd, S. (1996) Negative counter transference and suicide: an empirical evaluation. *Dissertation-Abstracts-International: Section B: The Sciences and Engineering*, 57(5-B), 3412.

Kleespies, P.M., Smith, M.R. and Becker, B.R. (1990) Psychology interns as patient suicide survivors: incidence, impact and recovery. *Professional Psychology: Research and Practice*, 21, 257–263.

Kolodny, S., Binder, R.L., Bronstein, A.A. and Friend, R.L. (1979) The working through of patients' suicides by four therapists. *Suicide and Life-Threatening Behavior*, 9(1), 33–46.

Levinson, P. (1972) On sudden death. *Psychiatry*, 35, 160–173.

Litman, R.E. (1965) When patients commit suicide. *American Journal of Psychotherapy*, 19(4), 570–576.

Pallin, V. (2004) Supporting staff and patients after a suicide, in D. Duffy and T. Ryan (eds) *New Approaches to Preventing Suicide: A manual for practitioners*. London: Jessica Kingsley Publishers.

Pope, K.S. and Tabachnick, B.G. (1993) Therapists' anger, hate, fear and sexual feelings: national survey of therapist responses, client characteristics, critical events, formal complaints and training. *Professional Psychology: Research and Practice*, 24(2), 142–152.

Sommers-Flanagan, J., Rothman, M. and Schwenkler, R. (2000) Training psychologists to become competent suicide assessment interviewers: commentary on Rosenberg's (1999) suicide prevention training model. *Professional Psychology: Research and Practice*, 31(1), 99–100.

Stone, A. (1971) Suicide precipitated by psychotherapy: a clinical contribution. *American Journal of Psychotherapy*, 25(1), 18–26.

Valente, S.M. (1994) Psychotherapist reactions to the suicide of a patient. *American Journal of Orthopsychiatry*, 64(4), 614–621.

Worden, J.W. (1991) *Grief Counselling and Grief Therapy* (2nd edn). London: Routledge.

Part III

Three therapeutic approaches to prevent suicide

9 Cognitive behavioural and rational emotive management of suicide

Wayne Froggatt and Stephen Palmer

In this chapter we focus on a unified cognitive behavioural model of suicidality, assessment procedures and a range of cognitive, imaginal and behavioural interventions. Therapist–client dialogue will be included to illustrate some of the techniques. A Personal Self-Harm Management Plan and assessment checklists have been included in Appendices 1 and 2 respectively, to be used in conjunction with the cognitive behavioural and rational emotive approach taken by this chapter.

What causes a wish to self-harm?

There are many explanations as to why human beings develop self-harm intentions. An often-asked question is: do people become suicidal because of *external* factors (e.g. their circumstances) or because of *internal* factors (their psychological state). The best answer to this question is: 'both'. It is clear that environmental factors such as social isolation, poor family support, sudden loss or abusive relationships increase suicide risk. However, not everyone exposed to such events and circumstances wishes to die. Factors internal to the individual clearly play a part. For example, suicide risk is increased by depression, high expectations of oneself, or a tendency to suppress emotions.

A psychological explanation with considerable research backing is provided by cognitive behavioural therapy (CBT). According to the two main variations of CBT – *rational emotive behaviour therapy* (REBT) developed by Albert Ellis, and *cognitive therapy* (CT) developed by Aaron Beck – suicide contemplation results from certain dysfunctional beliefs and attitudes.

Two key motivations

Writing from a cognitive therapy perspective, Williams and Wells (1989) state that there seems to be two main motivations for self-harm/suicide:

- *Communication*: the wish to send a message to someone or others who are perceived as not listening.

- *Escape*: the wish to escape from life, usually reflecting a perception that there are no more options left.

It is important to identify which motivation is operative, because each requires a different approach.

Two types of disturbance

REBT (Ellis, 1987) suggests there are two common themes which may lead to disturbed emotions and behaviours – self-hatred (known as ego disturbance) and low discomfort-tolerance (discomfort disturbance).

Ego disturbance involves an upset to the self-image resulting from demands about how one should be or behave, followed by global self-evaluation for not meeting these demanding standards. In relation to self-harm ideation, it is characterized by self-talk such as: 'Nobody cares about me, which shows that I'm no good' / 'I'm a failure, I deserve to die', coupled with 'I'll never be able to improve', this leads to 'I may as well kill myself'. Underlying these ideas will be core beliefs like: 'I need to achieve / have the approval of others', 'I can't stand failure / lack of approval', 'If I was not able to satisfy these needs, life would not be worth living'.

Discomfort disturbance involves a person's perception of threat to such issues as their safety, quality of life, emotional or physical pain and so on, coupled with excessive evaluations of the badness of negative events or circumstances and demands that they do not occur. In the case of self-harm ideation, it will result from self-talk like: 'My life is so bad / I feel so depressed / I can't bear this pain', coupled with 'There is no way out', this leads to: 'I may as well kill myself'. Underlying these ideas will be core beliefs like the following: 'Discomfort and misery are awful', 'I can't stand bad feelings and must avoid them at all costs', 'If I was helpless to do anything about bad feelings, the only solution would be to kill myself'.

There are four types of thinking that potentially underlie each disturbance. The most basic is demandingness: the individual believes that they or the world 'should' or 'must' be a certain way. Deriving from demands are the other three types: *awfulizing* – believing that something is awful, terrible or horrible because it is not as it 'should' or 'must' be; *discomfort intolerance* – viewing certain things as unbearable (known as 'can't-stand-it-itis'), and *self-rating* – viewing oneself (or other) as totally bad, stupid or incompetent.

For most people, ego and discomfort disturbance will coexist, but one or the other will tend to predominate. It is important to identify which is uppermost, because each requires different treatment. Note that ego and discomfort disturbance will not by themselves necessarily lead to suicidal inclinations. What is needed, as we shall see in a moment, is the added component of hopelessness: some kind of belief that oneself or one's circumstances are unlikely to ever improve.

Three directions of negative thinking

Beck (1967) points out that depressed people typically engage in highly negative thinking focused in three directions. It may be directed toward the self ('I'm no good') – this appears to be identical to Ellis' concept of ego disturbance – or toward the world ('The world is no good') – this would equate to discomfort disturbance.

The third direction is toward the future ('My future is no good'). Whichever of the first two is emphasized, a negative view of the future is the decisive element in depression and suicidality. A person may regard themselves or the world (or both) as no good, but they are less likely to become depressed or suicidal if they believe the situation is going to improve. However, if they see little or no hope for improvement, this provides fertile ground for the idea that the only solution is to terminate one's unworthy existence or presence in an unworthy world. It can be hypothesized that the degree of hopelessness determines the degree of suicidal ideation.

Beck outlines a further seven types of disturbed thinking (in addition to Ellis' list of four) that contribute to negative emotionality:

- All or Nothing thinking: 'I either do it perfectly or it's not worth doing at all.'
- Filtering: 'I can't see any positives in my life.'
- Overgeneralizing: 'Everything is going wrong in my life.'
- Mind-reading: 'They think I'm worthless.'
- Fortune-telling: 'Things can only get worse.'
- Emotional reasoning: 'I know I'm a failure – otherwise I wouldn't be feeling this way.'
- Personalizing: 'It must have been me that made her feel bad.'

A unified CBT model of suicidality

Ellis and Beck, the two main cognitive behavioural theorists, are often stating similar points, but using different words; further, where they do differ (for example, regarding the types of irrational thinking on which to focus) they tend to be complementary rather than contradictory. The model (see Figure 9.1) that combines their thinking in a unified understanding of why people become suicidal, incorporating as well the two key motivations for self-harm.

How does suicidal thinking come about? Both REBT and CT theorists agree that dysfunctional thinking has its origins in a combination of inherited biological temperament and learning that begins at birth and continues throughout the life cycle. This combination leads to the development of core beliefs or 'schema', which are enduring assumptions and rules about oneself, the world and how things 'ought' to be. They are usually held out of conscious awareness. When an individual is exposed to an adverse triggering event or circumstance (usually perceived by the individual as stressful), one or

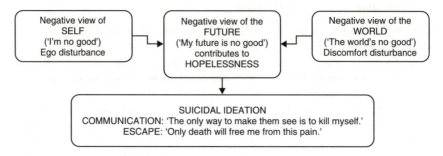

Figure 9.1 A model of suicide.

more of their core beliefs are activated, leading to current thinking. These negative 'automatic' thoughts (NATs), as they are sometimes called, then create emotional and behavioural consequences.

What follows is a model that illustrates all of the components referred to thus far. This is a version of Ellis' well-known ABC model, modified to reflect a broader CBT perspective:

'A' = Activating or triggering events

'B' = Beliefs

'C' = Consequences.

The example used is that of Anna, who was seen in hospital following an overdose of paracetamol. Anna had been moderately depressed for some months, not coping well with conflict in her relationship with Warren, who was expressing dissatisfaction and a desire to leave. Anna believed that she had to have a man for her life to have any meaning, but, because she had a very low opinion of herself, simultaneously believed that few men would ever want her. One afternoon she arrived at their flat to discover that Warren's clothes and belongings were gone. She took a number of paracetamol tablets, but shortly after, she reconsidered and rang the ambulance service, whereupon she was brought to hospital. Figure 9.2 highlights Anna's experience shown in the framework of the modified ABC model.

To summarize, when Anna's partner left, this *Activated* a long-held core *Belief* 'I'm nothing without a man'. She was not conscious of this belief, but was more aware of the current thinking that it stimulated: 'I'll never find another man who'll love me'. This 'automatic' thought in turn created her *Consequence:* a feeling of despair and the act of taking an overdose.

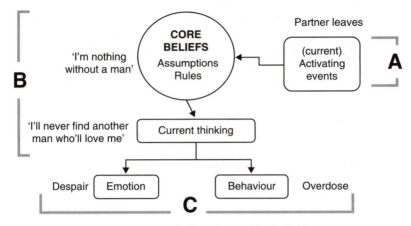

Figure 9.2 Anna's experience applied to the model of suicide.

Managing risk: overview and principles

Now we turn from theory to practice. The process of self-harm risk management can be summarized as follows:

1 Identify the presence of possible general risk factors.
2 Assess current risk.
3 Develop and implement a plan to reduce the risk level or protect the person if necessary.
4 Begin dealing with the client's underlying problems when the client is ready.

Before we look at each of these steps in detail, there are some general principles to keep in mind when working with suicidal clients, as follows.

First, *be as collaborative as possible*, given the client's mental and emotional state and level of risk. Do not take over any more than is necessary – this may only reinforce the client's belief in their inability to cope. As far as possible, involve the client in a dialogue about the assessment and proposed management. Model the approach of therapist and client working together as a team to problem-solve.

Second, while remaining collaborative, *be prepared in the early stages to supply initial energy* for a client who may be depressed and sees no options available to them. Avoid, for instance, aimlessly restating the client's problems, or vaguely discussing hopeless thinking without proposing any options. It is possible to combine appropriate directiveness with client involvement and collaboration. With suicidal clients, Socratic questioning is usually more appropriate than reflective listening.

Third, *consult*, as appropriate, the family doctor, other helping profession-als already involved with the client, specialist practitioners (e.g. psychiatrist), or other people significant to the client, including family members. Avoid acting alone with high-risk clients and if in private practice, consider if an appropriate referral to an inpatient setting may be more useful for the client.

We shall now take a closer look at the steps involved in assessment.

Identify the presence of possible general risk factors

The initial 'screening' phase involves identifying the presence of *general or demographic risk factors* – by reading previous notes, observing the person, and talking with them and with significant others (Simon and Hales, 2006). There are categories of risk span from low risk to very high risk (Cooper and Kapur, 2004). A list of key factors to look for, culled from statistical research, is on pages 243–245 (see 'Assessment checklists' in Appendix 2). Especially watch for the presence of *clinical depression*. If there have been previous self-harm episodes, ascertain the following:

- When was the last attempt?
- How frequent have they been?
- What were the circumstances triggering or surrounding the attempts?
- In the case of family self-harm history, have any attempts been successful?

Assess current risk

Ascertain whether the person is likely to harm themselves in the near future:

- Are they thinking of suicide now?
- How lethal is the proposed method (and what is the client's *perception* of lethality)?

    Higher ← firearms–hanging–gassing–cutting-wrists–pills → *Lower*

- Are there any preparations (giving away valued possessions, making a will, etc.)?
- What situations tend to trigger the suicidal ideation?
- What positives and alternative options can the person see in themselves or their circumstances?
- Watch especially for thoughts and feelings around the theme of *hope-lessness*, including the client's perception that there are no options for solving their problems.
- Find out what the person is trying to achieve (their *motivation*) – is it escape or communication? If the person says they would like to die, clarify this: do they just want to escape from their responsibilities for a while – or do they want to end their life?

- Note the presence or absence of *protective* factors. How much hope does the client see?
- Is good mental health care available? Would the client comply with this?
- Does the client consider they are needed by and have responsibility for children or other dependants?
- Does the client perceive they have strong social supports? Are competent caregivers available (parents, friends, etc.)?

How do you find out about suicidal thinking?

As stated in Chapter 5, do not be afraid to ask if the client is thinking about suicide – talking about it is likely to be a relief. This can be done sensitively. Start with general, minimally intrusive questions; moving, as necessary, to more specific queries, like the following example:

- How does the future seem to you?
- How hopeless does the situation seem to you?
- Does it sometimes seem that life isn't worth living?
- Have you ever thought of ending it?
- How would you go about it?
- Have you ever made moves toward doing this?
- Are you likely to at this point?

Clients who have already self-harmed

The same assessment process as described above applies with clients who have already self-harmed, with the addition of some questions designed to ascertain their intentions:

- What did they do? When? Where?
- Who was around? Did they expect to be found? Did they tell anyone before or after?
- Was the act planned or impulsive?
- What did they think would happen?
- What did they want to happen?
- What do they think/feel about what they did, and about being still alive?

Anna was seen by a mental health nurse from the crisis team shortly after her physical condition was stabilized in hospital. A number of background risk factors were identified: she was currently depressed, she had already made this one attempt, she had experienced what to her was a significant loss, she viewed herself quite negatively and did not see much hope that she would ever improve in the future. There were, though, some positives: she had support from her parents and several friends, there were no attempts previous to the current one, and she was willing to accept medication and psychological therapy for her depression.

The assessment of current risk (which also included detailed questioning about her overdose) revealed that though she lacked significant hope for the future, she was relieved to be still alive and embarrassed about what she had done. Although thoughts of death had been present for some weeks, there was no clear plan or consideration of the consequences prior to the overdose.

Anna's suicide risk was assessed as moderate. The most appropriate course of action was considered to be appraisal of her depression by a psychiatrist, followed by discharge from hospital with supervision and referral for psychological therapy.

Develop and implement a plan to reduce the risk level or protect the person if necessary

Planning

As the assessment proceeds, the plan for intervention will begin to develop. There are some general principles that will increase the effectiveness of the plan and its implementation. First, as far as possible, create the plan in consultation with the client, significant others, and appropriate professionals. Second, ensure that the plan is fully documented in a way that is accessible to other key practitioners. Third, notify the plan, level of risk, and supervision required to any others who may be involved with ongoing care of the client.

The discharge plan for Anna, worked out while she was still in hospital, was first discussed with her then checked with several key supporters. Copies of the plan were given to Anna, placed on the medical file, and sent to her family doctor, psychiatrist, and the community mental health team who would allocate a therapist for ongoing work. Relevant parts of the plan were communicated verbally to her friend Debbie, who was to call on her daily, and to her parents.

Intervention

Further intervention will depend on a number of factors, such as the motivation for suicide, the ongoing risk level, and the client's readiness for psychotherapy.

Take into account the client's motivation

If the wish to *communicate* predominates, find out what is being communicated to whom, then consider with the client how this can be done more functionally. This may involve, for example, relationship counselling or help to develop assertive responses.

If the wish to *escape* predominates, this may indicate a higher level of risk. Consider getting a second opinion if feasible, possibly via psychiatric assessment. It may be necessary for the person to be in a place of safety. There are some ways in which these options can be assessed and, while doing so, will, we hope, contribute to reducing the client's suicidal intentions.

Discuss the pros and cons of living and dying. A useful technique to aid this is the *benefits calculation* (described on page 154). This technique is an example of an intervention that can both assess the level of risk and at the same time, in many cases, reduce that risk.

As far as it is possible, make a careful assessment of the reality of the client's life situation, and of the cognitive framework they are using to interpret and evaluate that reality. Decide whether to *problem-solve* on their circumstances (see page 159), or work on dysfunctional thinking about those circumstances using strategies like *disputation* (page 161), *reframing* (page 162) or the *catastrophe scale* (page 163).

Initially, it will often be necessary to tackle thinking relating to hopelessness and lack of positive expectation. Cognitive techniques that can help here include *identifying reasons for living* (page 156), *identifying unfinished business* (page 156) and *generating alternatives* (page 157).

The circumstances of Anna's overdose might suggest, at first glance, a communication motive. However, on exploration, it became apparent that she was not trying to manipulate Warren into coming back – she really believed that the relationship was permanently over. Nor was it the so-called 'cry for help' – Anna saw little prospect for improvement, with or without help. As escape seemed to be the primary motivation, the crisis nurse assessed the level of risk by helping Anna carry out a *benefits calculation* (see the example on page 154); after this was completed, Anna decided that continuing to live was the preferable option.

Help the client problem-solve

Problem-solving, in the early stages of contact, involves helping the client to split up their various problems and look at solutions available, then plan how they will cope in the situations that lead to suicidal thoughts (also see Hawton and Kirk, 1989). *Problem-solving* is discussed on page 159. *Coping plans* (page 158) may also be relevant at this stage.

In Anna's case, some initial problem-solving around being alone in her flat was indicated, along with attention to some practical issues such as managing the rent on one income. The crisis nurse helped her prepare a coping grid (see page 159) for when she returned home.

Continue assessing the risk

The client's ability to cooperate with developing an appropriate intervention plan will provide further information about the level of risk. In particular, note any difficulty the client has in seeing options available to them.

Arrange support or monitoring as necessary

Identify a few resource people to whom the client can and will turn for help when feeling suicidal such as a parent, partner, friend, neighbour, members of the same religion, daycentre, volunteer, support group. List sources of emergency help such as the psychiatric emergency team, GP, telephone counselling service, police. Finally, check for and secure any substances, weapons, or other items the person had considered using.

Build a bridge to the next session

The most common way to help clients cope between contacts is to develop a personal self-harm management plan (see page 241). This may be enhanced (or replaced) by a coping plan (see page 158).

Obtain the client's agreement that:

- they will not harm themselves within a certain period, and
- if they are feeling suicidal, they will contact specified people.

Suggest to the client to regard their next episode of suicidal thinking as an opportunity to record the situation, their thoughts, and their feelings; and bring this data to the next session (see 'ABC diary' on page 161).

The crisis nurse helped Anna prepare a management plan to complement the coping grid mentioned earlier. Although she was unable to guarantee that she would not attempt self-harm before her next contact with the worker, she doubted that she would make further attempts before that time. She was also introduced to the ABC diary and the nurse helped her complete several entries as examples of what to do. They discussed the appropriateness of recording negative thoughts at this early stage, but Anna considered that it would be better for her to externalize and dispute these thoughts rather than just leave them buried.

Begin dealing with the client's underlying problems when the client is ready

As soon as the client is ready, address the factors that may keep them at risk of overreacting to the inevitable triggering events in their lives.

For ongoing therapeutic work, Anna was allocated a social worker trained in cognitive behavioural therapy. Early sessions involved a regular reassessment of Anna's suicide risk and the use of techniques to help reduce the suicidal ideation: Identifying reasons for living (page 156) and identifying unfinished business (page 156). Anna continued to keep the ABC diary, sharing the results at each session with the therapist, who was thus able to train Anna to more accurately identify dysfunctional thinking and increase her effectiveness in disputing it.

Within a few weeks, the focus was able to move from Anna's suicidal ideation to her underlying lack of self-acceptance, as indicated by her belief that, 'I am nothing without a man'. Ongoing therapy, involving the usual range of cognitive and behavioural techniques appropriate to any CBT programme, continued for a further eight months, with session frequency progressively decreasing from weekly to monthly.

An additional note: when the risk remains high

If supportive and therapeutic interventions are not enough to keep the person safe, then some further options may need to be considered. One is referral for psychiatric assessment, if not already carried out. For some, admission to or retention in hospital will be wise. In extreme cases, where the person is at high risk but rejects help, compulsory assessment and treatment may be necessary. Keep in mind that the higher the risk, the more important it is to involve other professionals in the helping process.

Inpatient treatment

Although the management of clients in hospital is beyond the scope of this chapter, most of the techniques already described are also relevant to that setting. There is a useful discussion of inpatient treatment in the guidelines issued by the New Zealand Ministry of Health (2003).

Note that while hospitalization will be needed for some high-risk clients, it will be inappropriate for many others. Admission may isolate them from family and support systems. Some will take on the 'patient role' and lose their sense of power and control. Placing someone in hospital when they could be managed in the community, just to 'be on the safe side', may actually retard their recovery.

Special issues

Working with clients from other cultures: developing cultural competence

When working with clients from cultural groups other than the practitioner's own, it is important to be conscious of the areas where modified approaches may be required (Palmer, 1999; Sewell, 2004). Be aware of differences, sometimes subtle, in meanings attached to particular words and concepts. Show sensitivity to any reluctance to disclose (which may be due to shame). For some cultures, there may be a greater expectation of and importance attached to involving the client's family in assessment and planning. Endeavour, where appropriate, to involve a specialist person such as a health worker from the person's own culture.

It is important to develop general cultural competence in assessment as the meaning of suicide from the client's viewpoint could represent a variety of things such as a social statement or sacrifice. A culturally bound therapist or health professional may not realize the significance to a client of what could be considered as minor incidents, such as disagreeing with one's family, parent or elders (see Horton, 2006; Wendler and Matthews, 2006).

Repetitive self-harm

Practitioners will sometimes work with individuals who engage in repetitive self-harm for reasons other than suicide. Histrionic behaviour, where the individual engages in attention-seeking acts, or dangerous behaviour to self-stimulate in response to anxiety or boredom is described by Freeman and White (1989). Borderline personality disorder, involving a complex set of factors including repetitive self-mutilation and threatened suicide, is discussed by Linehan et al. (1991). These conditions are beyond this chapter's scope, but some of the techniques already described can be used with such clients, and the references quoted will lead to more detailed recommendations.

Gaining the energy to commit suicide

Be aware that suicide risk may actually increase as depression improves. This is because a very depressed person lacks energy and motivation to do much about anything – but as their mood lifts, they may go through a stage where they develop the energy to plan and subsequently carry out suicidal intentions. Although their levels of depression are lower, their levels of hopelessness may still remain high. Thus the therapist may have conflicting scores on depression and hopelessness scales. Unfortunately, inexperienced therapists often focus on the assessment of depression and overlook hopelessness. A client's mood may also lift from severe depression when they have decided that suicide is the only strategy to cope with their current life or situation.

Fear of encouraging suicide

People are sometimes concerned that discussing the possibility of suicide may further stimulate suicidal thinking and intent. There is little evidence for this – in fact, talking about their suicidal ideation will usually be a relief to the client (as long as any questioning is done in a sensitive manner and the client is helped to see that there are valid alternatives to suicide).

Specific psychotherapeutic strategies and techniques

Now it is time to consider some of the many cognitive behavioural strategies that can be helpful with suicidal clients. Most of the techniques that follow are described in more detail in Freeman and White (1989), Ellis and Newman (1996), Curwen et al. (2000) and Froggatt (2003). For further reading of the cognitive behavioural approach we also recommend Rudd et al. (2001). Keep in mind that cognitive behavioural therapy is most effective when both client and therapist are in agreement to and clear about why they are using a specific technique or discussing a particular topic. A problem-solving approach is sometimes essential to help the client deal with specific life problems and issues (see Hawton and Kirk, 1989).

Helping the client to recognize the downward cognitive suicidal chain or spiral

Palmer (2005) focuses on encouraging long-term chronically depressed clients to note down the various cognitive and behavioural steps that trigger their suicidal ideation and thereby gain insight into managing their condition. By this process they can start to decentre or stand back from their thinking and hopefully take a more adaptive approach to limit the amount of time they experience suicidal ideation.

In the therapy session, the therapist and client note down on a whiteboard or paper the most recent downward cognitive suicidal chain or spiral the client experienced, starting with the triggering event, which can be external or internal in origin. It is important to include the client's behavioural responses as often modifying these and they are a necessary part of the intervention. This can be demonstrated with a brief case study.

Jayne had been depressed for two years; she was in her mid-thirties and in a relationship where she perceived her male partner as uncommitted to the relationship. She had been experiencing interpersonal difficulties at work too. The cognitive conceptualization (see Beck, 1995) in Figure 9.3 highlights the main personal and cognitive developmental issues.

When she became suicidal, she would start counting her sleeping pills and the paracetamol tablets she had hoarded. She would then avoid going to work or seeing friends for at least two or three days. This withdrawal

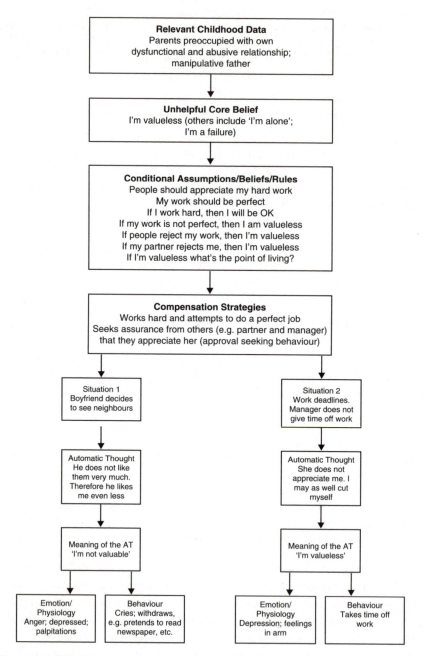

Figure 9.3 Cognitive conceptualization and focus of therapy.

from others helped to maintain her low mood and suicidal ideation for at least 48 hours' duration. With practice she was able to recognize a typical downward spiral and then behaviourally act in a more adaptive manner. Often the spiral was triggered by her perceiving herself as being rejected by a significant other such as her partner, manager or other organization such as a government department. A key idea that routinely exacerbated her levels of hopelessness and helplessness was, 'What's the fucking point?' This is illustrated in Figure 9.4.

She was anxious that she did not have enough sleeping pills, so her suicide might be painful. She then withdrew to her bedroom and lay on the bed. However, she still felt bad and described it as feeling 'like a void'. It was at this stage when she decided to take a proactive approach in dealing with her suicidal thoughts and feelings. This is the self-intervention or self-help stage. Figure 9.5 illustrates the interventions she applied.

In the early stages of therapy she became adept at recognizing and challenging her cognitive distortions; unfortunately, the underlying beliefs were activated which still led to her distressing suicidal ideation. Gradually her periods of low mood were less prolonged as she tackled her cognitions and behaviour related to the suicidal ideation. Therapy also consisted in helping her to challenge her core and intermediate beliefs and modify them.

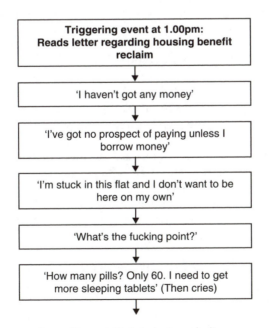

Figure 9.4 Downward cognitive suicidal chain (or spiral).

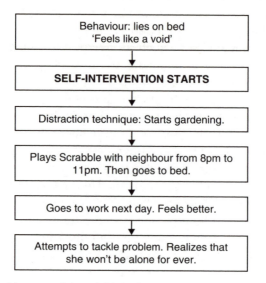

Figure 9.5 Climbing out of the suicidal spiral.

Changing the cost–benefit ratio: benefits calculation

Do a cost–benefit analysis with the client on their suicidal intentions: first, discuss reasons for dying (assess both pros and cons), and second, discuss reasons for living (again, assess both pros and cons). If the client has trouble thinking of reasons for living, ask questions like:

- What were your reasons for living before you became depressed?
- What would be your reasons for living if you weren't depressed now?
- What things have kept you going despite your problems?

Write up the calculation on a whiteboard or sheet of paper. A common format is to draw four boxes as shown in Table 9.1 (alternatively, each option could have a separate sheet of paper).

Sometimes the calculation can be enhanced by asking the client to decide how much value or benefit each item has to them, stating these values numerically, then adding up the numbers to see how the totals work out.

Note that advantages to the first option will often represent disadvantages of the second option, and vice versa. While this may seem like doubling up, in fact it aids clarification.

Having the client articulate the pros and cons in this way helps uncover negative thinking that can be worked on in sessions and for homework. This

Table 9.1 A suicide cost–benefit analysis

	Ending my life	*Staying alive*
Advantages	I'll stop being a burden to everyone.	I get the chance to work on myself and my problems.
	I will make up for all the bad things I have done.	I avoid causing huge pain to my family.
Disadvantages	Everyone will feel worse if I commit suicide.	I will keep on being a burden to everyone.
	I'll be dead – so I won't have the chance to behave better in the future.	I'll feel depressed for ever.

would involve, for example, checking out the reality of such beliefs as: 'Everyone will be better off without me' or 'I will never feel any better'. Disputation is discussed in more detail on page 161.

What if the client's calculation adds up in favour of suicide? In this case you will know that the risk level is probably higher than at first thought, so protective action may be indicated. Either way, the technique will be useful: it is hoped that the suicidality is reduced, if not, then a more accurate picture of the risk level is obtained.

Suicidal beliefs and counterarguments for older clients

Similar to the previous technique, Coon et al. (2004) demonstrate how suicidal beliefs can be addressed successfully by using counterarguments used with older clients using a two-column form. The counter belief is developed collaboratively with the client. Two examples are given here (Coon et al., 2004, p. 486):

Belief	Counterargument
Suicide represents a way for me to be reunited with deceased loved ones.	I run the risk that my concept of the afterlife is totally wrong. I have no guarantees that I will be reunited. Currently, I have my memories and pictures of them.
Suicide seems better than living with these health problems or disabilities that keep me from doing the activities I like. If I can't do what I used to do, I'd rather be dead.	I may not be able to do all the things I used to, but I can find ways to do some of them or a modified version of them. There are still many things I enjoy.

It is important that the client has a copy of the suicidal beliefs and the counterarguments so they can be used when they are by themselves, without assistance of the therapist or carers. With the client's permission, key workers, family members or carers could be aware of the list of beliefs and counterarguments and encourage their use when the client is feeling depressed or suicidal.

Questioning the advantages of suicide

This technique can be used alone, or as a follow-up to the 'advantages' of suicide the client listed in their benefits calculation. If this has not already been done, have the client list all of the perceived advantages to suicide they can think of. Then ask them to think of a catch to each 'advantage'. Table 9.2 is an example (adapted from Ellis and Newman, 1996).

Identifying reasons for living

Very depressed people tend to magnify the negatives in their lives and minimize the positives. A simple but often effective technique is to have them list reasons to live. This can be added to on a daily basis (Ellis and Newman, 1996). It will usually be helpful for therapist and client to start the list together; then the client can continue expanding the list for homework. (NB: if the client is unable to find many reasons for living, using this technique still serves a purpose by showing that the risk is higher than at first thought).

Identifying unfinished business

Here is a further technique that will help identify reasons for living. Have the client list unfinished business in their lives, using headings like the following (adapted from Ellis and Newman, 1996):

- Things I have been meaning to do or complete (list 3–10 key items).
- Why it is important for me to live to do these things (list 3–10 reasons).
- Unfinished business I will attend to now (list 2–3 items).

Table 9.2 The advantages of suicide

The Plus	The Catch
I won't be a burden to my family any more.	They will be devastated if I commit suicide.
I've failed at everything else – at least I will succeed at one thing: ending my life.	If I'm dead, I will never have the opportunity to succeed at anything in the future.
I won't feel bad any more.	I'll never feel good any more, either.

Although the client could undertake this technique by themselves as a between-session task, it is beneficial for this to be undertaken during a therapy session so that the therapist obtains further insight into their client's personal world and also assists the client in remembering or creating new goals the client wishes to achieve.

Generating alternatives

Work with the client to develop possible alternatives to suicide. 'Brainstorming' can be helpful here. Avoid directly suggesting that suicide is not an option – the client knows that it is always an option, and direct opposition by the therapist will serve only to damage rapport. The aim is to generate workable alternatives to suicide (see problem-solving on page 159).

Increasing the client's ability to cope

Imagery

The client can use the power of their imagination to challenge overly negative ways of thinking and practise new ways of coping (Palmer and Dryden, 1995). When using any of the techniques listed below, first run through the process several times in the interview, then get the client's agreement to practise several times a day at home (the repetition is important).

STRESS INOCULATION

Ask the client to visualize a crisis situation, to generate (within the session) feelings of hopelessness they feel in their everyday life. Then help them identify and change the cognitions which create the unwanted feelings.

REPLACEMENT IMAGERY

When the client is experiencing a repetitive dysfunctional image, have them bring the image to mind, then switch to a more functional replacement image (preferably one that you and the client have already worked out together). If, for example, the client keeps getting a picture of going to the garage and setting up the car to die by carbon monoxide poisoning, ask them first to experience the negative image, then second, visualize being in the garage, looking at the car, locking it, leaving the garage and locking that too, and going for a walk or engaging in some other pleasurable activity.

COPING IMAGERY

When the client is visualizing not coping with a particular situation, help them plan an alternative scenario where they do cope. Then have them visualize the situation, for example seeing other people being difficult, but seeing themselves coping in the more functional way worked out earlier (Palmer and Dryden, 1995).

Behaviour rehearsal

Therapist and client together can role-play or practise coping with interpersonal situations which the client thinks they cannot manage; for example, acting assertively with a partner, employer or friend. This can build the client's confidence in their ability to cope, and show them that there are alternatives available to deal with situations they previously saw as having no solution.

Activity scheduling

If the client thinks they are not able to cope with the demands of daily living or get motivated, help them plan how they will spend their time between sessions. The activity schedule provides a structure for this:

- Divide a sheet of paper into seven parts, one for each day of the week, each divided into hourly blocks.
- Help the client fill in each block with a task or pleasurable activity.
- As the client completes each activity, ask them to record next to it a rating of how much pleasure (P) they experienced, and the degree of mastery (M) they think they achieved (in each case using a 1–10 scale).
- At each interview, review how the client got on with their schedule for that week (see Table 9.3).

Coping plans

When the client lacks confidence they will be able to cope with their suicidal thoughts in particular situations, help them develop a list of strategies they

Table 9.3 Weekly activity plan and record

Weekly activity plan and record for week beginning: . . .			
	Monday	*Tuesday*	*Wednesday*
7–8	Eat breakfast P4 M8 Get dressed P5 M7		
8–9	Walk round garden P6 M9		
9–10	Debbie to visit P8 M9		

can use if and when the situation of concern occurs. There are two main types of strategy:

- Practising a self-help technique such as relaxation, postponing worry, doing a rational self-analysis, etc. (develop 4–6 of these).
- Carrying out specified activities such as mowing lawns, painting the house, etc. and engaging in pleasant activities like soaking in the bath, telephoning a friend, reading a novel, watching a video, and so on (ask the client to list 5–15 items).

Have the client write down the strategies before leaving the session. Ensure they know specifically what to do, and emphasize that the purpose is to simply cope with the situation – not be skilful with it.

The coping grid

A more structured variation of a coping plan is the 'coping grid'. There is a completed example in Table 9.4. The grid breaks the day into three manageable parts – day, evening and waking up from sleep – and then a plan is developed to deal with coping when alone or with people.

Encouraging problem-solving

Suicidal ideation, when oriented toward the 'exit' strategy, represents a perception that there is no hope of problems being solved in the future and that the only solution is to end one's life. Suicide may be seen as 'the solution to end all problems', a form of 'problem-solving'. The therapist needs to help the client see suicide for what it really is: 'the problem to end all solutions'.

Table 9.4 Coping grid

	What I can do when I am alone	*What I can do when with others*
During the day	Practise my relaxation technique. Go for a walk. Do a self-analysis. Ring Mum.	Get involved in whatever they are doing. If a close friend is there, alert them when I feel at risk. If at my place, make them a cup of coffee.
During the evening	Watch TV or a video. Ring Debbie or Jan. Read a magazine.	Same as for daytime.
If I wake during the night	Catch up on my letter writing. Do a self-analysis. If I feel really bad, phone Lifeline.	Not applicable.

Many of the techniques discussed thus far will help show that there are solutions other than suicide.

Problem-solving in general is discussed in Hawton et al. (1989) and Froggatt (1997, 2003); what follows is a brief summary of the standard process:

- Spell out problems in concrete, specific terms.
- Select one problem and express it in terms of a *goal*.
- Brainstorm alternative solution *strategies* aimed to achieve the goal.
- Consider each strategy (its possible results, how it fits with the client's values, its usefulness in achieving the goal), then decide which to pursue.
- Identify any blocks to carrying out the chosen strategies.
- Brainstorm specific *tactics* for carrying out the strategies.
- Select the tactics to use.
- Put the tactics into practice. Observe the results. If the desired outcome is not achieved, go through the steps again.

Increasing problem-solving confidence

This strategy for helping suicidal clients regain confidence that they can solve their problems (adapted from Ellis and Newman, 1996):

- Start by helping the client identify times when they have helped others with their problems: first, list names (it may help to list these under headings, e.g. older relative / sibling / spouse / child / friends / etc.), and second, state the type of problem they helped that person with.
- Next, have the client choose at least three people from the list and summarize, first, the problem they helped with, and second, what they said or did to help solve the problem.
- Finally, have the client list examples of how they have solved their own problems in the past (perhaps using a format like the following):

Problem situation (date / place / event /etc.)	The actions I took	The results of my actions

As this exercise progresses through each stage, Socratically assist clients to see that they do possess problem-solving skills that have been effective for themselves and others in the past. The third step will assist them to identify skills they can, perhaps, start using again now.

Identifying and changing dysfunctional thinking

ABC diary (also known as the Daily Thought Record)

Ask the client to record (between sessions) the following items, and bring their diary to the next session:

- The situations where they felt suicidal (the *Activating* events)
- What they were thinking (their *Beliefs* about the activating events)
- How they were feeling and/or what they did (their emotional and behavioural *Consequences*).

Keeping such a diary can help them see suicidal thoughts more clearly and also provide material to discuss with the therapist at the next session. (NB: use this approach only when the client is ready – if they are very disturbed, writing down their negative thoughts can sometimes simply make them feel worse.) Table 9.5 is an example of such a diary, with the addition of a section for replacing the old suicidal thinking.

Disputation or examination of beliefs

In the REBT literature, the term *disputation* is used. This forms the 'D' in Ellis' ABCDE model of emotional disturbance and management. It is sometimes misconstrued by neophyte therapists as arguing. In CBT therapists will work collaboratively with the client to examine their beliefs. It is important the process of 'disputation' or examination is undertaken in a sensitive manner by the therapist as arguing with clients is unlikely to be beneficial. The main strategy for disputing an irrational or unhelpful belief is through a

Table 9.5 Completed ABCD form

A Activating event / situation	B Beliefs / thoughts	C Consequence	D Disputation / rational response
Woke up feeling down	I can't stand feeling depressed	Exhausted 5/10	I don't like it, but it is not unbearable – I will feel better if I get myself moving.
Noticed that garden is full of weeds	I should be able to keep things up to date – I'm just useless	Self-downing 7/10	I'm not useless – I'm depressed at present. And while it is desirable to keep things up to date, it's not a Law of the Universe.

verbal dialogue between therapist and client. While this can be done didactically, it is usually more successful if the client is helped to check out the rationality of a belief 'Socratically' (i.e. through a series of leading questions), using three basic strategies:

- *Pragmatic* ('is this belief useful?'): the aim is to help the client see how an irrational belief leads to negative emotional and behavioural consequences. People are more likely to change a belief when they see that it is harmful to them and serves little or no useful purpose. It is often most effective to use pragmatic disputing first, before the other two strategies: 'What does telling yourself . . . do to you?' 'What effect does this belief have on the way you feel / behave?' 'What are the consequences for you of believing that . . .?'
- *Empirical* ('is this belief supported by the evidence?'): the goal here is to help the client see that their belief is inconsistent with reality, with little or no empirical evidence to support it: 'What evidence do you have for believing that . . . must happen?' 'Where is the evidence for thinking that you need . . .?' 'What evidence is there that may contradict this belief?' 'How reliable is the source of your information?' Ask the client to be very specific about the evidence they are using. Help them develop alternative explanations for events and circumstances.
- *Logical* ('does it follow?'): here you help the client examine and question the logic of their belief, helping them understand why it does not logically follow from the facts: 'How does it follow that because you want . . . to happen, therefore it must happen?' 'How does the fact that . . . is unpleasant make it unbearable?'

Time projection imagery

This technique is ideal for helping someone get a loss into perspective (Palmer and Dryden, 1995). Ask the client to begin by thinking about their loss; then visualize how they will be feeling and how their life will be at increasingly distant times in the future, e.g. in five days' time, five weeks, five months, five years. This can be even more effective if, as well as positive outcomes, the client also realistically foresees some potential problems – and visualizes being able to cope with them.

Keep the imagery going for as long as it seems helpful to capture a greater mood of optimism; then ask the client to come slowly back in time to the present, and perhaps attempt to plan the next few days.

Reframing

People with suicidal ideation may see actual or potential losses as catastrophic. Rather than trying to directly contradict this, Socratically help them see that they may be exaggerating the badness of events and circumstances.

One way to help the client get bad events into perspective is to re-evaluate them as 'disappointing', 'concerning' or 'uncomfortable' rather than as 'awful' or 'unbearable'. A variation of reframing is to help the client see that even negative events almost always have a positive side to them, listing all the positives the client can think of (this needs care, though, so that it does not come across as suggesting that a bad experience is really a good one).

Catastrophe scale

The catastrophe scale is a more elaborate way to get negative experiences into perspective:

- On a sheet of paper draw a line down the left side. Put 100 per cent at the top, 0 per cent at the bottom, and 10 per cent intervals in between. Have the client insert the event to which they are reacting at the applicable level.
- At each level, write in something the client thinks could legitimately be rated at that level. You might, for example, put 0 per cent – 'Having a quiet cup of coffee at home'; 20 per cent – 'Losing my purse'; 40 per cent – 'Being burgled'; 80 per cent – 'Being diagnosed with cancer'; 100 per cent – 'Being burned alive', and so on. The client will progressively alter the position of their 'activating event' on the scale, in relation to the other items, until they sense it is in perspective. Table 9.6 is an example of a catastrophe scale for Anna.

Dealing with self-image issues

Double-standard dispute

If the client is self-downing because they have behaved in a bad, stupid or incompetent manner, ask whether they would globally rate another person

Table 9.6 Completed catastrophe scale

CATASTROPHE SCALE Event: Boyfriend left me		
100	Burning alive	← original placing
90	Becoming a paraplegic	← 2nd placing
80	Being diagnosed with cancer	← 3rd placing
70	Having my car stolen	
60	Losing my job	
50	Being kicked out of my flat	
40	House burgled	
30	*Boyfriend leaving me*	← final placing
20	Losing my purse	
10	Catching a cold	
5	Missing my favourite TV programme	
0	Having a coffee at home	

(e.g. child, best friend, therapist, etc.) for doing the same thing. When they say 'No', then help them see that they are holding a double standard – which does not make sense. This technique can also be used with the 'shoulds' and 'musts' clients place on themselves, and is especially useful with resistant beliefs.

Big I, Little i

This technique, developed by Arnold Lazarus (1977) and described in detail in Palmer (1997), is a graphical way to help the client see how illogical it is to globally rate a human being: Draw a 'Big I' on the whiteboard or on paper (see Figure 9.6).

Ask the client to list various aspects about themselves, beginning with positives: 'If I asked your family or friends what are your good points, what do you think they would say?' For each item the client lists, draw a little '*i*' inside the big one. Point out that these little '*i*'s stand for the good points they have listed.

Now ask the client what negative aspects their family or friends might list. Again, draw little '*i*'s for each item. Then do the same for 'neutral' items. Discuss the end result with the client. Socratically help them see that human beings are a mixture of many positive, negative and neutral actions and characteristics, and that it is, therefore, impossible to rate a whole person.

This technique is most effective when, rather than simply pointing out didactically how illogical it is to rate a human being, the client is helped to an understanding of this through a process of Socratic questioning.

Ellis et al. (adapted 1997, pp. 112–114) provide an in-depth case study where they applied a range of cognitive interventions with a client who was suicidal. The following section describes how they used the Big I – little i technique. The therapist draws a 'Big I' on a whiteboard or sheet of paper (see Figure 9.6).

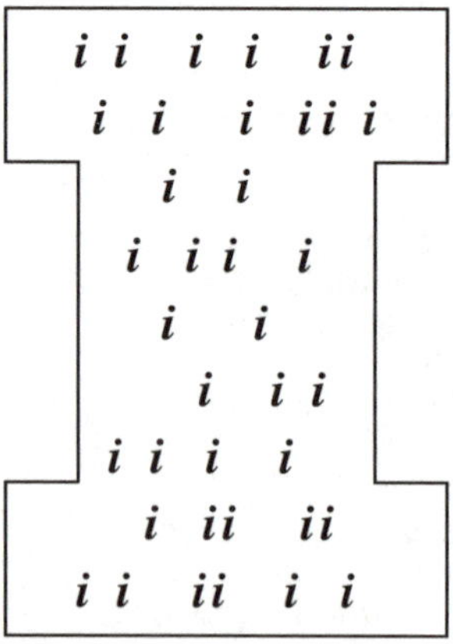

Figure 9.6 Big I, Little i.

Therapist: Now, this Big I represents you, your totality. And I'm going to fill it up in a minute with little '*i*'s which stand for various things about you, such as the way you smile, the kind of TV programme you like, and so on.

Client: I get you.

Therapist: OK. Now let's fill in this Big I with a few things about you. What would your family or friends say were some of your good points?

Client: Oh, well, I've got a good sense of humour, and let me see, I am kind-hearted, good to my children, I keep the house clean, I see that they're looked after properly . . . will that do (As the client was speaking the therapist drew small '*i*'s inside the Big I to represent different aspects about the client.)

Therapist: Each of these little '*i*'s stands for some aspect of you; this one (pointing to a little '*i*') stands for your good sense of humour, this other one stands for your kind-heartedness, and these other little '*i*'s represent all those other good points you mentioned you had.

Client: I understand.

Therapist: Now, these are some of the positive things. I'd imagine your friends and family may know you reasonably well.

Client: Yes.

Therapist: What negative things would they say about you?

Client: I easily get angry, I drive too fast . . . and I'm too trusting.

Therapist: (writing more little '*i*'s inside the big I) . . . Gets angry, drives too fast, too trusting. Now what about any neutral or indifferent things about yourself?

Client: Oh well, my dress sense isn't too bad; I can do alterations to the children's clothes and my house decorating ability is about average.

Therapist: (adding more little '*i*'s to represent the client's neutral points) If we spent all day on this and considered all the things you have done, including every thought or idea you've had since you were born, how many little '*i*'s do you think we would have?

Client: Loads! We'd easily fill up the Big I.

Therapist: Yes. Millions of different aspects of yourself, good, bad and neutral. Now let's return to your problem. When you fail at something, like picking your ex-boyfriend and then finding you've made a bad choice (therapist now circles one little '*i*' to denote this), you say, 'Because I picked this partner and I made a poor choice yet again, that proves I'm weak and an inadequate person'. Bearing in mind what we've been discussing in the last five minutes, are you actually being accurate?

Client: Well, I did make a big mistake when I picked him, and that's the fourth time I've been dumped after picking the wrong guy! Once again I failed to pick somebody who was right for me.

Therapist: (pointing to the little '*i*' he had circled inside the Big I) Agreed: you did fail to pick the right person. But how does that – this little '*i*' – make you (drawing a circle around the entire Big I) a total failure, and a totally weak and inadequate person?

Client: I suppose it doesn't.

Therapist: Granted that you may have some skills deficits when it comes to choosing the right partner and you may sometimes act in a weak and inadequate manner but as we can see from the diagram, this doesn't make you a total failure. When would we have all the facts in so we could really decide if you were a total failure and a totally weak and inadequate person?

Client: . . . When I die I suppose!

Therapist: You're absolutely right. On your deathbed, when you could have your own day of judgement. You could open up the big book (therapist opens his hands as if opening up a large book) and count up the number of times you had been a failure in your entire life. 'Yes, I was a failure on the 23rd of February in 1978; in 1983 I got a low grade in that exam; on four occasions I exhibited poor decision-making skills when I picked the wrong partners; my children weren't happy every day of their childhood; in 1985 I acted weakly; I lost my job, twice!'

Client: (laughing) Stop! Don't go on. It's ridiculous – to be a total failure I would have to be a failure all of my life, which is blatantly absurd.

Therapist: Could you summarize what point you think I'm attempting to make?

Client: I'm too complex to be rated as a total failure although you can rate the things I do such as acting weakly or picking the wrong partner four times.

Therapist: You're right. You can rate your traits, deeds, appearance, actions, skills or skills deficits but you are too complex to rate your entire self.

The therapist has to adapt the model depending upon what particular problem the client brings to therapy. With this technique, it is important to avoid just taking a didactic approach. By asking Socratic questions, clients usually become actively involved in the method and then provide challenges to dispute their self-downing beliefs. Ellis et al. (1977) recommended use of humorous over-exaggeration, which may also help some clients to see how absurd it is to globally rate themselves or others. However, this would have to be used with care when helping suicidal clients.

Complex as an amoeba

Dryden (1987, pp. 107–108) provides an example of a 'The "self" is too complex' intervention which helps to promote intellectual rational insight for clients who 'feel worthless'. In the case example provided the client is also suicidal:

Therapist: OK, so you say that you're worthless for cheating on your wife, is that right?

Client: Yes, that's what I believe.

Therapist: OK, but let's test that out. Are you saying that you are worthless, or what you've done is worthless?

Client: I'm saying that I'm worthless, not just what I did.

Therapist: OK, but let's see if that is logical. You know when you say 'I'm worthless' you are giving you, your personhood or your essence, a single rating. Can you see that?

Client: Yes.

Therapist: But let's see if you warrant that. You're 35. How many thoughts have you had from the day you were born till now?

Client: Countless, I guess.

Therapist: Add to that all your actions and throw in all your traits for good measure. From that time till now how many aspects of you are there?

Client: Millions, I guess.

Therapist: At least now when you say that Y-O-U ARE WORTHLESS you can see that you're implying that you are about as complex as a single-cell amoeba, and that this cell is worthless. Now is that true from what we've just been discussing?

Client: No, of course not.

Therapist: So do you, in all your complexity, merit a single rating?

Client: No, but I did do a pretty worthless thing and it was serious.

Therapist: Agreed, but what has greater validity, the belief, 'I'm worthless in all my essence' or the belief 'I am too complex to be rated, but I did do something lousy which I regret'?

Client: The second.

Therapist: Right and if you really worked on believing that would you still feel suicidal as you do now?

Client: No I wouldn't. I see what you mean.

When life really is bad

Sometimes the client's perception of their external problems may be based on reality. It is important that the therapist not be seen as minimizing these. It is better, in such cases, to acknowledge that the client does have significant problems, then help them see that:

- not all people with severe problems become suicidal
- suicidal feelings arise when a person adds to their original problem by self-blaming, catastrophizing, or demanding the problem not exist
- dealing first with such thinking will enable the individual to better solve their external problems.

Ellis and Newman (1996) present a useful discussion of so-called 'rational suicide', pointing out the problems with this concept. For clients facing unpleasant circumstances that cannot be changed, it may be helpful to introduce the principle of acceptance of reality (Froggatt, 1997, 2003). Acceptance is not the negative concept it may seem at first glance. To accept something does not mean that we have to agree with it: one can strongly wish or prefer that it did not exist, while realistically accepting there is no reason it should not exist. And acceptance is not 'resignation' – it does not mean we have 'given in' to things we dislike. We can continue to seek better solutions, but without the demand: 'Things must not be as they are', which induces hopelessness.

What is acceptance? To accept something is to acknowledge three issues: first, that it is a reality; second, that although it is unpleasant, it is bearable; and third, that even though it may be undesirable, there is no law of nature saying that it 'should' not be as it is. To increase one's tolerance for unpleasant realities that are difficult or impossible to change may be the ultimate protection from self-destruction.

Crisis counselling

McMullin (1986), who is an advocate of cognitive therapy, suggests that in a severe crisis, cognitive therapy could last for several hours and therapists could 'take no breaks. Flood the client with countering techniques; repeat them until the client comprehends their use . . . present an assured, self-confident manner. To enhance the client's feelings of support' (McMullin, 1986, p. 270). The client's reasons for committing suicide should be challenged by the therapist's arguments for staying alive (Neenan, 1996). Advocates of rational emotive behaviour therapy (REBT) appear to suggest a similar approach challenging suicide-inducing beliefs. Ellis stated:

> I almost always directly confront their irrational beliefs – particularly their strongly held beliefs that the unfavourable conditions of their lives are hopeless, that they will never be able to change them, and if that they continue to live they will not be able to be happy at all.
>
> (Ellis, 1987, p. 135)

A specific example in the REBT literature demonstrates the persistent challenging of the clients suicide-inducing beliefs (Neenan, 1996, pp. 9–10):

Client: I'm such a miserable failure, my family would be better off without me.

Therapist: But how will you know they are better off if you are dead? You won't be able to prove it.

Client: I just know they will be because I won't be an embarrassment or burden to them any longer.

Therapist: You see yourself this way because of your present depression, but your wife and family definitely do not share your opinion. They told me they would be devastated if you killed yourself. Is this what you mean by them being 'better off without me'?

Client: I'm sure they would quickly get over it and forget about me. They would be happier, I just know they would.

Therapist: Your family love you very much and they would suffer greatly if you committed suicide. There would be no quickly getting over it for them. Your suffering might stop but theirs would definitely start.

Client: I don't want them to suffer; I want them to be happy. I'm not sure what to do. I'm confused.

Therapist: Well, your family are waiting in the next room hopeful for some good news. Shall I tell them you are going to kill yourself in order to make them happier or that we are all going to work together to get you better?

Client: My family means so much to me, I never want to hurt them. They deserve better.

Therapist: So what shall I tell them?

Client: I don't want to die but I just can't see any light at the end of the tunnel.

Therapist: If you fight back against your depression with the love and support of your family, you will soon see the light dispel the darkness. If you really want to make your family better off, then chose to stay alive.

Client: Okay, I'll give it a try.

Therapist: Good. If it's all right with you, can I invite your family in so we can discuss what needs to be done.

Client: (slight elevation in mood) Yes, I would like to see my family now.

This dialogue highlights the therapist's persistent and unrelenting challenge of any beliefs that may lead to the client attempting suicide. Another aspect of this approach is involving the family or significant others if the therapist believes that this will be helpful and not counterproductive.

The therapist

Helping or supporting clients with suicidal ideation can be very difficult for counsellors, psychotherapists and other members of the helping professions. Often the practitioner will need to be aware of their own core beliefs, assumptions, rules or negative automatic thoughts (NATs) being activated when supporting such clients. The recognition and modification of one's own unhelpful beliefs will reduce our own anxiety triggered by suicidal clients. Being anxious about clients is likely to reduce our performance and not enhance it. Clinical supervision is strongly advised in these circumstances too.

Typical beliefs to be aware of include the following:

- I must perform well.
- I must succeed with all my clients.
- I am totally responsible for my client's actions.
- I'm useless.
- If I fail with my clients, this proves I'm a total failure.
- If I fail with my clients, my colleagues will know I'm a phony.
- The situation is totally hopeless.
- I can't stand this uncertainty about my client's condition.
- If I was in my client's situation I'd feel as bad as her/him.
- What's the point! My client won't improve whatever I do.

Practitioners can use the techniques previously discussed in this chapter to modify these beliefs.

Therapists who have not experienced suicidal clients yet may wish to use imagery to imagine counselling such a client and then note down any unhelpful beliefs that are triggered. Once obtained it would be useful to challenge and modify them.

Conclusion

This chapter provided a unified model of suicidality developed from a cognitive behavioural and rational emotive perspective. In addition to an assessment procedure, a range of strategies and techniques were highlighted that may help a therapist challenge the beliefs underpinning a suicidal client's depression, hopelessness and/or lack of self-acceptance. It should be noted that the techniques should be used within a therapeutic framework or model and not in isolation.

References

Beck, A. (1967) *Depression: Clinical, experimental and theoretical aspects.* New York: Harper & Row.

Beck, J.S. (1995) *Cognitive Therapy: Basics and beyond.* New York: Guilford.

Coon, D.W., DeVries, H.M. and Gallagher-Thompson, D. (2004) Cognitive behavioural therapy with suicidal older adults. *Behavioural and Cognitive Psychotherapy*, 32(4), 481–493.

Cooper, J. and Kapur, N. (2004) Assessing suicide risk, in D. Duffy and T. Ryan (eds) *New Approaches to Preventing Suicide: A manual for practitioners.* London: Jessica Kingsley Publishers.

Curwen, B., Palmer, S. and Ruddell, P. (2000) *Brief Cognitive Behaviour Therapy.* London: Sage.

Dryden, W. (1987) *Counselling Individuals: The rational emotive approach.* London: Taylor & Francis.

Ellis, A. (1987) A sadly neglected cognitive element in depression. *Cognitive Therapy and Research*, 11, 121–146.

Ellis, A., Gordon, J., Neenan, M. and Palmer, S. (1997) *Stress Counselling: a rational emotive behaviour approach.* London: Cassell.

Ellis, T.E. and Newman, C.F. (1996) *Choosing to Live: How to defeat suicide through cognitive therapy.* Oakland, CA: New Harbinger.

Freeman, A. and White, D.M. (1989) The treatment of suicidal behavior, in A. Freeman, K.M. Simon, L.E. Beutler and H. Arkowitz (eds) *Comprehensive Handbook of Cognitive Therapy.* New York: Plenum.

Froggatt, W. (1997) *GoodStress: The life that can be yours.* Auckland: HarperCollins.

Froggatt, W. (2003) *Choose to be Happy: Your step-by-step guide* (2nd edn). Auckland: HarperCollins.

Hawton, K. and Kirk, J. (1989) Problem-solving, in K. Hawton, P.M. Salkovskis, J. Kirk and D. Clarke (eds) *Cognitive Behaviour Therapy for Adult Psychiatric Problems.* Oxford: Oxford Medical Publications.

Horton, L. (2006) Social, cultural, and demographic factors in suicide, in R.I. Simon and R.E. Hales (eds) *Textbook of Suicide Assessment and Management.* Washington, DC: American Psychiatric Publishing.

Lazarus, A.A. (1977) Toward an egoless state of being, in A. Ellis and R. Grieger (eds) *Handbook of Rational-Emotive Therapy.* New York: McGraw-Hill.

Linehan, M., Armstrong, H., Suarez, A., Allmon, D. and Heard, H. (1991) Cognitive-behavioral treatment of chronically parasuicidal borderline patients. *Archives of General Psychiatry*, 48, 1060–1064.

McMullin, R.E. (1986) *Handbook of Cognitive Therapy Techniques*. New York: Norton.

Neenan, M. (1996) Tackling suicidal clients. *The Rational Emotive Behaviour Therapist*, 4(1), 8–11.

New Zealand Ministry of Health (2003) *The Assessment and Management of People at Risk of Suicide*. Wellington: Ministry of Health.

Palmer, S. (1997) Self-acceptance: concept, techniques and interventions. *The Rational Emotive Behaviour Therapist*, 5(1), 4–30.

Palmer, S. (1999) Developing an individual counselling programme: a multimodal perspective, in S. Palmer and P. Laungani (eds) *Counselling in a Multimodal Society*. London: Sage.

Palmer, S. (2005) *Suicide: myths, facts and prevention*. City Insight Lecture given at City University, London, April.

Palmer, S. and Dryden, W. (1995) *Counselling for Stress Problems*. London: Sage.

Rudd, M.D., Joiner, T. and Rajab, M.H. (2001) *Treating Suicidal Behaviour: An effective, time-limited approach*. New York: Guilford.

Sewell, H. (2004) Black and minority ethnic groups, in D. Duffy and T. Ryan (eds) *New Approaches to Preventing Suicide: A manual for practitioners*. London: Jessica Kingsley Publishers.

Simon, R.I. and Hales, R.E. (eds) (2006) *Textbook of Suicide Assessment and Management*. Washington, DC: American Psychiatric Publishing.

Wendler, S. and Matthews, D. (2006) Cultural competence in suicide risk assessment, in R.I. Simon and R.E. Hales (eds) *Textbook of Suicide Assessment and Management*. Washington, DC: American Psychiatric Publishing.

Williams, J.M.G. and Wells, J. (1989) Suicidal patients, in J. Scott, J.M.G. Williams and A.T. Beck (eds) *Cognitive Therapy in Clinical Practice: An illustrative casebook*. London: Routledge.

10 A psychodynamic approach to suicide

John Lees and Quentin Stimpson

This chapter begins by critically exploring Freudian and post-Freudian understandings of suicide, although due to limitations of space it is not comprehensive. Several examples drawn from clinical practice are then considered in relation to the theoretical ideas previously discussed. The chapter then moves on to reconsider psychodynamic approaches to suicidal clients from a Levinasian ethical position. The possibility that suicide may be a logical part of what it is to be human, rather than an indication of mental illness, is advanced.

> Freud's notion of the death instinct suggests, at its most minimal, that we want (or need) something we know nothing about, and that we are most drawn to what we think of ourselves as trying to avoid. That we are, essentially, idiosyncratic suicides, but not from despair, but because it is literally our nature to die.
>
> (Phillips, 1999, p. 110)

Suicide has been on the increase in the UK with the rate of suicide in men aged between 14 and 24 increasing by 78 per cent between 1980 and 1990 (Gask, 2000, p. 560). This has led to national suicide prevention strategies being set up to tackle the suicide rate (e.g. NIMHE, 2006). The possibility that a client may commit suicide is one of the reasons that a counsellor (as part of their duty of care) might decide to break confidentiality (Bond, 1993; British Association for Counselling and Psychotherapy (BACP), 1993). This reading of suicidal intention sees suicide as potentially linked with mental illness, hence it takes the view that the client may change their mind if they are mentally well, even if that goes against their immediate wishes.

This chapter explores a range of Freudian and post-Freudian perspectives on suicide and suicidal ideation. Although given that the psychodynamic church is a 'broad one' (Davies and Burton, 1996), and the limitations of space, it is in no way comprehensive. Various psychodynamic viewpoints are presented and these are then critically discussed in the light of some clinical examples. There then follows a re-examination of psychodynamic ideas pertaining to suicide in the light of Levinasian ethics, which it is suggested, raises some serious and important questions for practitioners in relation to how they think and work with a potentially suicidal client.

Theoretical understandings

Psychodynamic viewpoints on suicide accept that it may be linked with a depressive state, involving feelings of sadness, and they have also considered the narcissistic aspects of the suicidal act (e.g. Grunberger, 1990). However, the most predominant viewpoint held by psychodynamic therapists is that suicide is an aggressive act. Hence the psychodynamic point of view postulates that any attempt to understand suicide needs to also address the place of aggression within the human psyche. Freud's theorizing about the role and place of aggression went through various stages: originally he postulated that aggression was a derivative of the drive to (sexual) mastery (Freud, 1905), but by the time he wrote 'Instincts and their vicissitudes' in 1915 he had repositioned aggression as part of the self-preservative instinct.

Freud built on these earlier works in his seminal paper 'Mourning and melancholia' (Freud, 1917), in which he took up the view that the suicidal act is in fact a redirection of aggressive and murderous wishes towards another back onto the self. He thus still saw aggression as being principally directed towards others (or, in the language of psychoanalysis, an external object): that is to say, someone can kill themselves only if they have wanted to kill another person. Aggression 'represents the ego's original reaction to objects in the external world', (Freud, 1917, p. 252). For the person to be able to attempt suicide, Freud reasoned, they must have been 'overwhelmed by the object', i.e. the mental representation of an actual other person in the person's world (Freud, 1915, p. 252).

In order to get an overview of a psychodynamic approach to suicide, the notion of aggressive drives directed towards others thus needs to be supplemented by three other fundamental dynamic mechanisms: internalization, detachment from self and acting out. First, the aggression is internalized and brought to bear on the self. Second, the self establishes a particular relationship with itself. It, so to speak, detaches itself from itself: 'The ego can kill itself only if . . . it can treat itself as an object . . . if it is able to direct against itself the hostility which relates to an object' (Freud, 1917, p. 252). Finally, suicide is a form of acting out: the general psychodynamic view of this phenomenon is that the individual attempts to gain relief from a childhood trauma by re-enacting the trauma in the present. The acting out symbolizes the trauma, even though the individual is not aware of the link between the acting out and the original experience. Thus from the point of view of acting out, suicide would be seen as linked with unresolved childhood trauma.

Later work by Freud confirmed the centrality of the role of aggression in suicide. His ongoing explorations with patients led him to challenge his view of aggression as a form of the self-preservative (life) instinct and with the publication of 'Beyond the pleasure principle' (Freud, 1920) he introduced the concept of a separate aggressive drive (operative from birth) which he linked with the death (or destructive) instinct. The destructive instinct aims to 'undo connections and to destroy things . . . we may suppose that its final aim is to lead what is living into an inorganic state' (Freud, 1938, p. 148). Thus it has a suicidal aim. These earlier works not only lay the basis for psychodynamic views of suicide but also to some extent provide a direction for treatment through the technique of interpretation not only of the dynamic process itself, but also of any enactment (that is repetition compulsion) which may take place in the therapy. However these ideas, particularly ideas about the psychodynamic treatment of suicide, have been considerably enlarged by post-Freudian thinkers.

Melanie Klein did much to extend and develop Freud's concept of the death instinct and, while considering the important ameliorating effects of the life instincts upon the death instincts, she went on to emphasize the ways in which an infant's earliest experiences (usually with the mother) can help it to modify its innate destructive tendencies (e.g. Klein, 1946). Bion (1962) further developed these ideas about the importance of the earliest mother–infant relationship as the medium through which the infant is helped to manage its destructiveness through his concepts of the 'container' and 'contained' (Bion, 1962). Essentially for Bion, part of the mother's role is to be receptive to her infant's attempts at ridding itself of the unmanageable bits of its experience (e.g. its aggressive and destructive phantasies) through projective identification. By taking in the infant's projections (i.e. identifying with them) and detoxifying them through her maternal reverie she can then offer them back to her infant in a more manageable, digestible form.[1] However, it is often the case that the mother is unable to do this. She is unable to bear the infant's aggressiveness and thereby return it in a manageable form. Such traumatic infantile experiences may then manifest in later life in an acute susceptibility to rejection. As a result of the sense of rejection by the 'not good-enough' mother, the suicidal client may experience minor rejections in adult life as catastrophic blows. One way out of the ensuing psychic pain would be to regress to an earlier omnipotent state of existence where the self is merged with the parent. In adult life this manifests as a desire for annihilation and the obliteration of a separate existence. Therapeutically these dynamics may be reproduced and it is incumbent on the therapist to correct the emotional deficit – to become a 'container' who can bear the client's projections and return them in a manageable form.

Another psychodynamic perspective on suicide is that of Fenichel, who saw it as sometimes an attempt to escape the guilt arising from an over-harsh superego (Fenichel, 1990, p. 294), though he also acknowledged that behind the suicidal thoughts lay a wish to kill another (or others). Thus suicide was both a wish to kill off the superego (and the people it represented) as well as by so doing to gain their love/approval, and at root in suicide you found the re-emergence of '. . . the original annihilation of the deserted hungry baby . . .' (Fenichel, 1990, p. 400).

Fenichel's comments are reminiscent of Winnicott's words about break-down as something 'already experienced' in early life. Indeed Winnicott's ideas present yet another psychodynamic perspective on the phenomenon. He maintained that suicide may result from an internalization of aggression felt towards the mother, as for Winnicott the infant needed a certain amount of aggression in order to create a transitional space,[2] and so to begin to separate from the mother (Winnicott, 1956/1992, 1965, 1971). He thus sees suicidal desires/intentions as arising out of a failure to negotiate a natural developmental stage of life.

The work of Laufer and Laufer (1989; Laufer, 1995) around adolescent breakdown develops these Winnicottian themes. Suicide is seen as being either a way of gaining separateness from the object/other, or as an attempt to control the distance from the object/other (which has become identified with the suicide's body) whereby the suicidal act is seen as an attack on, or an abandonment of, the object/other.

The work of Scharff and Scharff (1992, p. 171) provides a broad object relations understanding of suicide and is a succinct summary of many of the ideas presented above. In essence they see suicide as potentially being about one or more of the following dynamics:

- an attack on the object with which the self has become identified
- an attack on the self to save the object (i.e. as an act of sacrifice)
- an attempt to separate the self from the object (when self and object are felt to be fused).

However, it should of course be noted that Scharff and Scharff's ideas pro-vide only a very broad, skeletal outline of psychodynamic thinking around suicide, lacking as they do any description (or consideration) of the rich detail and texture of the intricate interplay between inner and outer (usually early) experiences and the slippage between present and past time that the work of the theorists explored above offer. The other main area that Scharff and Scharff (1992) omit, which is arguably lacking in much object relations thinking, is the classical Freudian and Kleinian emphasis upon innate human aggressiveness (and its impact on the individual).

We will now illustrate the basic principles of the psychodynamic approach to suicide with reference to two clinical examples. The first one describes a client who threatened suicide and eventually succeeded in killing herself; the second describes a client who frequently threatened suicide and made several serious attempts to do so, but who ultimately failed to kill himself. Ethical consider-ations have been taken into account in order to protect the clients' identity.

Case examples

Ms M was a middle-aged woman who was a migrant to the United Kingdom from a developing country. She was the only child of a wealthy family. On ariving in the UK, she coped reasonably well. She worked and her job provided enough money to live a comfortable life. She thus seemed, on the surface, to have integrated well into western culture.

Ms M was seen for open-ended psychodynamic counselling. She presented with depression, isolation and loneliness. In addition to the counselling she was also seeing a psychiatrist, who prescribed medication for her. The details of her background remained obscure. The client was unable to speak about her childhood traumas and so we could only speculate about the cause of her problems. There was also the issue of her lack of cultural identity in the UK and her subsequent isolation and loneliness. Unfortunately, the help that she received from the counsellor and the psychiatrist was not enough and she succeeded in killing herself on the day that her counselling appointment was scheduled.

It is natural for a therapist, under such circumstances, to search for what we might have missed or to wonder if we could have done more. Indeed the difficulties posed by such a therapeutic experience for the therapist working psychodynamically – with its strong emphasis on containing powerful feelings based on a strong identification with the client – can result in a state of inner turmoil which may, in turn, lead to questioning whether we should continue to work as a therapist.

One significant factor in Ms M's story was that she managed to create a distance between herself and the members of her family by migrating to the UK. In view of the psychodynamic idea that suicide is ultimately based on aggression towards others one might thus speculate that she did this in order to keep her family safe from the effects of her own fury and murderous feelings. Indeed, in the therapy, she often spoke about her family, thinking and worrying about them much of the time in spite of the geographical distance she had placed between herself and them.

In spite of these concerns the therapeutic relationship gave at least the beginning of a new lease of life: she formed a strong identification with the counsellor. But when she realized that she could not possess the therapist in reality, she took her own life. She had often spoken about suicide to the counsellor, asking such questions as: 'What happens if I don't make it for the next session? What would you do?' In response the counsellor said: 'I would be very sorry. I would miss you, but I would carry on'. This was like a message from life to death saying, in effect, 'You might die, but I will continue'.

Both her reasons for migrating to the UK and her concern about the counsellor suggest that Ms M had some awareness of her murderous feelings towards others and she was thus concerned to mollify the effect of these. In Fenichel's (1990) terms she had a harsh superego and the suicide was, perhaps, a sacrificial act.

Mr H, in contrast to Ms M, frequently threatened suicide, and made several attempts, but never succeeded. He had had a traumatic and violent upbringing and, as a consequence of this, had lived in a succession of foster homes. He had also received psychiatric care. Unlike Ms M he was demonstrably angry: 'Don't trust the bastards' was his motto when dealing with any authority figures.

He frequently made violent threats during the sessions – both in regard to his own life and the lives of others – which were frightening for the counsellor. This was discussed fully in supervision and on balance it was decided that despite his anger Mr H actually was not an immediate threat to others. In fact apart from occasional angry outbursts with some people, he tended to do much more violence to himself and, on several occasions, had to be admitted to hospital after he had cut himself. In view of these developments, the therapeutic journey with the client was mentally and physically exhausting for the counsellor. It often felt like walking on thin ice or walking on a tightrope. The sheer weight of the verbal threats and projected aggression of the client led to a carelessness about personal safety. It led to the counsellor developing a strong impression that it is possible to get so used to that level of violence and aggression that it becomes hardly noticeable to the individual. It becomes the norm.

In view of the threats to the therapeutic alliance, from both the aggression of the client and the carelessness of the counsellor about personal safety, the management of the boundaries became an important aspect of the therapeutic work. Another important therapeutic focus was for the counsellor to sustain a sense of hope for the client even when all seemed hopeless. Furthermore, Mr H did not commit suicide, the counselling ended and Mr H managed to slowly pull together the threads of his life.

An unanswered question arising from this work was why the client did not end his life rather than continuing his tortuous and painful existence. The case perhaps illustrated some of the developmental aspects of aggression and suicidal feelings which have been discussed by Winnicott. But as in the case of Ms M, the work with Mr H raised questions rather than provided answers.

Theory and practice revisited: ethics and psychodynamic practice

The discussion has so far described some key aspects of the psychodynamic understanding of suicide and, from the point of view of practice, has commented on the theory and technique of interpretation and containment. It has tended to look at suicide as an aberration, for instance as arising out of a failure of maternal containment, and consequently viewed the therapist's task as one of repairing these failures. Having said this, it has also taken the view that dealing with suicide, and suicidal impulses, can raise as many questions as answers. So it is perhaps helpful to look at the other possibilities which might lie dormant within the psychodynamic approach to suicide.

In a fundamental sense we can raise the question of whether a reparative approach to suicide is consistent with psychodynamic theories about the death instinct. In the cases of Ms M and Mr H the level of identification between the counsellors and the clients can be possible only as a result of the counsellors being in touch with their own death instinct. However, if we take the notion of the death instinct seriously, then we have to consider the possibility that we all, in part, have a tendency towards our own destruction (or to borrow a phrase from Phillips (1999, p. 110) 'we are, essentially, idiosyncratic suicides'). An example of a case where the therapist has attempted to adopt this approach to the client may be found in one of the late Nina Coltart's published case histories where she says of her former client's suicide that she 'admired the dignity and forbearance of his silent departure' (Coltart, 1995, p. 38). Given the closeness of the publication of this study and Coltart's own suicide, the question of the extent to which the case study is actually autobiographical hangs in the air, but nevertheless it raises an important possibility: namely, whether we should allow the patient to decide to take their own life. This would require amending BACP's Code of Ethics and Practice for Counsellors and rethinking the principles of the counsellor's duty of care discussed earlier.

These considerations raise two possibilities. First, one logical outcome of contemporary psychodynamic Kleinian and post-Kleinian thinking is that the theory can be used to justify taking one's own life. Taken to its logical conclusion, the theory can become, so to speak, death affirming rather than life affirming (where death is viewed as an annihilation – a state of nothingness). Second, there is the question of ethics which, we will argue, goes beyond the counsellor's duty of care towards the client and raises fundamental questions about how engaged the counsellor should be with the client and how open they should be to the client's own desires and wishes. Psychodynamic counselling, as mentioned earlier, is a broad church: at one end of the spectrum a counsellor may be encouraged to adopt a standpoint of human engagement with his or her clients, at the other a position of detached neutrality.

A prominent proponent of adopting a standpoint of human engagement is Peter Lomas who encourages 'ordinary human decency' in his practice (Lomas, 1999, pp. 15–37).

Lomas recalls once sitting with a client who 'had got stuck and was in a bad way'. He responded by saying 'look, if you won't do it for yourself, what about me?' (Morgan, 1999, p. 29). This, of course, fits with Lomas' observation that even though research seems to suggest that the therapeutic relationship is the most important factor in therapy, we still don't know what sort of a relationship is best. Therefore it seems strange that much therapeutic training advocates that their trainees learn how to adopt a detached, clinical-professional approach to their clients, rather than a more ordinary one where a human concern for the other is dominant.

The techniques of human engagement – and neutrality – are, however, problematic when we examine them closely. Heaton (1999), for instance, takes an uncompromising view of the notion of neutrality:

> To be neutral to a person is morally monstrous as it denies his/her personhood, it shuts people out of the human community where moral language makes sense and it enables us to control them pretending it is for their good.
>
> (Heaton, 1999, pp. 65–66)

Indeed, it could be argued that both the humanly engaged standpoint of Lomas and the classical analytic attitude of neutrality are essentially unethical as both actually deny the personhood of the client, arising as they do from the theoretical and/or personal leanings of the counsellor. They do not allow for the client in their otherness (i.e. difference) from both the counsellor and his/her theories (noting that counsellor's theory choice and usage is essentially a highly subjective and idiosyncratic affair: see e.g. Marks, 1978; Cornsweet, 1983; Johnson et al., 1988; Vasco et al., 1993; Vasco and Dryden, 1994; Feltham, 1999).

We suggested earlier that the issue of suicide raised more questions than answers for the psychodynamic counsellor. Indeed, this is even more so when we consider the ethics of working with someone who is suicidal. Is it ethical for the counsellor to break confidentiality if they believe that a client is in danger of taking their life? Is suicide automatically the act of a mentally ill person or is it an act which can be understood as arising naturally out of the human condition, and one that can be undertaken rationally and even justified theoretically? Is it ethical for a counsellor to allow clients to take their life? Is it more ethical to see the human aspects of the therapeutic relationship as paramount? Is it ethical to adopt a therapeutic stance of detached neutrality? What is an appropriate ethical standpoint to take in relation to suicide? Gordon (1999), drawing upon the work of the philosopher Levinas, puts forward a particular response to such questions as these:

> Ethics, in the very particular sense that Levinas gives it, is at the heart of psychotherapy, but ethics in this sense requires . . . an attitude or position of radical openness towards the other in all his strangeness which avoids reducing the other to what is already known to us.
>
> (Gordon, 1999, p. 47)

Thus the question becomes: is it possible to respond to the client in an ethical, non-neutralizing way which allows for their own, unique truth? Although we have come upon this question through the consideration of suicide it is a fundamental one which weaves its way through all psychotherapeutic practice and confronts us all as practitioners.

Lacan was a notable exception to the resistance to considering the practice of psychotherapy as being fundamentally an ethical one, devoting a whole year (1959–1960) to it in his famous seminars where he maintained that 'ethical thought is at the centre of our work as analysts' (Porter, 1992, p. 38). As such he may provide a way forward in addressing the above dilemma, even though this offers no clear answer to the bewilderment and difficulties often encountered by a counsellor who has worked with a client who has committed suicide, such as Ms M. But then Lacan never aimed to provide clear, or indeed comfortable, answers. For Lacan the analyst's task is to enable the patient's 'own unique truth [to] emerge in the treatment, a truth that is absolutely different to that of the analyst' (Evans, 1996, p. 39). Analysts must not align themselves with society's morality as this is seen as being pathogenic (which in this respect could include society's tendency to locate suicide as being pathological per se), but neither should the analyst advocate that the client adopt a libertine approach to themselves and their problems. Instead the analyst must challenge the patient to address the fundamental question that Lacan formulates as: 'Have you acted in conformity with the desire that is in you?' (Porter, 1992, p. 314). The aim of therapy being for the client to articulate their relationship to their own desire. Then, perhaps we can meet clients in an ethical and human way that honours them in their uniqueness.

Perhaps this, in a psychodynamic sense (if we are true to the theory) is what both Ms M and Mr H achieved.

Conclusion

As discussed in the case examples, working with suicidal clients raises difficult questions and difficult potential answers. Indeed, while a psychodynamic viewpoint provides ways of understanding the causes of the urge to commit suicide, the violence of the act leaves the psychodynamic counsellor – and the relatives and acquaintances – with unanswered questions. A powerful after-effect of having worked with a client who has committed suicide can be an emptiness, a feeling of not knowing. These feelings can be explained to some extent by psychodynamic perspectives on working with disturbed clients (e.g. the work of Bion and his notions about attacks on thinking and the place of not knowing in the therapeutic encounter).[3] But as we have also seen, this may not always have to be the case as some psychodynamic thinking (taken to its logical conclusion) also suggests that desiring our own death may be a fundamental part of what it is to be alive.

Notes

1 Bion suggested that babies use their mothers as places to put the undigestible parts of their experiences (e.g. their aggressive and destructive phantasies).By being receptive to their baby's projections the mother becomes the container of the baby's unconscious, undigestible phantasies and through her ability to process, i.e. think about, what the baby has put into her so the mother is able to lessen the power (or detoxify) the baby's destructive and aggressive phantasies. The mother is then in a position to make sense of her baby's formerly unthinkable experiences/phantatsies and to offer them back to the baby in a modified, digestible form (Symington and Symington, 1996, pp. 50–58).

2 Transitional space is, for Winnicott, the space that developmentally gradually opens up between the mother and her baby, and it relates to the baby's acknowledgement that there is a separation between it and its mother. It is the place of all human creativity (Newman, 1995, pp. 336–342).

3 Bion suggests that there are parts of the personality that attack and destroy logical thinking processes, seen at their extreme in the personality of the psychotic (Bion, 1959; Symington and Symington, 1996, pp. 143–165). Bion writes about the importance of approaching the therapeutic work from a position of not-knowing, or 'negative capability' (Bion, 1970; Symington and Symington, 1996, pp. 166–174).

References

Bion, W.R. (1959) Attacks on linking. *International Journal of Psychoanalysis*, 40, 308–315.

Bion, W.R. (1962) *Learning from Experience*. London: Karnac.

Bion, W.R. (1970) *Attention and Interpretation*. London: Tavistock.

Bond, T. (1993) *Standards and Ethics for Counselling in Action*. London: Sage.

British Association for Counselling and Psychotherapy (BACP) (1993) *Code of Ethics and Practice for Counsellors*. Rugby: BACP.

Coltart, N. (1995) A philosopher and his mind, in E.G. Corrigan and P.E. Gordon (eds) *The Mind Object: Precocity and pathology of self-sufficiency*. London: Karnac.

Cornsweet, C. (1983) Nonspecific factors and theoretical choice. *Psychotherapy: Theory, Research and Practice*, 20(3), 307–313.

Davies, T. and Burton, M. (1996) The psychodynamic paradigm, in W. Dryden and R. Woolfe (eds) *Handbook of Counselling Psychology*. London: Sage.

Evans, D. (1996) *An Introductory Dictionary of Lacanian Psychoanalysis*. London: Routledge.

Feltham, C. (1999) Against and beyond core theoretical models, in C. Feltham (ed.) *Controversies in Psychotherapy and Counselling*. London: Sage.

Fenichel, O. (1990) *The Psychoanalytic Theory of Neurosis*. London: Routledge.

Freud, S. (1905) Three essays on the theory of sexuality, in *Standard Edition*, 7, 125–245. London: Hogarth Press.

Freud, S. (1915) Instincts and their vicissitudes, in *Standard Edition*, 14, 109–140. London: Hogarth Press.

Freud, S. (1917) Mourning and melancholia, in *Standard Edition*, 14, 237–260. London: Hogarth Press.

Freud, S. (1920) Beyond the pleasure principle, in *Standard Edition*, 18, 3–64. London: Hogarth Press.

Freud, S. (1938) An outline of psycho-analysis, in *Standard Edition, 23*, 141–207. London: Hogarth Press.

Gask, L. (2000) Suicide and deliberate self-harm, in C. Feltham and I. Horton (eds) *Handbook of Counselling and Psychotherapy*. London: Sage.

Gordon, P. (1999) *Face to Face: Therapy as ethics*. London: Constable.

Grunberger, B. (1990) Suicide of melancholics, in B. Grunberger, *Narcissism: Psycho-analytic essays*. Madison, CT: International Universities Press.

Heaton, J. (1999) The ordinary, in L. King (ed.) *Committed Uncertainty in Psycho-therapy: Essays in honour of Peter Lomas*. London: Whurr.

Johnson, J.A., Germer, C.K., Efran, J.S. and Overton, W.F. (1988) Personality as the basis for theoretical predilections. *Journal of Personality and Social Psychology, 55* (5), 824–835.

Klein, M. (1946) Notes on some schizoid mechanisms, in *Envy and Gratitude and Other Works, 1946–1963*. New York: Delta.

Laufer, M. (ed.) (1995) *The Suicidal Adolescent*. London: Karnac.

Laufer, M. and Laufer, M.E. (1989) *Developmental Breakdown and Psychoanalytic Treatment in Adolescence: Clinical studies*. New Haven, CT: Yale University Press.

Lomas, P. (1999) *Doing Good? Psychotherapy out of its depth*. Oxford: Oxford University Press.

Marks, M.J. (1978) Conscious/unconscious selection of the psychotherapist's theor-etical orientation. *Psychotherapy: Theory, Research and Practice*, 15(4), 354–358.

Morgan, S. (1999) Interview with Peter Lomas, in L. King (ed.) *Committed Uncertainty in Psychotherapy: Essays in honour of Peter Lomas*. London: Whurr.

Newman, A. (1995) *Non-compliance in Winnicott's Words*. London: Free Association Books.

NIMHE (2006) *National Suicide Prevention Strategy for England: Annual report on progress 2005*. Leeds: Care Services Improvement Partnership, National Institute for Mental Health in England.

Phillips, A. (1999) *Darwin's Worms*. London: Faber & Faber.

Porter, D. (trans.) (1992) *Jacques Lacan: The seminar. Book VII: The ethics of psycho-analysis, 1959–60*. London: Routledge.

Scharff, J.S. and Scharff, D.E. (1992) *Scharff Notes: A primer of object relations therapy*. New York: Jason Aronson.

Symington, J. and Symington, N. (1996) *The Clinical Thinking of Wilfred Bion*. London: Routledge.

Vasco, A.B. and Dryden, W. (1994) The development of psychotherapists' theoretical orientation and clinical practice. *British Journal of Guidance and Counselling*, 22(3), 327–341.

Vasco, A.B., Garcia-Marques, L. and Dryden, W. (1993) 'Psychotherapist know thy-self!': Dissonance between metatheoretical and personal values in psychotherapists of different theoretical orientations. *Psychotherapy Research*, 3(3), 181–196.

Winnicott, D.W. (1956/1992) Primary maternal preoccupation, in D.W. Winnicott, *Through Paediatrics to Psycho-analysis*. London: Karnac.

Winnicott, D.W. (1965) *The Maturational Processes and the Facilitating Environment*. London: Hogarth Press.

Winnicott, D.W. (1971) *Playing and Reality*. London: Tavistock.

11 A solution-focused approach

*John Sharry, Melissa Darmody and
Brendan Madden*

Self-harm and suicide are among the most challenging and frightening problems that you can encounter as a professional in the course of your work. The
risk of clients harming themselves can debilitate you from acting creatively
and collaboratively, and make your actions defensive, focused solely on risk
assessment rather than therapeutic change. Yet it is precisely a creative and
collaborative response, such as that engendered by solution-focused and
other strengths-based therapies that is the most likely to facilitate change
and re-empower clients to take back charge of their lives. This chapter
describes some principles of a solution-focused approach to working with
suicidal clients, which can be used in conjunction with traditional approaches
and which focuses on establishing safety as well as assessing risk. Working
from this model the clinician shifts to identifying client strengths and coping
skills, to collaborating with the client to establish meaningful goals and to
helping the client envision a positive future. Arguably, such an approach
can increase collaboration between therapist and client and lead to a more
client-centred safety plan.

Suicidal behaviour: a serious problem

Self-harm and suicide are serious problems which affect large numbers of
people in the western world. Particularly alarming are the recent increases in
suicide and suicide attempts by young people and teenagers, especially young
men (Cantor, 2000). There are specific differences in the rates of suicide and
attempted suicide between young men and women. Young women are more
likely to attempt suicide, but less likely to be successful and more likely to seek
the support of family, friends and mental health services. Young men are
more likely to choose lethal means, less likely to seek support and thus much
more likely to complete suicide (Carr, 1999). Depression and suicide are
highly correlated in that studies have shown that between 29 and 88 per cent
of people who committed suicide were depressed and about half of all people
with a diagnosis of depression report having suicidal ideation (Lonnqvist,
2000). However, it is important to note that not all people who attempt
suicide report being depressed. Other factors such as drug and alcohol use,

risk-taking and impulsive behaviour are all very significant contributors to a decision to make a suicide attempt. Although for some people a suicide attempt is a once-off event, studies have shown that 50 per cent are likely to repeat an attempt within the following twelve months and some of these are successful (Carr, 1999).

A significant number of people at risk of suicide do not seek professional help, (especially young men: Pfeffer, 2000), but some studies have shown that over half of those who attempt suicide are already in contact with mental health services (Hawkes et al., 1998). This puts an onus on mental health professionals to find therapeutic ways of reducing the risk of the many suicidal and depressed clients who come to the attention of services, while also finding creative ways of reaching out to the significant groups of young people who are at risk and who avoid professional contact. Traditionally, the professional response has consisted of risk assessment and management, followed by treatment interventions such as medication or psychotherapy (Carr, 1999; Hawton and van Heeringen, 2000). Alarmingly, there has been little empirical research to suggest that either medication or psychotherapy-based interventions, in their current format, are effective in reducing the risk of suicide, when compared to a non-treatment control group (Heard, 2000; Verkes and Cowen, 2000). (This is partly due to the ethical and practical difficulties in conducting such research.) Cognitive and problem-solving therapies, however, which focus on helping the young person and their family solve practical and relationship problems, show the most promise (Hazell, 2000).

In addition, many of the techniques used by practitioners, such as entering into a no-suicide contract with clients during treatment, are not as effective as commonly believed. For example, in a postal survey of clinicians, examining the rates of suicidal attempts following treatment, Kroll (2000) found that 41 per cent of respondents had treated people who committed or made a serious attempt *after* entering into a no-suicide contract with the clinician. While this tells us nothing of the efficacy of contracting relative to not contracting, it does indicate that no clinician should take excessive comfort from the fact that a suicidal person agrees to contract for safety. Indeed it suggests that we should continue to be searching for more effective ways of working with this high-risk client group.

Solution-focused therapy: a strengths-based approach

Solution-focused therapy (SFT) is a collaborative and non-pathological approach to therapy developed by de Shazer and others from the 1980s (de Shazer et al., 1986; O'Hanlon and Weiner-Davies, 1989; Berg, 1991; Sharry, 2001; Sharry et al., 2004). Belonging to the social constructionist school of thought, the approach questions the usefulness of many of the traditional assumptions about psychotherapy such as that problems need to be always understood before solutions can be reached, or that symptoms mask underlying deeper problems which have specific causes, or that real therapeutic change takes time and is invariably resisted by clients. From a postmodern perspective such assumptions are not true or false. They do, however, direct the course of the therapeutic conversation, selecting what therapists listen to and guiding the thrust of their questions and therapeutic techniques.

SFT proposes that strengths-based assumptions are more *useful* in guiding therapeutic conversations. For example, in contrast to the above assumptions it is arguably more useful to conceive that solutions need to be understood and elaborated rather than problems, that therapeutic change can be brief and pivotal, and that 'resistance' occurs only when therapists misunderstand the client's individual way of cooperating.

In practical terms, SFT is a reorientation from a problem-focused to a solution-focused approach to therapy. The focus is on working with client strengths, rather than deficits, on analysing positive exceptions rather than problem patterns and on elaborating preferred futures and goals rather than problem pasts. In a nutshell, the focus is on where clients want to go, rather than where they have been. The role of the therapist is to clear his or her head of hypotheses about the nature of the problem (or the solution) and to adopt an 'unknowing position' viewing the client as the expert. From a stance of respectful curiosity towards clients and their life situations, the therapist asks questions that aim to facilitate the client in generating their own solutions to the problems that brought them to therapy.

Suicide risk and solution-focused therapy

In recent years many practitioners have been exploring how solution-focused therapy can apply to work with clients who are suicidal or who have a history of self-harm (Hawkes et al., 1998; Softas-Nall and Francis, 1998a; Calcott and MacKenzie, 2001; Hawkes, 2003). In particular the authors have explored how solution-focused ideas, particularly scaling questions can be used to enhance traditional approaches to suicide risk assessment in order to establish a safety plan with clients and their families. Although there is a growing body of research for solution-focused therapy in general (George et al., 1999), there is as yet no empirical evidence for the effectiveness of the approach with suicidal clients. There is however some evidence that the strengths-based orientation that solution-focused therapy engenders may be a fruitful one. For example, Malone et al. (2000) studied eighty-four depressed individuals, many with a prior history of suicide attempts. Depressed individuals who had *no* history of suicide attempts had greater survival and coping beliefs, more moral objections to suicide, and more reasons for living. While being far from definitive, these results suggest that rather than exclusively carrying out risk assessment, clinicians should also spend time doing the things that might prevent depressed individuals from attempting suicide, such as highlighting their coping skills, exploring their reasons for living and helping them envision a more hopeful and optimistic future.

In addition, there have been a number or suicide prevention programmes in the USA, which have raised awareness about suicide among teenagers and have focused on helping teenagers identify the warning signs in themselves and others, as well as teaching them how to access help and support. Follow-up empirical studies, however, have not shown a decrease in suicidal behaviour and alarmingly there has been some evidence that risk has been increased (Schaffer and Gould, 2000). One hypothesis is that this is due to the usual problem-focused nature of the interventions, which may increase the appeal to teenagers. Indeed, many studies have shown that there is an increase in suicides when a prominent figure in youth culture (such as a pop or movie star) commits suicide and this is well publicized in the media (Schmidtke and Schaller, 2000). For this reason, it is likely that prevention programmes that focus on wellness and health, teaching young people social and coping skills are more likely to be more successful. Indeed, some studies suggest that these health-focused interventions are the most promising in reducing suicidal intention among teenagers, though further evaluation is needed (Klingman and Hochdorf, 1993). This underpinning wellness philosophy resonates with the strengths and goal focus of solution-focused therapy and is where a contribution can be made.

Solution-focused therapy is not unique in engendering a strengths-based collaborative approach to working with suicidal clients and the ideas strongly resonate with other brief interventions particularly those from the cognitive behavioural tradition. For example, the SNAP programme (Miller et al., 1992), a cognitive behavioural intervention for adolescent suicide attempters and their families, has much in common with solution-focused therapy, in that it focuses on establishing practical goals, encouraging strengths-based communication between family members and using scaling questions to assess risk and to establish safety plans.

Some people have expressed caution about using a strengths-based approach with suicidal clients, especially given an implicit lack of emphasis on risk assessment. Indeed a strict application of strengths-based techniques, without taking into account the dangers that clients could be in, would be an unethical way of practising as clearly there will be times when the therapist has to take unilateral action to ensure a client's safety (such as informing other family members, the family doctor or arranging an involuntary inpatient stay). However, there are also dangers from being excessively problem or risk focused in that this can close down the possibility of therapy. Clients will simply not talk to you if they feel you are going to react in a specific way without consulting or listening to them first. For example, many people will not disclose just how depressed or hopeless they feel for fear someone will 'lock them up'. Ironically, it is these clients, who are without a person with whom they can supportively communicate, who are at the most risk of harming themselves. In their model combining the benefits of the solution-focused therapy model with the caution of risk assessment, Hawkes et al. (1998) have recommended using the standard solution-focused therapeutic interview as the starting point of engagement with the client. Safety can be explored using some of the model's techniques, notably scaling questions (as we shall see later). If concerns still exist about safety, for the therapist or client, then the therapy stops and a management plan is negotiated. The overriding concern is the safety of the client.

Using the ideas in practice

In the remainder of this chapter, we describe the application of a number of solution-focused techniques to working with suicidal clients and their families as follows:

- listening for strengths
- finding exceptions
- exploring how clients cope
- moving from problems to goals
- using scaling questions.

We conclude the chapter with the important area of how suicide risk can be assessed and managed from a solution-focused perspective in particular by using scaling questions.

Listening for strengths

Clients who have attempted suicide can experience a lot of blame and anger from those around them. Their family and friends can be upset and angry at what has happened and the clients themselves can feel guilty at what they have done and fear that they must be 'losing it' or going mad. The suicide attempt is often experienced as a shameful event for the clients and their families. In the case of a young person living at home, parents can feel guilty that they did not protect their son or daughter and be anxious and hypervigilant about there being a repeat attempt. Many parents have described the situation immediately after a suicide attempt as being like 'walking on eggshells' as the parents fear saying or doing anything that might provoke another attempt.

When faced with the above web of blame and guilt, the therapist must find a way of not adding to these negative feelings but of establishing an alliance with clients and their family. A strengths-based approach to listening has a lot to contribute to this process. Consider the differing impacts of the two possible opening questions to a young person and to a family member in a post-suicide attempt interview.

To the client

Therapist: What made you do what you did?

OR

Therapist: You must have had a pretty good reason for doing what you
did?

To the family member

Therapist: What has been happening in the family just prior to what
Roger did?

OR

Therapist: I'm sure you have been coping with quite a lot since what
happened with Roger?

In both cases, the first questions can inadvertently communicate a judgement
or make the client feel defensive. In the case of the client, he may be surrounded by family and friends asking him this question, who implicitly blame
him for what happened. By the therapist asking the same question, he may feel
that the therapist blames him also. In the case of the family member, the first
question may reinforce a person who already feels at fault and guilty that
something amiss in the family 'caused' the suicide attempt. The second opening statements are more empathetic, disarming and non-judgemental. It is
difficult for people to disagree with them and they implicitly assume a positive
strengths-based view of the individuals, for example that the client acts reasonably and with good cause, and that the family member takes action to cope
with difficult events. In this way strengths-based listening has begun and both
the client and the family member are gently invited to tell more of their stories.

How we listen and communicate with clients and their families, after the
suicide attempt, helps construct how the event is understood by them and
thus their expectations and actions as they go forward. For example, the event
could be understood by the client as 'a further example of the hopelessness he
feels' or as 'a turning point in his life when things changed positively for him'.
Or the family members could perceive the attempt as the beginning of a
downward slide to even more serious problems or they could view the event
as a 'lucky escape' which gave them an opportunity to get closer to their son
or daughter and to make a difference in the future.

While therapists cannot control how families and communicate with each
other and come to understand what has happened, they are highly influential
and co-authors with the theme of the process. Helping the client and family
communicate supportively with one another and create a strengths-based
and possibility-focused understanding of what has happened, *which fits with
all the evidence and the unique experience of the family*, is likely to be the
best protective factor going forward. This means bracketing our negative
expectations and predictions about the family (many of which can flow from

professional theories about the problem) and genuinely seeking to under-stand the family in a different and more constructive light. It also means actively searching with the family for signs of change and hope and helping them to use the difficult event of the suicide attempt as an opportunity to learn from one another and to constructively move forward.

Consider the following example of this strengths-based listening with a teenage mother who has had suicidal thoughts and a near-fatal attempt.

Therapist: How did you pull back at the last moment [from the suicide attempt]?

Client: (thinks) Well, I thought of my children.

Therapist: I see, what did you think about them?

Client: I thought of how alone they would be if I killed myself, of how much they need me.

Therapist: Sounds like you have a lot of love for them . . . that you really want to be there for them.

Client: (a little tearful) Yes.

Therapist: What does that say about you as a person . . . that you want to be there for your children . . . even despite the pain you feel yourself?

Client: (pause) . . . It means that I want to be the best mother I can be for them.

Therapist: I can really see that.

The shift to a strengths-based conversation starts with the therapist thinking positively about the clients and their actions and beginning to reflect this back to them. For example, when faced by a family who have come to therapy because of a suicide attempt, rather than seeing them simply as having dys-functional communication patterns, the therapist can reflect about the cour-age and organization it took to come to therapy and state:

Therapist: You're the type of family that doesn't sweep problems under the carpet, but faces them bravely and takes steps to sort them out . . . I think it also shows a great willingness to change and learn, the fact that you all got here today.

Or rather than reflecting about the action of a suicide attempt, the therapist can reflect back to the client the underlying motivation that underpins it, stating for example:

Therapist: I'm struck by how desperately you must want things to change for the better, given that you were prepared to consider ending your life.

The focus on strengths, skills and resources is not about simple 'positive thinking' or about denying or minimizing the problem. A strengths-based approach is not problem or pain phobic. Clients need to feel that their problems and difficulties are taken seriously, that their suffering is acknowledged and that they are not blamed for the problem. A good strengths-based therapist communicates this empathic understanding, while also communicating a belief in the strengths of the client and in the possibility that they can influence things for the better. Therapy should both provide the client with compassion and understanding about their difficulties as well as encouragement and inspiration that things could be made better.

Finding exceptions

An essential aspect to SFT is the belief that there are always exceptions to problems (de Shazer et al., 1986). Problem patterns are never rigidly fixed through time and different situations. There are always times and situations when the problem occurs slightly less or even not at all. Indeed, the fact that a person is aware that there is a problem suggests that they are making a comparison to another time or situation when the problem did not exist. For example, a woman who feels depressed knows this only if she has a sense of other times when she was happier.

These exceptions are often forgotten, ignored or considered to be 'flukes'. Solution-focused therapists, however, believe that exceptions deserve the closest attention in therapy. They signify examples of 'micro-solutions' already occurring within clients' experience and ways in which clients have applied their existing resources. They can be conceived of as chinks in the armour of the problem. If understood and explored they can be amplified and repeated, ultimately leading to the eventual dismantling of the problem. Consider the following questions designed to elicit exceptions:

Therapist: You were saying that you didn't always feel suicidal, that it has only come upon you since autumn . . . How were things different for you then, say during the summer before the problems started?

Therapist: You were saying that the weekends are the worst for you . . . that then you feel all alone, and the negative thoughts get in on you . . . (client nods) . . . so presumably things are a little better for you midweek . . . so how are things better then?

Once an exception has been identified it should be explored in detail with follow-up questions such as: In what way are things different for you then? What do other people notice? What else? What else? The more concrete and meaningful the detail to the client, the more likely it is to facilitate change. Consider the following sequence:

Therapist: When, over the last few months, has the pain lifted, even a little bit?

Client: (silence) I don't think it ever lifted . . . well, maybe a bit, after my boyfriend found the pills, I just had them hidden in case I needed them, I hadn't taken them yet, but Ben he found the pills and went mad, well, first he went mad and then he started crying and told me how much he loved me and that he wouldn't know what to do if I was gone. It was really strange, but for a while after that I felt better . . .

Therapist: You felt better . . . how do you explain that?

Client: I guess, because I know he cared that much about me, it made a difference . . . I think I felt closer to him after we talked.

Therapist: So when you talk to your boyfriend or when you feel cared for, that can make a real difference to you . . .

Exploring how clients cope

Suicide attempts and depression are serious problems and can have a devastating impact on individuals and families. Although solution-focused therapists take these problems seriously, they are less interested in exploring the effects or damage inflicted by the problem and more interested in exploring how clients have responded to and coped with what has happened. Such a focus can be more empowering in helping clients identify strengths and resources to manage the problem more effectively. To identify coping skills the therapist can use questions such as the following:

- How do you get through the times when the suicidal thoughts are bothering you?
- How do you cope with your depression?
- What keeps you going on a daily basis?
- Who is your greatest support, when faced by a bout of depression? What do they do that is helpful?
- What gives you the strength to keep going?

Searching for the client's coping responses to their problems can often require a gentle persistence on the part of the therapist. Immersed in the grip of the problem, it is easy to forget how one has coped in the past. The role of the therapist is to help clients 'remember' and reaccess these coping skills and often this can lead to unexpected strengths and resources. Consider the following example:

Therapist: How have you managed to deal with your depression on a daily basis?

Client: Well, I don't think I have, I feel like I'm falling apart, it has been so hard.

Therapist: I understand it has been really difficult . . . Yet you still got here today . . . Somehow you have been managing even though it is pretty tough . . . What has helped ?

(Silence)

Client: Well, my friends have been good, I mean they all know I've been down and they call and send little text messages to me, sometimes this helps and sometimes . . . I don't know, it's too much.

Therapist: So sometimes their support can be too much, but other times it can be helpful . . . When is it helpful?

Client: I guess, when they don't push too much, when they simply are there for me.

Therapist: Which friend is best at doing this?

Client: I think Alison is.

Therapist: So Alison is a good support . . . What other things in your life are a support to you?

Client: Sometimes I like being on my own and just writing. I have this journal that I've been keeping, poetry and things like that. It helps, when I want to be alone and just think and write, it keeps me sane.

Therapist: Really, tell me more about how the diary helps.

Client: I feel like I can get it out, you know get out the madness in my head and just write it out. It helps me and I hope it will help others one day, I have this idea that my writing might help other girls who have been through what I have.

When we explore clients' coping we can often discover that they have engaged in many creative ways of managing their problems, some of which are recommended by various therapeutic models. In the above case example the therapist discovered that the client kept a journal as a way of coping, a technique which is suggested by many therapists for different problems (e.g. Dolan, 1991). Setting out to first discover clients' own methods of coping rather than suggesting new ones is much more effective as these are much more likely to be built upon and carried out on an ongoing basis.

Moving from problems to goals

Suicidal thoughts and suicide attempts are serious problems but they are not goals. Suicide is more of a means to an end rather the end or goal in itself.

Clients who see suicide as an option, desperately want things to be different in their lives, whether this is ending the hurt they feel or ensuring other people take notice. Although it is a drastic course of action, they feel hopeless and believe that suicide is the only way to achieve these goals. The aim of therapy is to uncover with the client the positive goals and intentions which underpin their suicidal actions and to explore with them how they can achieve these by other means. For example, if clients say that they wish to die, the therapist becomes interested in what they hope to be different by this. The question becomes 'How do you hope that being dead will help or be different for you?' Consider the following more elaborate example.

Therapist: Things must have been really difficult for you, for you to consider harming yourself . . . You must really want things to be different in your life?

Client: Yeah, I want an end to the pain I'm feeling.

Therapist: I see, you don't want to feel this pain any more, you'd prefer to feel a bit . . .?

Client: . . . a bit better

Therapist: Ah ha, how are things for you when they are better?

Client: Well, I wouldn't wake up with this dark cloud over me . . . I'd wake up and feel lighter.

Therapist: So when things are better, you wake up in the morning feeling lighter . . . maybe rather than a dark cloud there would be . . .

Client: sunshine

Therapist: Ahh . . . so you would like more sunshine in your life?

Client: Yeah that is it.

Therapist: (curious) Tell me then, what would you be doing differently if there was more sunshine in your life?

Client: Hum . . . I guess I would be able to go back to work, it has been a while since I went to work . . . feeling so down and all.

Therapist: What else?

Client: Well, I guess I would not feel like ending it, I would feel like there was something to live for.

Therapist: Like?

Client: That people cared, you know, I would know that people cared, it just seems that they don't any more.

Therapist: So it is pretty important for you to know people care . . . When was the last time you had that feeling?

The therapist attempts to help the client articulate clear, positive goals, defined in terms of things the client wants rather than what he or she does not want. For example, it is not sufficient to know that the client does not want to be depressed any more, the therapist wants to know what will be present in his or her life when the depression is gone – what will the client be feeling or doing when the depression is gone? The more concrete and detailed the goal is, the better. The aim is to help the client envision a future where the problem has been eliminated and to describe this in detail.

Goals for the therapy

As well as uncovering the positive goals that underpin clients' suicidal intentions, the solution-focused therapist is interested in establishing an agreed goal for the therapy with the client. The question is not 'What problem brings you to therapy?' but 'What would you like to achieve by coming to therapy?' Or as Iveson (2000) frames it, 'What is your best hope for these meetings? Establishing goals with children and parents is a tricky business as they often have goals that appear directly in conflict and this is especially the case when dealing with a serious and frightening problem like suicide, though the discovery of an agreed goal marks a critical step towards change. Consider the following sequence, taken from a family session with a teenager who had attempted suicide.

Therapist: (addressing whole family) So what would you hope to get out of coming to these meetings?

Father: We're here for Tina.

Therapist: You're here for your daughter.

Father: I don't want anything bad to happen to her . . . I want to help her.

Therapist: You want her to be safe and well . . . and you want to find a way of helping her.

Father: Yeah.

Therapist: What do you think of what your Dad is saying?

Tina: (shrugs) Dunno!

Therapist: (addressing Tina) What would you hope for coming down to this meeting?

Tina: I just wish everyone would stop making a fuss and leave me alone

Therapist: Yeah . . . you'd like some space?

Tina: Yeah, I wish they'd trust me again.

Therapist: You'd like your parents to trust you and give you some space?

Therapist: (addressing the mother) What do you think? What would you like to happen?

Mother: I'd just like to get the old Tina back.

Therapist: What do you like about the old Tina?
Mother: Well, she'd smile a lot more.
Therapist: I see, you'd like to see a lot more smiles.

By helping the family formulate goals rather than problems the therapist helps the family members to transcend their conflict and work together on individual and shared aspirations.

When the client sees suicide as the goal?

Establishing goals with clients often isn't easy and it can be especially challenging with clients who initially describe 'suicide as the goal'. While as a professional you can't ethically agree with such a goal, arguing with, confronting or trying to persuade clients to have a different goal is usually an ineffective way forward. It can be more fruitful to explore with them what life would be like after the suicide has happened and thereby begin to discover the underlying goals and positive intentions that are distinct from the suicidal act. Consider the two following sample questions that can often work well when they are put as a challenge to clients (especially teenagers) who are initially resistant to envisioning alternatives:

Therapist: I've got an unusual question now . . . but I'm not sure you'd be able to or want to answer it.
Client: Go on, try me.
Therapist: OK, supposing you've done it and gone through with the suicide . . . and suppose your spirit survives and is hovering above looking down, what would be different?

OR

Therapist: Suppose that after you die you find yourself at the pearly gates. You are greeted by an angel who informs you that you have been granted a second chance. When you return to earth you find that all your problems are gone and your life is very satisfactory. How would life be for you then?

(Calcott and MacKenzie, 2001)

In other instances an honest revelation of the professional's goals for the work, can sometimes create the circumstances where you can negotiate a realistic goal (that doesn't involve suicide). Consider the following example where the client, who is in an inpatient ward, feels very hopeless and sees no other way out but suicide:

Therapist: So what are your best hopes for these meetings?
Client: I dunno, I don't see any other way out. I just can't bear the pain any more.

Therapist:	Things sound really hard for you at the moment.
Client:	Yeah, I just want to end it all. And that is what I'm going to do when I leave here. They can't keep me in forever.
Therapist:	You're pretty serious about trying to kill yourself?
Client:	And I don't think coming to meet you can change my mind.
Therapist:	You're not sure yet what we can achieve in these meetings.

(Pause)

Therapist:	Can I make a proposal to you?
Client:	OK.
Therapist:	I'm sorry that you are in so much pain, so much so that you feel like ending your life. And I'd like to be of help to you, but I don't want to see you killing yourself. Would you be interested in talking with me about how things could be different, how you could end the pain without ending your life. You can then decide if it is helpful to you. Even if we don't come up with anything new, you can still go back to your old option, but I think we might be able to find something helpful. Would you like to give this a try?

The aim is to invite clients into conversation about alternative perspectives on the problems they are facing and to open up the possibility of a future where life is better for them, with suicide sidelined as a potential method of moving forward.

Using scaling questions

The solution-focused therapist is interested in discovering how change happens in clients' lives and in helping them understand and build on this. Scaling questions provide powerful and versatile ways of measuring change and breaking goals down to small achievable steps and are used in many other therapies and models such as cognitive behavioural therapy (e.g. Miller et al., 1992). Consider the following example:

> On a scale of one to ten, where ten is the happiest you ever felt (or where you have achieved your goal for therapy), and one is the worst you ever felt, where would you say you are now?

Depending on where clients place themselves, the therapist has a series of important follow-up questions to elicit progress and plan next steps. For example, suppose a client says he is at three on the scale, the therapist can ask:

- What has got you to three on the scale?
- What is different being at three rather than two? (What else is different? What would other people notice?)
- What is the highest point you have reached on the scale? (What was that like? What were you doing then?)
- What would be different if you moved to four on the scale?
- When was the last time you were at four?
- What needs to happen so you can move to four?

When working with families or couples, scaling questions can be very useful in helping family members communicate positively and to identify what they want from one another (Softas-Nall and Francis, 1998b). For example, suppose a teenage girl, who had attempted suicide, rated herself at two on the scale (where ten was 'feeling happy and safe') but she had in the past been at six, the therapist could explore how the family could help in the following way:

Therapist: What was happening when you were at a six? What were things like in your family then? What were you doing differently? What were your parents doing differently? What did you feel about those times?

In addition, the therapist could ask the parents corresponding questions:

Therapist: What do you remember about the time when things were six in the family? What did you notice about your daughter then? What was she doing differently? What were you doing differently?

Even if a client scores very low on the scale, follow-up questions can be used to elicit what next steps need to be taken. For example if the client states they are at one on the scale – the lowest point they have ever felt – the therapist can respond:

Therapist: I'm sorry to hear, things are so low for you at the moment . . . Supposing things were to be a little better for you, say you were to move one point (or half a point) forward on the scale . . . What would that be like? What would you first notice, that would tell you that things were beginning to improve?

Assessing safety using scaling questions

As distinct from working with other clients we have a responsibility, when working with suicidal clients, to assess the suicide risk and to take action if clients are in danger. Some therapists have explored how solution-focused therapy can complement more traditional forms of risk assessment, by using scaling questions to collaboratively establish with clients the level of risk and the safety action needed (Hawkes et al., 1998; Softas-Nall and Francis, 1998b; Calcott and MacKenzie, 2001). Useful questions are as follows:

Therapist: On a scale of one to ten, how confident are you that you will be able to get through the weekend without attempting to harm yourself, where one means you feel you have no chance and ten means you are totally confident? What makes you that confident? What needs to happen to make you more confident . . . to move one point forward on the scale?

Therapist: Suppose over the weekend your mood drops two points on the scale, what will you do to ensure you get back on track? What would help to get you back up to six on the scale?

Where appropriate, other family members should be involved in safety discussions, and often they can provide great resources in helping the client be safe. Questions can be addressed to them as follows:

Therapist: On the same scale, how confident are you that your son will be safe this weekend? What makes you that confident? What needs to happen to make you more confident . . . to move one point forward on the scale?

In order to work safely in a therapeutic contract, clients ideally should be able to give some sort of guarantee that they will not harm themselves between sessions. If this is not the case, therapists may need to consider other options. Consider the following example:

Therapist: On a scale between one and ten, when ten is you can 100 per cent guarantee me you will be able to keep yourself safe until we meet again and one is after our meeting you think you are definitely going to end things, where would you say you are now?

Client: Two.

Therapist: What would help you feel more confident that you would be able to be safe until next week?

Client: Don't know, I guess I just feel so out of control again, I had been doing really well, but recently it is just scary . . . Maybe I have to go back into the hospital, I hate to say this, but it would be the only place I would feel safe at the moment. If I am on my own, I just couldn't promise anything.

Therapist: It sounds pretty scary at the moment. Should we call your GP and see if he can arrange for you to go in hospital.

In the above example, although the therapist has to take action (i.e. contacting the GP) to ensure the safety of the client, this is done in as collaborative a way as possible to preserve the client's sense of self-efficacy in deciding the resources needed to protect him or herself. If the client was not able to cooperate and demonstrated a high level of risk, then the therapist would have to consider taking unilateral action (e.g. in extreme cases arranging for the client be detained involuntarily). It can be acknowledged with the client that you cannot simply do nothing if they intend to harm themselves, that you have a duty of care to protect them and do what you can to preserve life. As Hawkes et al. (1998) state, this is the point where therapy should stop and case management should begin, although this should be done in as respectful and collaborative way as possible.

Conclusion

Traditionally, professional responses to suicidal and self-harming clients have consisted of risk assessment and case management. In recent times there has been a growing interest in exploring more collaborative and strengths-based approaches such as solution-focused therapy to working with this client group. In this chapter we have outlined how the principles of listening for strengths, finding exceptions, exploring coping, reframing problems as goals and using scaling questions can be applied to working with clients who are suicidal and/or at risk of harming themselves. The approach can be best conceived as enhancing and complementing traditional approaches and it is not a replacement for solid risk assessment and management. The aim of such a therapeutic approach is to move away from an exclusive focus on the problem and to help clients envision a positive future where suicide is not an option.

References

Berg, I.K. (1991) *Family Preservation: A brief therapy workbook*. London: Brief Therapy Press.

Calcott, A. and MacKenzie, J. (2001) *Solution-focused approaches with people who have self-harmed*. Paper presented at Community Psychiatric Nurses' Association (CPNA) Conference, Antrim, May.

Cantor, C.H. (2000) Suicide in the western world, in K. Hawton and K. van Heeringen (eds) *The International Handbook of Suicide and Attempted Suicide*. Chichester: Wiley.

Carr, A. (1999) *Handbook of Clinical Psychology: A contextual approach*. London: Routledge.

de Shazer, S., Berg, I.K., Lipchik, E., Nunnally, F., Molnar, A., Gingeich, W.J. and Weiner-Davis, M. (1986) Brief therapy: focused solution development. *Family Process*, 25, 207–221.

Dolan, Y.M. (1991) *Resolving Sexual Abuse: Solution-focused therapy and Ericksonian hypnosis for adult survivors*. New York: Norton.

George, E., Iveson, C. and Ratner, H. (1999) *Problem to Solution: Brief therapy with individuals and families* (2nd edn). London: Brief Therapy Press.

Hawkes, D. (2003) A solution-focused approach to psychosis, in B. O'Connell and S. Palmer (eds) *Handbook of Solution-Focused Therapy*. London: Sage.

Hawkes, D., Marsh, T.I. and Wilgosh, R. (1998) *Solution Focused Therapy: A handbook for health care professionals*. Oxford: Butterworth-Heinemann.

Hawton, K. and van Heeringen, K. (2000) *The International Handbook of Suicide and Attempted Suicide*. Chichester: Wiley.

Hazell, P. (2000) Treatment strategies for adolescent suicide attempters, in K. Hawton and K. van Heeringen (eds) *The International Handbook of Suicide and Attempted Suicide*. Chichester: Wiley.

Heard, H.L. (2000) Psychtherapeutic approaches to suicidal ideation and behaviour, in K. Hawton and K. van Heeringen (eds) *The International Handbook of Suicide and Attempted Suicide*. Chichester: Wiley.

Iveson, C. (2000) *Solutions for everyone: brief therapy in clinical practice and beyond.* Paper presented at Brief Therapy Group Conference, Dublin.

Klingman, A. and Hochdorf, Z. (1993) Coping with distress and self-harm: the impact of a primary prevention program among adolescents. *Journal of Adolescence*, 16(2), 121–140.

Kroll, J. (2000) Use of no-suicide contracts by psychiatrists in Minnesota. *American Journal of Psychiatry*, 157(10), 1684–1686.

Lonnqvist, J.K. (2000) Psychiatric aspects of suicidal behaviour: depression, in K. Hawton and K. van Heeringen (eds) *The International Handbook of Suicide and Attempted Suicide*. Chichester: Wiley.

Malone, K.M., Oquendo, M., Haas, G., Ellis, S., Li, S. and Mann, J. (2000) Protective factors against suicide acts in a major depression: reasons for living. *American Journal of Psychiatry*, 157(7), 1084–1088.

Miller, S., Rotheram-Borus, M.J., Piacentini, J., Graae, F. and Castro-Blanco, D. (1992) *SNAP: A brief cognitive-behavioral family therapy manual for adolescent suicide attempters and their families*. Columbia, OH: Department of Child Psychiatry, Columbia University.

O'Hanlon, W.H. and Weiner-Davies, M. (1989) *In Search of Solutions: A new direction in psychotherapy*. New York: Norton.

Pfeffer, C.R. (2000) Suicidal behaviour in children: an emphasis on developmental influences, in K. Hawton and K. van Heeringen (eds) *The International Handbook of Suicide and Attempted Suicide*. Chichester: Wiley.

Schaffer, D. and Gould, M. (2000) Suicide prevention in schools, in K. Hawton and K. van Heeringen (eds) *The International Handbook of Suicide and Attempted Suicide*. Chichester: Wiley.

Schmidtke, A. and Schaller, S. (2000) The role of mass media in suicide prevention, in K. Hawton and K. van Heeringen (eds) *The International Handbook of Suicide and Attempted Suicide*. Chichester: Wiley.

Sharry, J. (2001) *Solution Focused Groupwork*. London: Sage.

Sharry, J., Madden, B. and Darmody, M. (2004) *Becoming a Solution-Focused Detective: Identifying your client strengths in brief therapy*. New York: Haworth.

Softas-Nall, B.C. and Francis, P.C. (1998a) A solution-focused approach to a family with a suicidal member. *The Family Journal: Counseling and Therapy for Couples and Families*, 6(3), 227–230.

Softas-Nall, B.C. and Francis, P.C. (1998b) A solution-focused approach to suicide assessment and intervention with families. *The Family Journal: Counseling and Therapy for Couples and Families*, 6(1), 64–66.

Verkes, R.J. and Cowen, P.J. (2000) Pharmacotherapy of suicidal ideation and behaviour, in K. Hawton and K. van Heeringen (eds) *The International Handbook of Suicide and Attempted Suicide*. Chichester: Wiley.

Part IV

Group interventions

12 Support groups

Minna Pietilä

The distinctive nature of suicide bereavement

In late modern western society, psychological theorizing has largely replaced other belief systems such as religion in explaining and managing personal experiences (Kivivuori, 1992), also bereavement (Clark, 1999). In this chapter, I intend to challenge the currently dominant psychological understanding of suicide bereavement as (purely) an individual's 'inner' experience by pointing out that even if people feel that their experiences are thoroughly true and authentic, talking about bereavement – in research occasions or otherwise – is an utterly social action in which people use culturally and historically specific resources that construct moral orders.

Psychologically, 'reclaiming' oneself after a loss is thought to require 'going through' an intense phase of mourning (Giddens, 1991). Psychological perceptions of bereavement are best represented in stage and task theories concerning 'the grief process', which lay people have been also found to use in their descriptions of emotions after a loss (Wambach, 1985–1986; Peräkylä, 1990). People may experience psychological explanations as empowering because they suggest, for example, that all difficulties can be overcome with the right kind of attitude. Seale (1998) notes that the stages and tasks of grief can work as a classificatory system enabling people to organize their disturbing experiences as normal. This can also often be seen to happen in bereavement support groups.

The stages of the grief process have been described as involving initial shock, disbelief and denial, unreal feelings, despair after realizing the factuality of death, 'bargaining', being angry and blaming others, feeling ashamed and guilty, and experiencing abandonment and depression before the eventual acceptance of and adjustment to what has happened (e.g. Scheff, 1990; Littlewood, 1992; Pritchard, 1995). The resemblance of this description to the stage theory of dying (originally presented in Kübler-Ross, 1970) can be seen to emerge from applying the psychoanalytic model of attachment and loss to both dying and bereavement (Seale, 1998). The expected achievements of grieving have been outlined in task models of grief (e.g. Moore and Freeman, 1995) in which bereaved people are encouraged to accept the reality of their loss, experience the pain, let go of the deceased person, adjust to life without them and either reinvest their emotional energy into other relationships or internalize the lost person as a part of themselves (Littlewood, 1992; Walter, 1996). According to Valente et al. (1988), successfully accomplished bereavement enables 'personal growth and improved coping strategies', whereas unresolved grief can cause susceptibility to such problems as 'psychosis, social decompensation, substance abuse, deviant identity, accidents, psychosomatic illness, and career failure'. The task of bereavement support groups is obviously to enhance recovery from the loss.

Suicide bereavement in the family has been studied quite extensively in psychology and psychiatry. Many of these studies (e.g. Calhoun and Allen, 1991; Moore and Freeman, 1995; Pritchard, 1995) suggest that suicide is a particularly painful loss as compared to other kinds of bereavement (however, on the basis of several studies, McIntosh (1996) reports having found more similarities than differences with regard to experiencing different kinds of bereavement). Suicide is usually considered a sudden, unanticipated and untimely death, leaving the bereaved person with a lot of hurt and confusion because there was no chance to settle things, evaluate mutual roles and reach a conclusion about the relationship (Achté et al., 1985; Pritchard, 1995). The bereaved person may try to do this afterwards in individual counselling or support groups. Suicide can be experienced differently from dying of, for example, an illness or an accident which were in no ways 'deliberate', or of old age, which can be seen to complete the 'trajectory' of life (Pritchard, 1995). Murphy (1996) argues that problems in coping with suicide can be so enduring as to be barely possible to accommodate. In particular, parents of suicides are seen to be subject to pressures of 'unresolved conflicts and unexpressed emotions' (Miles and Demi, 1991–1992; see also Littlewood, 1992; Pritchard, 1995), because the relationship between parents and children is considered especially close.

It is often pointed out that a moral stigma has been traditionally attached to a suicide's family (Achté, 1996; Young and Papadatou, 1997). Some psychological studies (Lester et al., 1991–1992) have found that people still strongly disapprove of both suicide and the family involved. The most typical feelings after a family member's suicide – guilt, anger, depression and shame (Douglas, 1967; Trolley, 1993; Saarinen et al., 1997) – are considered to be particularly intensive and disruptive if bereaved people blame themselves or someone else for having contributed to the deceased person's troubles, or if others blame them (Pritchard, 1995). Depression and guilt are said to easily become chronic complications of the grief process, because bereaved people can perceive themselves as 'disloyal' with respect to the deceased person when they start to feel better (Saarinen et al., 1997). In bereavement support groups, participants are encouraged and expected to 'share' with each other whatever experiences and emotions they may have.

Talking and support groups in assisting bereavement

It has been suggested (Littlewood, 1992) that, instead of any forced customs, only measures that people create or adopt themselves are sufficient for dealing with bereavement. However, people always choose their ways to act from a socially available, historically particular repertoire. In contrast to the earlier communal and religious rites, in nineteenth-century western societies bereavement became mainly a private family matter as a consequence of increased individualism and emphasis on separateness of families from their community (e.g. Gillis, 1997; Minois, 1999). The aftermath of death started to focus 'on the needs of the bereaved' (Hockey, 1997), and today bereaved people are offered such specialized coping practices as individual counselling, psychotherapy and support groups. Support groups well represent typical contemporary thinking about bereavement, which is considered to be an individual's experience benefiting from sharing with 'fellow sufferers', that is, a private as well as a public matter. The narratives of support groups may now actually serve as the main ritual for the living to remember the deceased (Petty, 2000). Since grief is perceived as a normal rather than pathological psychological reaction to death, support groups are often regarded as more suitable than therapy for those bereaved by suicide (Moore and Freeman, 1995).

All psychological support practices seem to consider talking about the deceased person and emotions associated with the loss to greatly accelerate the bereaved person's adjustment to their situation (Littlewood, 1992; Marttunen et al., 1993) due to narrativity, which brings 'the self' efficiently 'into discourse' (Seale, 1998). Interactive talk is thought of as a vital means for successful accomplishment of the grief process, because seeing other people's reactions is considered to speed up evaluation of, and finding meanings for, one's own situation (Kleinman, 1988; Walter, 1996). Traditional individual psychotherapy has sometimes been dismissed for being of little value to distressed people exactly because it cannot offer them the same emotional rewards as does talking with 'honest and accepting' others (Aldridge, 1998).

It is frequently reported (e.g. Riches and Dawson, 1997) that people consider only those who have similar experiences to be really able to understand them and engage in their situation. Therefore, the most significant aspect about bereavement support groups may be the realization that, in the given situation, people share similar experiences and go through more or less the same process (Seale and Davey, 1996; Walter, 1996; Seale, 1998). As Petty (2000) puts it, 'one has to have "been there" ' to know what an experience is about. Complete outsiders may be perceived as only superficially interested and unable to really comprehend the nature of the questions involved. However, sometimes it can also be accepted – or even demanded – that outsiders should not try to involve themselves in issues that they know nothing about (Good, 1994; Moore and Freeman, 1995; Lillrank, 1998). People may keep up even their 'deviant status' by implying that, due to their exceptional experiences, they are not just equal to but actually better than others (Goffman, 1963; Scambler, 1984; Seale, 1996).

People with a similar kind of experience of loss often regard each other as living proof of a successful negotiation of the loss and as 'honorary experts' who are in a unique position to understand, as well as offer relevant advice and information to, one another (Littlewood, 1992). In bereavement support groups, sharing one's experiences with others through talking is considered important because it is seen to enable explicit recognition and validation of those experiences (Lee, 1994). Together, bereaved individuals can 'ratify' each other's understandings and perceive even their most intense reactions as normal (Scheff, 1990; Moore and Freeman, 1995). Experiences of 'solidarity' and 'togetherness' (Seale, 1996a) in the groups are hoped to ease members' possible social stigma and help them redefine and empower their role in relation to other people (also Atkinson, 1996). According to Moore and Freeman (1995), bereavement support groups have proved effective since 'healing is well served by membership in a group that allows a specified time and place for grieving'. Littlewood (1992) argues that people who have participated in support groups have a higher self-esteem and a better ability to experience and express their grief than others. Riches and Dawson (1997) note that at least group members have become better aware of the ways in which other people understand coping with grief. Sometimes support groups are described to have also caused participants severe emotional confusion (Littlewood, 1992), mainly due to poor group dynamics or unprofessional leaders. For example, in Harmanen's (1997) study, the commonest reasons for members to leave support groups were being uncomfortable about handling their experiences publicly and about the contradicting rights of the individual and the group, such as taking turns in speech and listening to others.

Data and method

This chapter is based on a study of sixteen qualitative interviews with parents and (adult) children concerning their experience of a (respective) family member's suicide. The data were analysed by applying membership categorization device (MCD) analysis (Sacks, 1992), which studies the routine methods of members' (participants in a situation) everyday interaction to make the production of their actions observable and to enable investigation of social order. MCD analysis examines social order by exploring talk as local collaboration and by analysing how people do descriptions in their categorization work. The units of MCD analysis appear as collections of categories which members make existing and relevant in their descriptions as analyses and explanations of what is going on in the situation and how the actions of the parties involved should be evaluated (Baker, 1997; Frith and Kitzinger, 1998). MCDs link categories together through culturally based relationships that refer to regular modes of interaction between and within these categories (Sacks, 1992). Even if some collections appear to be culturally relatively permanent, different versions of them can be constructed in local talk by characterizing their structures differently. In the following, I take examples of the interviewees' talk in order to demonstrate how they handled their expectations of other people's and bereavement support groups' roles with respect to their experience of their family member's suicide.

Rights and responsibilities of other people

In their talk, the interviewees regulated other people's participation in their experience of their family member's suicide by creating a hierarchical order of rights and responsibilities based on others' estimated proximity to or distance from the experience. Other people were considered to either have a partial access to the experience as 'the own' (Goffman, 1963; for example, 'fellow sufferers' in bereavement support groups) or 'the wise' (Goffman, 1963; sympathetic others), or to have no access at all. Thus, potential problems in sharing the experience with others occurred not only due to their refusal to talk about suicide or the like, but also because not everybody was entitled to the right to talk – or even know – about the incident.

The interviewees implied that basically everybody should have been told the truth about their family member's death as suicide, which constructed them (and the deceased person) as morally acceptable people with nothing to hide, while concealing the matter could have been understood as, for example, a sign of shame. However, the interviewees said also that in practice they had chosen with whom to share their experience in order to protect themselves, their families, the deceased person or others. Their accounts involved another contradiction in describing both wanting other people to help them and disqualifying them from helping. Some interviewees considered other people as something to defend themselves against if they had been judgemental, rejecting or intrusive, which the mother below described in talking about her son's suicide twelve years earlier:

> So that in such, such a really great agony and despair, that, that if they [other people] still, like, judge [a suicide], that's then indeed a truly horrible double burden also to the relatives.

This mother said that other people's condemnation of suicide would be 'a truly horrible double burden' to the deceased person's relatives because they, in any case, experienced 'great agony and despair' after the suicide. She thereby implied that condemnation of suicide would be a morally unacceptable thing for others to do. Some interviewees described having carefully considered what to do and say also to avoid shocking or burdening other people. However, once others got involved, the interviewees regarded themselves as not responsible for them or the possible distress caused to them. For example, a year after her mother's suicide, her daughter claimed she, rather than others, had the right to 'comfort' because she considered she was the one having the real problems:

> I don't myself, like, of course I cannot, am not able to start to comfort anybody when they get shocked, like, because of that [the suicide], because I'm the one who's in deep shit there.

By saying 'of course I cannot', this daughter marked her experience as self-evidently something she alone 'owned' and nobody else had the same right to 'get shocked' about, which constructed her as a deeply grieving, morally adequate family member. Owning the suicide experience in such a (jealous) way gave the deceased person and the lost relationship a 'sacred' meaning, because nobody else could really comprehend or interfere with it. The father below described this in talking about his son's suicide two years earlier:

> Then there is also that, there is that funny attitude, there comes just this chemistry, that who, who can talk about it [the suicide], who else except us [he and his wife]. So that, that too, that becomes then too, that not everybody, not everybody can talk about it in any case, or we wouldn't accept it if they did.

This father implied that he and his wife were the only people who had an unquestionable right to talk about their son's suicide and characterized this 'family feeling' as 'chemistry', which made it appear as something innate and natural. It also marked their family as a self-sufficient unit separate from other people and dealing with its internal affairs on its own. The interviewees expected those who were denied access to their experience to be still respectful and encounter the bereaved individuals as normal people. If they did not, their behaviour was described as completely inappropriate and unhelpful.

The daughter below described this in talking about her father's suicide six months earlier:

> I think it's important that . . . in continuity you'd just encounter this person [the bereaved] as a human being then . . . when you meet there in the everyday, so that you won't start avoiding them or don't dare to go and say something . . . I believe that one should just go and say . . . just that . . . just anything.

This daughter expected others to confirm for bereaved people that they were still essentially normal 'human beings' by just 'going and saying something' to them. Others had failed to perform the sympathetic and supportive role if they had not said and done the proper things in the situation but had become too involved or not involved enough.

For example, in talking about his 16-year-old son's suicide two years earlier, the father below implied that the experience was impossible to share with others because they did not discuss topics like suicide:

> Almost everybody [in the support group] had the feeling that those who were not really close, that their attitude [to the suicide] was rejecting, this embarrassment, perhaps exactly just that, that embarrassment perhaps best describes it.

This father said that other people's typical reaction to the bereaved person's experience was 'embarrassment' and confirmed this to be also other support group members' opinion. Those others who were allowed a partial access to the interviewees' experience were expected to show not only compassion and willingness to talk and share the experience but also to acknowledge the unavoidably limited nature of their participation, since they did not 'own' exactly the same experience. They were expected to be sensitive to the special nature of the interviewees' bereavement and to offer support by listening without patronizing, which the mother below described in discussing her son's suicide a year earlier:

> She [a friend] has taken care of me quite a lot in a very discreet way. So that she doesn't say that 'pull your socks up now' or 'you should do this or that now'.

This mother appreciated a friend who had 'taken care of [her] . . . in a very discreet way', because this had not introduced any inappropriate expectations for her to do this or that, which she could not have fulfilled anyway.

Talking in support groups

Half of the interviewees had participated in bereavement support groups, acting as storytellers and recipients of other people's stories, which undoubtedly influenced their understandings of their own family member's suicide and bereavement. In their descriptions, the interviewees largely appreciated talking in support groups as a therapeutic measure, since sharing what they were going through with 'fellow sufferers' had efficiently validated their own experience as normal. They did not seem to have the need to defend themselves against other support group members as sometimes appeared to have been the case with people outside the experience, or to protect them as they had done with their families. They described how group members had, at best, formed a safety net among themselves. Therefore, in terms of identifying with others in their group, the interviewees seemed, first and foremost, to consider themselves as people bereaved by suicide. For example, their specific family relationship to the deceased person – and, thus, their particular experience of suicide – did not appear as the most important aspect about the group's successfulness.

In talking about his son's suicide two years earlier, the father below described the mode of death as the decisive factor for him and his wife to identify with their support group:

> We didn't get anything out of that, that, that [parish's support] group. And then again, we were the only ones in that bereavement, bereavement group who had, like . . . a suicide in the background, so that then this [another] group where we were now, so it was . . . there everybody had a relative who had committed suicide, like, so that there it was, it was easier to talk there.

The interviewees described how, after talking with other group members, they were capable of understanding even themselves and their own experiences better than before. The father below said that he and his wife had learnt from other bereaved people in support groups in which they had participated after their son's suicide twelve years earlier:

> I now understand those people better who have the same experience especially because, for example, this kind of grief seminar and all where we've been [with his wife], so they've then made us richer since we have, have been able to participate, like, three times in the process of a group like this.

In an 'anonymous' group of people with similar experiences, the interviewees had found it obviously easier to be just one of the many, particularly in contrast to their family in which they had to perform also other social roles and show their attendant feelings. Only in support groups it seemed to have been possible for them to talk about their suicide bereavement as individuals, without taking into account the emotions and experiences of their intimate circle. Other people's approving support seemed to have been particularly important for the parents in their responsible roles, which the father below referred to in talking about his son's suicide a year earlier:

> All alone, it would have been absolutely horrific indeed if there was nothing, nobody with whom to chew over the issue. At least, yeah, well, it's really nothing more than that there's somebody listening and and and, well, well, exchanging opinions too, actually.

This father implied that other people's company had been beneficial for him because it had enabled him to 'chew over' his son's suicide. By describing the possible scenario of having to deal with the suicide 'all alone' as 'absolutely horrific', he indicated that his understanding of his son's act had developed in collaboration with others who had 'listened' and 'exchanged opinions' with him. He further specified what kind of interaction was supportive:

> I then opened the discussion there soon after we [he and some friends] had sat down and exchanged a bit of news, and then we handled this, this [the suicide] for the rest of the evening. And he [one of the friends] is of that sort who is capable of handling such things without avoidance. There are few people of this, this kind, but, but, well, you do welcome the few.

The father said that in order to be helpful, people had to be 'capable of handling such things [as his son's suicide] without avoidance' and 'for [a whole] evening', if need be. However, in his experience there were only a few such people.

The interviewees said that sharing their suicide experience was most helpful with people who had been in 'the same situation' and, therefore, were really able to comprehend it, as the daughter below implied when she described her husband's inability to ever understand her experience of her father's suicide a year earlier:

> I think that he [her husband] cannot, like, he cannot ever understand and comprehend it, like, in a completely similar manner to somebody who's been in exactly the same situation.

Therefore, even if nobody could ever fully share one's particular experience, the company of those with a similar experience was valuable. The interviewees described other people in a similar situation to have made them see their own experiences in a different light, as did the daughter below in talking about her father's suicide twenty-four years earlier:

> If there are these phases . . . of one's own life in the background and and then I empathetically live these moments with some people to whom they exist now, which have existed for me . . . sometime . . . then that is indeed a chance for me too to understand . . . understand, or in some way it changes one's viewpoint of that . . . that one's own [experience] sometime back then, or one can see and notice more things in it now.

The interviewees produced a sense of mutual acceptance and togetherness by describing their experiences as similar to those of other group members, which the daughter below discussed in talking about her mother's suicide a year earlier:

> The thing I liked about the group was that there you could, like, exchange thoughts with people, that the people are in the same situation as I am. And, well, then, there you could, like, talk yourself but also listen.

Those interviewees who had participated in support groups thus described becoming also a member of a relevant, accepting group of people through talking and expressing their emotions. The slogan of suicide survivors' community could indeed be 'We are different but normal with our experience'. The interviewees implied that they should have been able to help others with a similar experience, because the help they had received themselves challenged them morally to try to return it. The wish to be 'strong' enough 'one day' to support others that the daughter below described in talking about her mother's suicide sixteen years earlier was quite typical:

> If only one could be so strong as one day to go and somehow help if these kinds of situations [suicide aftermath] should occur.

Besides being generally 'good people', accounts of wishing to help others constructed the interviewees as morally adequate family members who tried to learn something from their experience so that it would not go all wasted. Some of the interviewees said that even though they had initially worried about showing their feelings to others or had found it difficult to talk about the suicide, this had all changed in the support group, as did the daughter below in talking about her mother's suicide a year earlier:

> People quite openly, like, cried there [in the group] and nobody was in any way afraid of showing any feelings, so that there was crying and rage and laughter and whatever. So that it was good in that way.

This daughter described her support group in the way in which psychotherapeutic approaches intend them to be, that is, a place for uninhibited expression of all possible emotions. Also, a father said that the best thing about going to a support group had been enabling his feelings to 'come out' without restrictions. However, due to the principle of 'owning experience' according to which people emphasize the importance of their own particular experience expecting others to recognize its priority status and the fact that all group members were in the same situation in this sense, the interviewees had found it sometimes difficult to share their experience with the group. These different moral orders, one concerning the individual and another the group, created a tension in the interviewees' otherwise positive accounts of their groups. Talking in groups was also described to easily turn into repetitive 'chewing over' the same issues, particularly if the group continued for a long time.

Emotions and bereavement support in sociological framework

Psychological considerations of suicide bereavement and support groups that have been discussed in this chapter have several restrictions. For one thing, instead of any universal truths, people's problems and the ways in which they are tackled can be seen as culturally and historically particular productions. For example, rather than being 'natural', the ways of grieving which are considered normal in present-day western societies seem to derive from white middle-class ideals (Field et al., 1997), surrounded by fear of failing to do what is socially expected (Lee, 1994). In particular, the stage and task theories of grief have been criticized for assuming similarity in experiences, coherence of processes and eventual integration (Petty, 2000), while these expectations can be seen to have created coercive rules for normal grieving, that is, moral order that threatens to label any deviation disagreeable and pathological (Littlewood, 1992).

Asserting individuals' need for expressing their 'natural' feelings and cele-brating emotions as 'a powerful [inner] force' (Lutz, 1996) that reveal a per-son's 'true' character (Landman, 1996) are also late modern phenomena rather than any universal human condition. In talking about their emotions, people try to produce themselves as credible and comprehensible with respect to social expectations. In the essentialistic psychological discourse, talking about one's authentic emotions has become the most significant way of marking one's unique individuality and the moral adequacy of one's acts (also Walter, 2001). Authentic emotions appeal to a romantic ideal of human nature in relation to which the 'social self' is often considered as somehow false, repressed or threatening (Fridlund and Duchaine, 1996). For example, Lee (1994) notes that bereaved people may want to talk about the uniqueness of their own experience and get it recognized by others before they can 'go on to draw comfort from the fact that in some sense it is not [unique]'. Since people are considered to 'own' their personal experiences as a significant part of their separate, authentic selves, they are seen to have only a limited access to each other's experiences. Yet, due to emotional experiences being defined simultaneously as unique to the particular individual and as something emer-ging from a subconscious bio-psychological structure beyond any specific person, the same 'sacred' emotions both ascribe people with profound indi-viduality and rid them of personal control over their life events. Thus people are, after all, seen as only partially capable of 'owning' their experiences. Understanding death as a subjective psychological experience may have actu-ally created 'threats of personal meaninglessness' (Mellor, 1993) because those experiences do not appear to connect to anything outside the individuals facing them.

Contemporary western individuals are expected to construct and com-municate their 'inner worlds' in psychologically orientated ways. Therefore, also bereavement support group activities can be understood as resulting from socially functional interaction instead of a (metaphysical) connection between individual 'psyches'. It can be claimed that, rather than emerging from inside of them, people gain their experiences through the process of generalization which takes place in exchanging similar stories with others (Sacks, 1992). Petty (2000) suggests that the 'mutual understanding and recovery', which are said to take place in suicide bereavement groups, actually rely on certain kinds of perceptions of suicide and grieving with which the members can construct themselves as 'having experienced this particular loss'. She notes that, instead of talking being a 'universal human response to traumatic loss', support group activities may 'support or produce patho-logical symptoms' because members who are initially unsure about their 'anger' or 'guilt' can start to produce accounts of these sentiments soon after joining.

If emotional experiences are understood to occur unavoidably they are separated from the culturally and historically established social relationships within which they actually take place (also Lee, 1994; Seale, 1998). For example, in order to perform oneself favourably to others one has to demon-strate right kinds of emotions at the right time. Statements about emotions thus rather interpret behaviour than describe it (Bedford, 1986). Bereaved people's expressions of their feelings after a suicide should, therefore, be considered not only as reflections of their inner experiences but also in terms of such 'dramaturgical' social roles as those within their family (Hockey, 1993; see also Riches and Dawson, 1997). Acknowledging the social nature of emotional expressions does not mean claiming that everything people do, think and express is entirely determined by the social context in which they find themselves. For example, there may be a lot of 'unstructured' emotion around in bereaved people's experiences of a family member's suicide which never gets socially organized in terms of verbal accounts.

When expressing emotions is examined as a tool with which people can understand and manage their relationships, emotional expressions become observable as constructions of local moral orders that concern some specific events (Denzin, 1984; Warner, 1986; Lutz, 1988). Values attached to different emotional 'performances' function as the community's moral indicators that emerge from and reorganize the social order, because social control works efficiently through emotions that identify people's moral reputation. Persons who fail to communicate appropriate amounts of proper sentiments in a situation are likely to be judged more harshly than others (Taylor, 1985). For example, the western family's typical expectations of affection and love may, after a family member's suicide, necessitate also expressions of guilt (Finch, 1989; Scheff, 1990; Parrott and Harré, 1996), because people are supposed to share their family members' experiences and, at least to some extent, be responsible for them. Those who do not demonstrate this can be considered, for example, cold and indifferent. Thus, suicide bereavement can be perceived as social action in which people consult relevant stocks of expert knowledge to act in ways which make them socially comprehensible and acceptable.

Conclusions for suicide bereavement practices

As for the practical contributions of this chapter, I hope it can offer useful insights for suicide bereavement studies and work because it takes a different view of bereavement from ordinary psychological approaches in which people's lived experiences are often understood exclusively as individuals' inner sensations. I wish that the approach adopted here may add to empirically based sociological thinking about the social nature of human action by showing how people engage in representing and creating cultural knowledge in and through their interaction even in relation to something that is often considered their most individual and personal act, talking about their own experiences and emotions. Thus, in late modern suicide bereavement there is, on the one hand, the feeling individual with his or her lived experiences and, on the other, the social world with its ideals and expectations in which this individual negotiates the meanings of those experiences, producing social order through moral talk. I further hope that the findings presented here could help bereaved people realize that, rather than uncontrollably 'bursting out' from inside of them, their thoughts and emotions are, to an extent, based on their socially produced analysis of the situation in which they find themselves which, again, is linked to their cultural understandings of how things work in the world. Additionally, I hope that people working with bereaved families may use the outcomes of this study to help bereaved people in understanding their 'own' experiences as also being social phenomena.

References

Achté, K. (1996) Kunnian ja häpeän kysymyksiä (Questions of pride and shame), in T. Heiskanen (ed.) *Särkynyt sydän: Omainen ja itsemurha (A Broken Heart: Relatives and suicide)*. Jyväskylä, Finland: Gummerus.

Achté, K., Lönnqvist, J. and Pentikäinen, J. (1985) Vanha suomalainen kuolemankulttuuri (The old Finnish culture of death), in J.E. Ruth and P. Heiskanen (eds) *Kuolema elämän keskellä (Death at the Centre of Life)*. Keuruu, Finland: Otava.

Aldridge, D. (1998) *Suicide: The tragedy of hopelessness*. London: Jessica Kingsley Publishers.

Atkinson, J. (1996) Schizophrenia, in B. Davey and C. Seale (eds) *Experiencing and Explaining Disease*. Buckingham: Open University Press.

Baker, C. (1997) Membership categorization and interview accounts, in D. Silverman (ed.) *Qualitative Research: Theory, method and practice*. London: Sage.

Bedford, E. (1986) Emotions and statements about them, in R. Harré (ed.) *The Social Construction of Emotions*. Oxford: Basil Blackwell.

Calhoun, L.G. and Allen, B.G. (1991) Social reactions to the survivor of a suicide in the family: a review of the literature. *Omega*, 23, 95–107.

Clark, D. (1999) Series editor's preface, in T. Walter (ed.) *On Bereavement: The culture of grief*. Buckingham: Open University Press.

Denzin, N.K. (1984) *On Understanding Emotion*. San Francisco, CA: Jossey-Bass.

Douglas, J.D. (1967) *The Social Meanings of Suicide*. Princeton, NJ: Princeton University Press.

Field, D., Hockey, J. and Small, N. (eds) (1997) *Death, Gender and Ethnicity*. London: Routledge.

Finch, J. (1989) *Family Obligations and Social Change*. Cambridge: Polity Press and Basil Blackwell.

Fridlund, A.J. and Duchaine, B. (1996) 'Facial expressions of emotion' and the delusion of the hermetic self, in R. Harré and W.G. Parrott (eds) *The Emotions: Social, cultural and biological dimensions*. London: Sage.

Frith, H. and Kitzinger, C. (1998) 'Emotion work' as a participant resource: a feminist analysis of young women's talk-in-interaction. *Sociology*, 32, 299–320.

Giddens, A. (1991) *Modernity and Self-Identity: Self and society in the late modern age*. Cambridge: Polity Press.

Gillis, J.R. (1997) *A World of their Own Making: A history of myth and ritual in family life*. Oxford: Oxford University Press.

Goffman, E. (1963) *Stigma: Notes on the management of spoiled identity*. New York: Penguin.

Good, B.J. (1994) *Medicine, Rationality, and Experience: An Anthropological Perspective*. Cambridge: Cambridge University Press.

Harmanen, E. (1997) *Sielunhoito sururyhmässä: Tutkimus ryhmän ohjaajan näkökulmasta Suomen evankelis-luterilaisessa kirkossa* (*Healing the Soul in a Bereavement Support Group: A study of the counsellor's viewpoint in the Evangelic-Lutheran Church of Finland*). Helsinki: Suomalaisen teologisen kirjallisuusseuran julkaisuja 207.

Hockey, J. (1993) The acceptable face of human grieving? The clergy's role in managing emotional expression during funerals, in D. Clark (ed.) *The Sociology of Death: Theory, culture, practice*. Oxford: Blackwell.

Hockey, J. (1997) Women in grief: cultural representation and social practice, in D. Field, J. Hockey and N. Small (eds) *Death, Gender and Ethnicity*. London: Routledge.

Kivivuori, J. (1992) *Psykokulttuuri: Sosiologinen näkökulma arjen psykologisoitumisen prosessiin* (*Psychoculture: A sociological perspective to the process of psychologization of everyday life*). Helsinki: Hanki ja Jää.

Kleinman, A. (1988) *The Illness Narratives: Suffering, healing, and the human condition*. New York: Basic Books.

Kübler-Ross, E. (1970) *On Death and Dying*. London: Tavistock.

Landman, J. (1996) Social control of 'negative' emotions: the case of regret, in R. Harré and W.G. Parrott (eds) *The Emotions: Social, cultural and biological dimensions*. London: Sage.

Lee, C. (1994) *Good Grief: Experiencing loss*. London: Fourth Estate.

Lester, D., McCabe, C. and Cameron, M. (1991–1992) Judging the appropriateness of completed suicide, attempted suicide and suicidal ideation. *Omega*, 24, 75–79.

Lillrank, A. (1998) *Living One Day at a Time: Parental dilemmas of managing the experience and the care of childhood cancer*. Jyväskylä, Finland: Gummerus.

Littlewood, J. (1992) *Aspects of Grief: Bereavement in adult life*. London: Routledge.

Lutz, C.A. (1988) *Unnatural Emotions: Everyday sentiments on a Micronesian atoll and their challenge to western theory*. London: University of Chicago Press.

Lutz, C.A. (1996) Engendered emotion: gender, power, and the rhetoric of emotional control in American discourse, in R. Harré and W.G. Parrott (eds) *The Emotions: Social, cultural and biological dimensions*. London: Sage.

McIntosh, J.L. (1996) Survivors of suicide: a comprehensive bibliography update, 1986–1995. *Omega*, 33, 147–175.

Marttunen, M., Aro, H., Henriksson, M. and Lönnqvist, J. (1993) Omaisten tuen tarve itsemurhan jälkeen (Relatives' need of support after a suicide), in J. Lönnqvist, H. Aro and M. Marttunen (eds) *Itsemurhat Suomessa 1987 projekti* (*Suicides in Finland 1987 Project*). Jyväskylä, Finland: Gummerus.

Mellor, P.A. (1993) Death in high modernity: the contemporary presence and absence of death, in D. Clark (ed.) *The Sociology of Death: Theory, culture, practice*. Oxford: Blackwell.

Miles, M.S. and Demi, A.S. (1991–1992) A comparison of guilt in bereaved parents whose children died by suicide, accident, or chronic disease. *Omega*, 23, 203–215.

Minois, G. (1999) *History of Suicide: Voluntary death in western culture*. London: Johns Hopkins University Press.

Moore, M.M. and Freeman, S.J. (1995) Counselling survivors of suicide: implications for group postvention. *Journal for Specialists in Group Work*, 20, 40–48.

Murphy, S.A. (1996) Parent bereavement stress and preventive intervention following the violent deaths of adolescent or young adult children. *Death Studies*, 20, 441–452.

Parrott, W.G. and Harré, R. (1996) Overview, in R. Harré and W. G. Parrott (eds) *The Emotions: Social, Cultural and Biological Dimensions*. London: Sage.

Peräkylä, A. (1990) *Kuoleman monet kasvot: Identiteetin tuottaminen kuolevan potilaan hoidossa* (*Death's Many Faces: Producing identity in caring for the dying patient*). Tampere, Finland: Vastapaino.

Petty, M.S. (2000) SOS and the retelling of suicide. *Health*, 4, 288–308.

Pritchard, C. (1995) *Suicide – the Ultimate Rejection? A psycho-social study*. Buckingham: Open University Press.

Riches, G. and Dawson, P. (1997) 'Shoring up the walls of heartache': parental responses to the death of a child, in D. Field, J. Hockey and N. Small (eds) *Death, Gender and Ethnicity*. London: Routledge.

Saarinen, P., Viinamäki, H., Lehtonen, J. and Lönnqvist, J. (1997) Omaisten psyykkinen tilanne ja ammattiavun tarve läheisen itsemurhan jälkeen (Relatives' psychical condition and need of professional help after a suicide in the family). *Suomen Lääkärilehti*, 52, 981–986.

Sacks, H. (1992) *Lectures on Conversation, volumes I and II*. Oxford: Blackwell.

Scambler, G. (1984) Perceiving and coping with stigmatising illness, in R. Fitzpatrick (ed.) *The Experience of Illness*. London: Tavistock.

Scheff, T.J. (1990) *Microsociology: Discourse, emotion, and social structure*. London: University of Chicago Press.

Seale, C. (1996) Stigma and normality, in B. Davey and C. Seale (eds) *Experiencing and Explaining Disease*. Buckingham: Open University Press.

Seale, C. (1998) *Constructing Death: The sociology of dying and bereavement*. Cambridge: Cambridge University Press.

Seale, C. and Davey, B. (1996) Experiencing and explaining disease: some conclusions, in B. Davey and C. Seale (eds) *Experiencing and Explaining Disease*. Buckingham: Open University Press.

Taylor, C. (1985) The person, in M. Carrithers, S. Collins and S. Lukes (eds) *The Category of the Person: Anthropology, philosophy, history*. Cambridge: Cambridge University Press.

Trolley, B.C. (1993) Kaleidoscope of aid for parents whose child died by suicidal and sudden, non-suicidal means. *Omega*, 27, 239–250.

Valente, S., Saunders, J. and Street, R. (1988) Adolescent bereavement following suicide: an examination of relevant literature. *Journal of Counseling and Development*, 67(3), 174–177.

Walter, T. (1996) A new model of grief: bereavement and biography. *Mortality*, 1, 7–25.

Walter, T. (2001) Reincarnation, modernity and identity. *Sociology*, 35, 21–38.

Wambach, J.A. (1985–1986). The grief process as a social construct. *Omega*, 16, 201–211.

Warner, C.T. (1986) Anger and similar delusions, in R. Harré (ed.) *The Social Construction of Emotions*. Oxford: Basil Blackwell.

Young, B. and Papadatou, D. (1997) Childhood death and bereavement across cultures, in C.M. Parkes, P. Laungani and B. Young (eds) *Death and Bereavement Across Cultures*. London: Routledge.

13 A group intervention for adolescents and young adults with recurrent suicide attempts

*Monique Séguin, Ginette Goulard,
Yvonne Bergmans and Paul S. Links*

Every indicator confirms the alarming magnitude of the health and social consequences of suicide. Suicide attempters are estimated to have a risk of dying from suicide that is more than 100 times higher than that in the general population (Hawton and Fagg, 1988). Approximately 15 per cent of attempters will reattempt suicide within the first year following their attempt (Schmidtke et al., 1996; Van der Sande et al., 1997).

Psychological autopsy studies over the last decades have consistently shown that the vast majority of suicide cases are associated with current and lifetime mental disorders, especially depressive disorders, substance abuse/dependence, borderline and antisocial personality disorders, all of which tend to occur with remarkably high levels of comorbidity (Lesage et al., 1994). In different psychological autopsy studies done since the mid-1980s (Murphy and Wetzel, 1982; Isometsa et al., 1996; Séguin et al., 2003) most confirm the importance of personality disorders, especially borderline personality disorder (BPD) as a risk factor observed in approximately 40 per cent of people deceased by suicide.

Hengeveld et al. (1996) found a significant relationship between major repeaters (with five or more lifetime suicide attempts) versus minor repeaters (fewer than five attempts) and the risk of recurrent suicide attempts over a one-year follow-up (76 per cent versus 39 per cent; $p = 0.0002$). However, Hengeveld et al. (1996, p. 272) acknowledged that based on current knowledge, 'it is not possible to disentangle factors that lead to the first suicide attempt, factors that lead to repetition of suicide attempts and factors that maintain the recurrence of this behaviour.' For example, recurrent suicide attempts are related to Axis II diagnoses such as borderline personality disorder (Hengeveld et al., 1996; Davis et al., 1999). However, it is not clear whether the number of recurrent attempts predicts the subsequent morbidity and mortality as well as the treatment response independent of the diagnosis.

This points to the importance of creating structures of services that address the needs of people who self-harm and make recurrent suicidal attempts.

Specific characteristics with adolescents

Even if we must be careful in making a diagnosis of a personality disorder in adolescents because their personality is still developing (see APA Guidelines, 1994), it is essential to recognize the pathological development in personality if we wish to intervene earlier in the course of the disorder. A diagnosis of borderline personality disorder, as with most personality disorder diagnoses, is often avoided in child and adolescent psychiatry. If clinicians are often hesitant to make the diagnosis in adults because of stigma, insurance denial or inadequate training, the situation is even more frequent in child and adolescent psychiatry.

Not only is the diagnosis of borderline personality disorder avoided, but also some clinicians believe that you cannot make a diagnosis of a personality disorder before the age of 18. Therefore, these very troubled adolescents often get misdiagnosed and inappropriately treated.

Personality disorders may be diagnosed in children and adolescents who have shown stable maladaptive features that have been present for at least one year. These maladaptive patterns of functioning must be present in the following spheres: cognition, affect, interpersonal functioning and impulse control (APA, 1994: DSM-IV). By avoiding making an early diagnosis and providing adequate treatment, we are putting them at risk of developing these maladaptive patterns even further.

The self-injury and suicidal attempts seen in borderline patients usually start in adolescence. Self-injury, sometimes referred to as self-harm or self-mutilation, may be defined as deliberate behaviour which causes tissue damage or marks lasting for several hours or more, and does not include autistic body modification, such as piercing (Favazza, 2003). Contrary to popular belief, individuals with a borderline personality disorder (BPD) who have a history of self-mutilation are much at risk of death by suicide (Stanley, 2001). It is proposed that early maladaptive schema of a self-harm or suicidal crisis may sensitize suicide-related thoughts or behaviour that will then become more active and accessible (Beck, 1996). The self-harm thoughts and behaviours are then more easily triggered and the episodes can become more severe (Joiner, 2000). The lifetime risk of suicide for BPD is as high as 10 per cent (Paris, 2002). The patients who self-mutilate are often perceived as attention seeking or manipulative but research has shown that these patients tend to be more depressed, anxious and impulsive and tend to underestimate the lethality of their suicidal attempts (Stanley, 2001). Most patients who self-mutilate have made at least one suicide attempt. Therefore it is of extreme importance to address these patients early in their illness. By intervening early and before the personality disorder has fully crystallized, we hope to provide patients with more adaptive patterns of behaviour.

Levine et al. (1997) described individuals suffering from BPD as having difficulty identifying the emotions of others and for themselves. Fredrickson and Joiner (2002) and others speak of the cognitive rigidity experienced by individuals in suicidal crisis suffering from depression. This rigidity creates deficits in social problem-solving, in the confidence they have of being able to solve problems, and in the capacity of generating alternative solutions in order to solve the problems they face. McLeavey et al. (1994), Rotheram-Borus et al. (1994) and Hawton and Kirk (1998) all point to deficits in the realm of problem-solving and the necessity for developing skills in this area in order to manage suicidal crisis.

O'Leary (2000), after an extensive review of the neuropsychological literature, suggests that memory problems for those suffering from BPD may arise from difficulties retrieving learned material rather than encoding processes. McLeod et al. (1998) suggest that suicidal clients showed deficits in positive thinking.

Interpersonal deficits have been noted in many areas. Livesley (2000) reports deficits in the capacity for intimacy and mature attachment, and Kjellander (1998) notes instability in interpersonal relationships as being a factor consistent for those suffering from BPD. Recurrent suicide attempters suffer a wide variety of psychopathologies and it is not infrequent to hear that the majority have experienced trauma in their lifetime (Wheelis and Gunderson, 1998).

Psychosocial group intervention: background

Given the need to develop effective interventions that will decrease the risk for suicide or subsequent suicidal behaviour in suicide attempters, Hawton et al. (1998) completed a systematic review of all randomized controlled trails of psychosocial and physical treatments targeted at preventing the repetition of deliberate self-harm or suicide attempts in individuals who had engaged in deliberate self-harm shortly before their enrolment into the study.

The studies have been grouped according to the use of common therapeutic strategies. In the first grouping, subjects were offered a form of problem-solving therapy compared to standard aftercare. In terms of preventing recurrence of self-harm behaviour, there were no significant differences between problem-solving therapy and standard care (odds ratio = 0.70; 59 per cent CI 0.45, 1.11). However, the problem-solving therapy was found to be significantly more effective in reducing depression, hopelessness and improving patients' problems than the standard aftercare (Townsend et al., 2001). The second group of studies involved outreach approaches or improved access to therapists rather than standard aftercare. These intensive interventions did not significantly reduce the rate of recurrence versus standard care (odds ratio = 0.84; 95 per cent CI 0.62, 1.15). The third grouping of studies included interventions that offered twenty-four-hour access to psychiatric advice versus standard aftercare. Once again, the emergency access interventions did not significantly reduce the rate of recurrence compared to standard care and one study suggested that easier access to emergency services increased the repetition in those subjects with recurrent suicidal behaviour compared to standard care.

Hawton et al. (1998) reported on one of the published trials of dialectical behaviour therapy versus standard aftercare in subjects with borderline personality disorder and parasuicidal behaviour. This study demonstrated a significant reduction in the repetition of parasuicidal behaviour versus the comparison group. This study has now been replicated by Linehan's group and two other investigators (Evans et al., 1999). Unfortunately, dialectical behaviour therapy has limited application to many settings because of the intensity of the intervention, the complexity of the model particularly for individuals with limited education and the lack of demonstrated efficacy with males. The authors identified the need for interventions that were more trans- ferable and applicable to general psychiatric settings, that were efficient for men and that examined other outcomes beyond the repetition of deliberate self-harm such as problem-solving or the regulation of emotions.

As for adolescent treatment, we know from adult data that inpatient hospi- talization is generally not helpful in the treatment of personality disorders (Paris, 2002) but often this is where the adolescents with the most severe personality disorders are treated, because the suicidal risk becomes impos- sible for the family or foster care to tolerate. The family environment is often very unstable as the families of these patients have significantly greater rates of psychopathology (Goldman et al., 1993). The risk of borderline personal- ity disorder is five times more common in first degree relatives. Ideally, family intervention should be of primary importance but in practice it is not always possible (Villeneuve and Roux, 1995). Many of these patients are no longer living with their biological parents and in many cases a family reintegration is not recommended due to the severe family pathology.

Apart from day treatment and hospitalization, few treatment programmes exist for these adolescents. Despite the importance of repeated self-harm among adolescents, very little is known regarding how it should be managed. Group therapy shows promise as a treatment for this population (Wood et al., 2001).

The group represents a setting to repair their maladaptive patterns of interpersonal functioning. Most social learning takes place by observing others and the results of their actions (Bandura, 1989). The group can pro- vide the safety needed to re-establish a better adapted mode of interpersonal functioning and at the same time improve their affective regulation and impulse control. The trait of impulsivity is associated with repeated suicide attempters and is an important therapeutic target for prevention of future suicide attempts (Brodsky et al., 2001).

Rationale of our group therapy with adolescents

Literature linking work on attachment with theories of borderline pathology has stressed the common characteristics shared by ambivalently attached/ preoccupied and borderline groups 'to check for proximity, signalling to establish contact by pleading or other calls for attention of help, and clinging behaviours' (Fonagy et al., 2000, p. 103). Gunderson (1996) highlights the theme of intolerance of aloneness and terror of abandonment in such patients, which has been claimed to account for many of the clinical features observed in this group of patients.

Childhood trauma may be a common pathway to serious high suicide risk, comorbid combinations of borderline personality disorder and major depression. Patients who have been physically, sexually or emotionally abused also frequently come from backgrounds in which abandonment and neglect are common (Sabo et al., 1995). As children, such individuals frequently had caregivers who were themselves within the so-called borderline spectrum of severe BPD (Belsky et al., 1995). The literature about abused and neglected patients emphasizes the patient's need for safety and the relevance of addressing this in the context of psychotherapy (Herman, 1992). In sexually abused patients, the risk of suicidal behaviour was additionally increased by antisocial features, hopelessness and comorbid depression (Brodsky et al., 2001; Soloff et al., 2002).

Most of these patients did not experience protectiveness and a sense of safety in infancy and have difficulty protecting themselves. A constellation of problems creates this difficulty in protection: the feeling of aloneness, the need–fear dilemma and guilt (Adler, 1994). For Adler, the aloneness issue relates to their inability to count on their own internal resources to soothe and hold themselves at times of stress and separation. The fear of losing the other person and the urge for fusion/entanglement with someone because of the intense longings creates the need–fear dilemma. Finally, Adler (1994) identifies the intense guilt as a manifestation of their all-or-nothing thinking style, manifested by their feeling of being bad and hateful at one moment and that the other person is bad or hates them at the next.

Psychotherapy aimed at addressing the distorted interpersonal boundaries, the self-blame and guilt is appropriate (Thedford Lambert, 2003). Supportive psychotherapy, cognitive behavioural therapy and group therapy benefit many patients with unstable personalities. A study of borderline patients has demonstrated the efficacy of group therapy in reducing the rate of completed suicides (Wilberg et al., 1998).

Psychotherapy, such as Linehan's (1992) dialectic behaviour therapy protocol, Clarkin et al.'s (2006) recommendation for psychoanalytic psychotherapy or Ryle and McCutcheon's (2006) cognitive analytic therapy, all aim, first, to establish an attachment relationship with the patient, second, to use this to create an interpersonal context where understanding of mental states becomes a focus, and third, to attempt to create a situation in which the self is recognized as intentional (see Fonagy et al., 2000).

In order to protect themselves, patients need to learn to

- enhance their protective abilities, enhance their capacity for self-protection, soothe and distract themselves in order to contain the feelings of aloneness and abandonment in time of stress

- understand and respect their interpersonal boundaries, and be aware of their personal boundaries and other people's boundaries to gradually avoid the need–fear dilemma
- learn to understand their mental state
- enhance affect regulation, identify the emotion and realize that behaviour is a choice in order to recognize the self as intentional
- learn strategies to help de-escalate a stressful situation, be aware of the intensity and the rapidity of their escalation, in order to count on their own internal resources to hold themselves.

Intervention content: a multimodal approach

Livesley (2000) indicates that a comprehensive treatment most likely requires multiple interventions from diverse schools of thought. The current intervention being proposed is a psychosocial/psychoeducational approach adapted to adolescents with recurrent suicide attempts, that addresses the core issue of protection, in regards to their own ability for self protection and keeping safe.

Group structure

Psychosocial/psychoeducational intervention for persons with recurrent suicide attempts (PISA) was developed as an intervention for adults with recurrent suicide attempts (Bergmans and Links, 2002; Links et al., 2003). From 1999 until 2001, young adults were integrated into multi-age groups. Because of their distinct stage of psychosocial development, sometimes the content of the group needed to be modified and adjusted for them. It was then decided the intervention would be offered in an adapted version for the adolescent and young adult population. The model proposed attracted interest and the PISA programme for adolescents and young adults is presently a multisite intervention project offered in two Canadian provinces in the two official languages of French and English. The primary focus of the intervention with this younger group is concentrated on improving their capacity to protect themselves; keeping safe and establishing safe interpersonal boundaries.

The twenty week outpatient group intervention was developed for individuals with a lifetime history of two or more suicide attempts. Referrals come from family physicians, community allied health professionals, inpatient psychiatrists, and emergency and crisis intervention staff typically after a recent suicidal crisis. The groups are held at the hospital's Outpatient Services. Clients participate on a weekly basis for ninety minutes in the group intervention. Groups consist of six to eight members, with three co-therapists.

Each week is organized around a skill which is the focus of the session. The intervention consists of five modules of skill and strategy development. Each group member is provided with a journal, notebook and pens. Snacks of juice, coffee and cookies are provided at each session. Sessions follow a basic structure of handing out minutes from the previous week's session, and giving clients an opportunity to review and comment. Weekly minutes provide an ongoing documented collection of issues, strategies and concepts discussed throughout our time together which clients can refer to when outside the session.

After this opening, patients are asked to identify a specific challenge they have met during the week and how they have attempted to overcome it in a safe way. Group discussion is encouraged and support is provided by the peers and therapists. Each group participant gets the chance to participate. The opportunity to review and consolidate previous concepts and skills arises out of this discussion and is the opening to teaching new content. This more informal discussion and sharing time is then followed by the teaching of a new concept, skill or strategy. Process versus content is a regular struggle for therapists, knowledge of content for the entire intervention and flexibility is necessary. The process of each session is to maintain a balance between issues that clients bring, and skills teaching that are relevant to the issues raised.

The introduction of the weekly skill training is organized around presentation of new material, handouts, role playing, and so on. This gives opportunity to the patients to receive positive feedback and reinforcement from therapists and co-members of the group.

At the end of the twenty week programme, patients receive an individual certificate and therapists give personal feedback to patients on their own progress, especially on their own ability in keeping safe.

Modules and content

Protective ability and personal safety

In the first session, members identify what 'safe' means for them, individually and as a group. This gives us the foundation for developing group ground rules regarding disclosure, confidentiality and behaviours within the group. It also allows for a discussion of the group's purpose: to develop strategies for living life more safely and making safer choices when in distress. Emphasis is placed on the fact that participants may not have been protected while growing up but they have to learn to protect themselves. It is a foundation that is repeatedly returned to during group sessions.

Clients regularly tell us how 'unsafe' they feel in the many parts of their lives. Some clients, based on life experiences, do not believe they have the right to feel safe. Clients are invited into a process of developing a visualization of an actual or imaginary safe place. This later becomes part of their repertoire of grounding exercises and self-soothing practices. A list of alternatives to self-harm is generated by all members and strategies to soothe and distract themselves are discussed and encouraged: deep breathing, muscle relaxation, sleep hygiene, and emotional memory/flashback management are also taught in this module. The identification of networks, both professional and personal, are drawn up by clients. A list of local resources for crisis services and distress lines is given.

Personal boundaries and interpersonal relationships

The fear of losing and the urge of fusion/entanglement with someone together with the intense longing put some of the patients at risk in their interpersonal relationships. Many of them have experienced conflict in relationships with friends and intimate partners, which is consistent with an ambivalent type of attachment relationship (Main et al., 1985; Crittenden, 1994).

Boundaries are identified as a means of protection. Clear communication is essential to developing boundaries, with rehearsal taking place through role play; anticipatory emotional reactions and personal choices are discussed during the session. Goals for relationship management are discussed using a modified version of Linehan's (1993) work.

Education: understanding their mental state

The module on education relays the concept that diagnoses are a means to identifying the suffering. Clients are often unclear how the features of their diagnosis may exacerbate a situation. Others believe that the diagnosis defies any sense of hope toward living life differently. Education regarding diagnosis provides a language with which clients can communicate some of their distress to other caregivers. Some report the education providing relief, and some report it gives them some sense of control.

Affect regulation

Affect regulation and tolerance is an often noted difficulty with this clientele (Linehan, 1992; Deiter et al., 2000). Levine et al. (1997) noted significantly lower levels of emotional awareness of self and others being found in their study of individuals living with BPD. Thus members are encouraged to identify emotions while in session. This leads to discussion regarding their all or nothing thinking. By becoming more aware of the extremes of feelings, and by developing a greater ability to identify other types of emotions, a greater awareness of a variety of emotions and needs may be enhanced. The teaching process is to encourage identification of the emotions leading up to the behaviour. The module begins with the above distinctions and then clients develop a scale of intensity, similar to Rotheram-Borus et al.'s (1994) thermometer. Other sessions are devoted to early warning signs.

Problem-solving and strategies to de-escalate

Problem-solving as a module includes the teaching and utilization of the steps to problem-solving developed by Rotheram-Borus et al. (1994) and

Hawton and Kirk (1998). It is raised formally in the last part of the intervention. Clients are reminded of their level of emotional intensity and distortion as interfering with successful problem-solving. Concepts of time and place to finding solutions for problems is taught, as well as coming to accept that some problems will never be solved, or not right now. In the height of emotional distress, safety is of key importance, with the primary options including self-soothing, distracting or reaching out to de-escalate, utilizing one's network support, reality checking and then reviewing the situation for other problem-solving strategies.

In facilitating this intervention and working with a high risk group, it is important that care providers maintain regular supervision to remain on target with the core intervention and to manage their own transference/countertransference responses. Each team maintains weekly supervision and the adherence to the intervention protocol is maintained through regular telephone discussions and two visits each year with parts of or the entire facilitation/supervision teams.

Case example

Milly was referred to the PISA group after a serious drug overdose following a break-up with her boyfriend of two weeks. Milly at 17 years of age was no stranger to psychiatric emergency rooms and the psychiatric inpatient units. She had multiple emergency visits for self-harm and suicidal attempts including lacerations, drug overdoses and asphyxiation. She had two lengthy hospital inpatients stays for a total of 106 days. She lived at different periods of time with her father, her mother, foster homes and group homes. Her only brother was also in foster care.

Her personal history included abandonment by her alcohol-dependent mother at the age of 3. She was then raised by a violent father who also misused alcohol. In elementary schools she moved four times and was never able to make friends in her new schools. An early diagnosis of attention deficit disorder (ADD) and learning disorder were made through the school system. She made the first of many suicide attempts at the age of 13. Her long departed mother, hearing about Milly's difficulties through relatives, came into the picture to 'rescue' her daughter. But three months later she dropped her off at the local hospital, stating she could not understand her 'crazy' daughter, who was then cutting her arms on a regular basis.

Other diagnoses made in the course of her treatment included conduct disorder, major depressive disorder, bipolar disorder, social anxiety disorder, eating disorder, and substance abuse disorder.

Ninth week

At the ninth week of the group, Milly shared with the group her fears regarding the approaching Christmas holidays. Her father, who lived out of town, had called her the week before and told her he expected her to be home for Christmas. Milly had not seen her father in over six months. During the last two visits, he had been drinking excessively. Milly had experienced severe mood swings and had been drinking and self-mutilating every day of her last visits at her father's home. Milly did not want to go but felt that she could not refuse her father's demand. With the help of the group, she explored how she could feel 'safer' and she decided she would go for only two days and would ask her grandmother if she could sleep at her house. Her grandmother agreed. After the holidays, Milly told the group that her father was still drinking but she was able to leave his house early after dinner and did not self-harm during her short stay at home.

Twentieth week

At the twentieth week of the group, Milly told the group she had decided to enter a long-term drug rehab programme the following month. She had struggled with drug use for the last three years and felt that she could not stop on her own. For the first time, she was able to admit it was a problem and able to accept the support given to her by the other members of the group. She was still having episodes of cutting her arms and abdomen but these were reduced in frequency and intensity. She had not made any suicidal attempt since the start of the PISA programme. The week following the end of the programme, Milly was admitted to a six months community-based drug rehab programme.

Outcome and feedback

Of three completed groups for participants between the ages of 14 and 25, thirty young women started the groups and twenty completed. All had an Axis I and Axis II diagnosis, all had a comorbid diagnosis which consisted primarily of borderline personality disorder, mood disorder, post-traumatic stress disorder (PTSD), drug and alcohol abuse/dependence and conduct disorder. All were being treated with psychoactive medication for their disorders. Of the total group, twenty-six had been previously hospitalized for psychiatric treatment. All had multiple suicidal thoughts, gestures and attempts. (In one group, participants had a mean number of seven attempts; mean age of first being aware they wanted to die was

13 years, and mean age at first attempt was 14.) All participants were encouraged to pursue their individual treatment with their therapist and to discuss their participation in the group with their therapist or interveners.

Of the thirty participants, only two lived with both their biological parents, three were living with their mother at the time of the group, three with their father and one with an aunt. Nine were living in group homes, six in small apartments, two in shelters, three in school residences and one was in a hospital setting.

Ten out of thirty dropped out of the groups for various reasons: one got a job, two moved, five gave up because they were too emotionally distressed by the group and two were forced to participate by their educators and we gave them permission not to come. The dropouts happened very early in the group process most of them during the first two sessions. Only one participant dropped out much later because she moved to another province.

For those who stayed, all believed it had been worth it and attendance was excellent over the twenty-week period. Participants were rarely absent, even if some had to travel long distances to participate. When they were absent, they usually called to justify their absence. At the end of the groups, most of the participants expressed a wish to repeat the group. End of group comments and initial pre-post data indicate that clients feel the group intervention is a valuable experience.

Results

The initial goals when creating the groups were to decrease the duration, intensity and frequency of suicide attempts. It became clear that change, in the areas of the affective, cognitive and behavioural skills contributing to suicidal behaviour, is a slow process. The lives of many of these clients are extremely chaotic, with many never having developed the skill to keep themselves safe. The groups for individuals under the age of 25 are in their initial stages of development. Data presented at this time is limited not only due to the small number of groups completed, but also because of the resistance in filling out self-report measures even if participants have been more than willing to give their feedback verbally.

The concept of safety is paramount both in the environment in which the groups take place, through modeling and in the skills content. Participants reported feeling 'listened to', 'respected' and the facilitators 'bother to get to know you'. They noted that within the context of a group, they were 'able to speak up', or saw the group as being, 'a place to come for support'. One member identified, 'I learned a lot about relationship patterns'. Feeling understood and having a place to belong is reflected in the comments: 'I feel I've made friends with other group members that understand me well' and 'I am not alone'. They reported that it felt different from other groups in that it was 'non-competitive', 'non-judgemental' and they felt they were 'treated like people not diseases', noting 'the issues here are more relevant'. They reported that humour was a necessary component to aid in titrating both the emotional content and intensity of the sessions. The titrating was important given that the most frequently named fear at the start of the intervention, was 'to be triggered' or 'overwhelmed' when in the group.

Participants reported that their feeling of hope, although still a struggle, was better than when they began the group six months earlier. This was consistent with the Beck Hopelessness Scale pre-post mean measures (N = 24; z = 2.049; asymp. sig. (two-tailed) = 0.041). A member reflected this changed when she stated: 'I feel like I'm going some place: I'm not as stuck', and another member reflected: 'I learned to not be so hard on myself . . . I used to feel like I was a failure or stupid but I don't feel this way any more'.

Participants reported changes in self-harm with respect to either a decrease in frequency and intensity. Client feedback regarding self-injury and suicide included comments such as

- 'There is something different about my headspace when I do it, it's not as deep.'
- 'I argue with myself more, I know I have some coping skills.'
- 'I came here to learn tricks, I didn't learn any tricks but I stopped hurting myself and I like coming.'
- 'I don't know if it's the group or you (pointing to the therapist) but even if I still pierce myself, I don't self-harm and I don't have any desire to kill myself.'

At the same time, one member reported no change, and no one reported it 'getting worse'.

Preliminary results using Linehan's Suicidal Behaviour Questionnaire (Linehan et al., 1991) show suicidal ideation means dropping from pre-group 44.8 to post-group 42.62 (N =15–8) and suicidal threats means from pre-group 17.0 to 13.2857 post-intervention (N = 14–7) with a preliminary and cautionary significance in suicidal ideation (N = 6; z = 2.032; asymp. sig. (two-tailed) = 0.042). Sample size pre-post completed measures significantly hampers further discussion at this time.

Emotional literacy, one of the targets of the intervention, being measured by using the Toronto Alexithymia Scale (TAS–20), interestingly showed little change in the group under the age of 25. The ability to identify, describe or to externalize feelings remains in the seriously alexithymic range at pre- and post-group with little to no change. This is a substantial difference from the aggregate group that includes adults where changes in alexithymia were significant for both the total score and the externalization of feelings (N = 50; Total mean asymp. sig. (two-tailed) = 0.020; Difficulty Externalizing Feelings Sig: = 0.018 for the entire group). Participants reported that after the intervention, they were aware that emotions are 'not bad [they're] normal', 'can be controlled', and that they had some training in how to name them and to cope with them.

Members reported sharing information and being able to ask for help as significant positive steps for themselves that occurred within the first half of participating in the intervention. They reported that when not in the group, they found it 'hard to share feeling outside of group'; 'worry-[ing] about letting others down' and coming to their own acceptance 'that there are times when I can't be at my best and that I really do have a legitimate reason'.

Conclusion

Early results show that PISA is a promising approach for young patients suffering from severe comorbid disorders at high risk of suicide. It offers hope that maladaptive patterns of functioning can perhaps be transformed and that the quality of life of these patients can possibly be augmented by early intervention. It will be difficult to verify how much the group intervention is responsible for the improvement seen in the patients without additional longer controlled studies.

Until then, it will be important for physicians and other health care professionals to recognize and properly identify early signs of psychopathology in adolescents who self-harm or attempt suicide. Identification is only the first step, we must continue to develop and study more specific treatment programmes, such as PISA for these high risk adolescents.

Another important impact of this group is that it may change the way clinicians see their patients. Clinicians usually see these patients in crisis, a time during which the interaction may be stressful. The group intervention may allow a more positive view of these difficult patients.

References

Adler, G. (1994) Transference, countertransference and abuse in psychotherapy. *Harvard Review of Psychiatry*, 2, 151–159.

American Psychiatric Association (APA) (1994) *Diagnostic and Statistical Manual of Mental Disorders, Fourth Edition* (DSM-IV). Washington, DC: APA.

Bandura, A. (1989) Social cognitive theory, in V.R. Greenwich (ed.) *Annals of Child Development*. Greenwich, CT: JAI Press.

Beck, A.T. (1996) Beyond belief: a theory of modes, personality and psychopathology, in P.M. Salkovskis (ed.) *Frontiers of Cognitive Therapy*. New York: Guilford.

Belsky, J., Rosenberger, K. and Crnic, K. (1995) The origins of attachment security: classical and contextual determinants, in S. Goldberg, R. Muir and J. Kerr (eds) *John Bowlby's Attachment Theory: Historical, clinical and social significance*. Hillsdale, NJ: Analytic Press.

Bergmans, Y. and Links, P.S. (2002) A description of a psychosocial/psychoeducational intervention for persons with recurrent suicide attempts. *Crisis*, 23(4), 7–12.

Brodsky, B.S., Oquendo, M., Ellis, S.P., Haas, G.L., Malone, K.M. and Mann, J.J. (2001) The relationship of childhood abuse to impulsivity and suicidal behavior in adults with major depression. *American Journal of Psychiatry*, 158, 1871–1877.

Clarkin, J.F., Yeomans, F.E. and Kernberg, O.F. (2006) *Psychotherapy for Borderline Personality: Focusing on Object Relations*. Washington, DC: American Psychiatric Publishing.

Crittenden, P.M. (1994) Family patterns of relationship in normative and dysfunctional families. *Development and Psychopathology*, 3, 491–512.

Davis, T., Gunderson, J. and Myers, M. (1999) Borderline personality disorder, in D.G. Jacobs (ed.) *The Harvard Medical School Guide to Suicide Assessment and Intervention*. San Francisco, CA: Jossey-Bass.

Deiter, P.J., Nicholls, S.S. and Pearlman, L.A. (2000) Self injury and self capacities: assisting an individual in crisis. *Journal of Clinical Psychology*, 56, 1173–1191.

Evans, K., Tyrer, P., Catalan, J. and Schmidt, U. (1999) Manual-assisted cognitive behaviour therapy (MACT): a randomized controlled trial of a brief intervention with bibliotherapy in the treatment of recurrent self-harm. *Psychological Medicine*, 29, 19–25.

Favazza, A.R. (2003) *Self mutilation and body modification*. Rounds given at Centre for Addiction and Mental Health, Toronto, Ontario, April.

Fonagy, P., Target, M. and Gergely, G. (2000) Attachment and borderline personality disorder: a theory and some evidence. *Psychiatric Clinic*, 23, 103–122.

Fredrickson, B.L. and Joiner, T. (2002) Positive emotions trigger upwards spiral towards emotional well-being. *Psychological Sciences*, 13, 172–175.

Goldman, S., D'Angelo, E. and DeMaso, D. (1993) Psychopathology in the families of children and adolescents with borderline personality disorder. *American Journal of Psychiatry*, 150, 1832–1835.

Gunderson, J.G. (1996) The borderline patient's intolerance of aloneness: insecure attachments and therapist availability. *American Journal of Psychiatry*, 153, 752–758.

Hawton, K. and Fagg, J. (1988) Suicide, and other causes of death, following attempted suicide. *British Journal of Psychiatry*, 152, 751–761.

Hawton, K. and Kirk, J. (1998) Problem-solving, in. K. Hawton, P.M. Salkovskis, J. Kirk and D.M. Clark (eds) *Cognitive Behaviour Therapy for Psychiatric Problems: A practical guide*. New York: Oxford Medical Publications.

Hawton, K., Arensman, E., Townsend, E. Bremner, S., Feldman, E., Goldney, R. et al. (1998) Deliberate self-harm: systematic review of the efficacy of psychosocial and pharmacological treatments in preventing repetition. *British Medical Journal*, 317, 441–447.

Hengeveld, M.W., Jonker, D.J.L. and Rooijmans, H.G.M. (1996) A pilot study of a short cognitive-behavioural group treatment for female recurrent suicide attempters. *International Journal of Psychiatry in Medicine*, 6, 83–91.

Herman, J. L. (1992) *Trauma and Recovery*. New York: Basic Books.

Isometsa, E.T., Henriksson, M.M., Heikkinen, M.E., Aro, H.M., Marttunen, M.J., Kuoppasalmi, K.I. and Lonnqvist, J.K. (1996) Suicide among subjects with personality disorders. *American Journal of Psychiatry*, 153, 667–673.

Joiner, T.E., Rudd, D., Rouleau, M. and Wager, K. (2000) Parameters of suicidal crises vary as a function of previous suicide attempts in youth inpatients. *Journal of the American Academy of Child and Adolescent Psychiatry*, 39(7), 876–880.

Kjellander, C., Bongar, B. and King, A. (1998) Suicidality in borderline personality disorder. *Crisis*, 19, 125–135.

Lesage, A.D., Boyer, R., Grunberg, F., Vanier, C., Morissette, R., Ménard-Buteau, C. and Loyer, M. (1994) Suicide and mental disorders: a case-control study of young adult males. *American Journal of Psychiatry*, 151, 1063–1068.

Levine, D., Marziali, E. and Hood, J. (1997) Emotion processing in borderline personality disorders. *Journal of Nervous and Mental Disease*, 185, 240–246.

Linehan, M. (1992) Behaviour therapy, dialectics and the treatment of borderline personality disorder, in D. Silver and M. Rosenbluth (eds) *Handbook of Borderline Disorders*. Madison, CT: International Universities Press.

Linehan, M. (1993) *Cognitive Behavioral Treatment of Borderline Personality Disorder*. New York: Guilford.

Linehan, M., Armstrong, H.E., Suarez, A., Allmon, D. and Heard, H. (1991) Cognitive-behavioural treatment of chronically parasuicidal borderline patients. *Archives of General Psychiatry*, 48, 1060–1064.

Links, P., Bergmans, Y. and Cook, M. (2003) Psychotherapeutic interventions to prevent repeated suicidal behavior. *Brief Treatment Crisis Intervention*, 3, 445–464.

Livesley, W.J. (2000) A practical approach to the treatment of patients with borderline personality disorder. *Psychiatric Clinics of North America*, 23, 211–232.

McLeavey, B.C., Daly, R.J., Ludgate, J.W. and Murray, C.M. (1994) Interpersonal problem-solving skills training in the treatment of self poisoning patients. *Suicide and Life-Threatening Behavior*, 24, 383–394.

McLeod, A.K., Tata, P., Evans, K., Tyrer, P., Schmidt, U., Davidson, K. et al. (1998) Recovery of positive future thinking within a high-risk parasuicide group: results from a pilot randomized control trial. *British Journal of Clinical Psychology*, 37, 371–379.

Main, M., Kaplan, N. and Cassiday, J. (1985) Security in infancy, childhood, and adulthood: a move to the level of representation. *Monographs of the Society for Research in Child Development*, 50, 66–104.

Murphy, G.E. and Wetzel, R.D. (1982) Family history of suicidal behaviour among suicide attempters. *Journal of Nervous and Mental Disease*, 170, 86–90.

O'Leary, K. (2000) Neuropsychological testing results. *Psychiatric Clinics of North America*, 23, 41–60.

Paris, J. (2002) Chronic suicidality among patients with borderline personality disorder. *Psychiatric Services*, 53, 738–742.

Rotheram-Borus, M.J., Piacentini, J., Miller, S., Graae, F. and Castro-Blanco, D. (1994) Brief cognitive-behavioural treatment for adolescent suicide attempters and their families. *Journal of the American Academy of Child and Adolescent Psychiatry*, 33, 508–517.

Ryle, A. and McCutcheon, L. (2006) Cognitive analytic therapy, in G. Stricker and J. Gold (eds) *A Casebook of Psychotherapy Integration*. Washington, DC: American Psychological Association.

Sabo, A.N., Gunderson, J.G., Najavits, L.M., et al. (1995) Changes in self-destructiveness of borderline patients in psychotherapy: a prospective follow-up. *Journal of Nervous and Mental Disorder*, 183, 370–376.

Schmidtke, A., Bille-Brahe, U., De Leo, D., Kerkhof, A., Bjerke, T., Crepet, P. et al. (1996) Attempted suicide in Europe: rates, trends, and sociodemographic characteristics of suicide attempters during the period 1989–1992. Results of the WHO/EURO Multicentre Study on Parasuicide. *Acta Psychiatrica Scandinavica*, 93, 327–338.

Séguin, M., Lesage, A., Tousignant, M., Chawky, N., Turecki, G., Rouleau, G. et al. (2003) Stratégie de recherche sur le suicide : identification des causes multiples. *Journal des Psychologues*, 212, 22–26.

Soloff, P.H., Lynch, K.G. and Kelly, T.M. (2002) Childhood abuse as a risk factor for suicidal behavior in borderline personality disorder. *Journal of Personality Disorders*, 16, 201–214.

Stanley, B., Gameroff, M., Michalsen, V. and Mann, J. (2001) Are suicide attempters who self-mutilate a unique population. *American Journal of Psychiatry*, 158, 427–432.

Thedford Lambert, M. (2003) Suicide risk assessment and management: focus on personality disorders. *Current Opinion in Psychiatry*, 16, 71–76.

Townsend, E., Hawton, K., Altman, D.G., Arensman, E., Gunnell, D., Hazell, P. et al. (2001) The efficacy of problem-solving treatments after deliberate self-harm: meta-analysis of randomized controlled trials with respect to depression, hopelessness and improvement in problems. *Psychological Medicine*, 31(6), 979–988.

Van der Sande, R., Buskens, E., Allart, E., van der Graaf, Y. and van Engeland, H. (1997) Psychosocial intervention following suicide attempt: a systematic review of treatment interventions. *Acta Psychiatrica Scandinavica*, 96(1), 43–50.

Villeneuve, D. and Roux, N. (1995) Family therapy and some personality disorders in adolescence. *Adolescent Psychiatry*, 20: 365–380.

Wheelis, J. and Gunderson, J.G. (1998) A little cream and sugar: psychotherapy with a borderline patient. *American Journal of Psychiatry*, 155, 114–122.

Wilberg, T., Friis, S. and Karterud, S. (1998) Outpatient group psychotherapy: a valuable continuation treatment for patient with borderline personality disorder treated in a day hospital. A 3 year follow-up study. *Nordic Journal of Psychiatry*, 52, 213–221.

Wood, A., Trainor, G., Rothwell, J., Moore, A. and Harrington, R. (2001) Randomized trial of group therapy for repeated deliberate self-harm in adolescents. *Journal of the American Academy of Child and Adolescent Psychiatry*, 40, 1246–1253.

Postscript

Why did I choose to edit a journal symposium and then a book on suicide? On reflection I now realize that there was one main reason: a young friend, who I had known since his childhood, became distressed about current overwhelming life issues and then committed suicide (see Palmer, 1997). Another sad experience reinforced my interest: on a Boxing Day (26 December) in the 1990s, my family and I watched a person commit suicide by walking fully clothed into the rough and cold Atlantic. He was only 500 yards away from help but it might as well have been miles. Unlike the fictional BBC television sitcom character, Reggie Perrin, he did not return alive. By the time the helicopter crew from the nearby naval base came to rescue him, he was dying. They had arrived within minutes and put their lives at risk in the rescue bid. In response the local community wanted the access steps to the beach restored. Probably this would have made little difference. In both of these cases, I felt powerless to intervene. In parallel with these experiences I had already been to Beijing, China, on two different occasions to give a paper and run a workshop on suicide prevention. It is now easy to see how my experiences focused my mind on suicide.

I hope that the strategies and interventions we have covered in this book help the helpers to reduce or prevent suicide in their client groups, workplaces and communities.

Reference

Palmer, S. (1997) Multimodal therapy, in C. Feltham (ed.) *Which Psychotherapy?* London: Sage.

Part V

Appendices

Appendix 1: Personal Self-Harm Management Plan

For: ....   Date: ....

In the event of suicidal feelings or thoughts, I will do the following:

- Write down and analyse the thoughts about self-harm.

- Do something physical (e.g. go for a walk, exercise, etc.) as follows:

_____

_____

_____

_____

- Call and talk with a friend or someone else, such as (list names and phone numbers):

_____

_____

_____

_____

- Do something that I usually enjoy (whether or not it seems enjoyable now) – like the following:

_____

_____

_____

_____

_____

If feelings of self-harm persist, I will make contact with the following:

(list names and phone numbers)
- My counsellor: _____
- My doctor: _____
- Doctor's after hours service: _____
- Psychiatric emergency service: _____
- Telephone counselling service: _____
- Psychiatric Unit: _____
- Hospital Accident and Emergency: _____
- Police: _____
- Other:

_____

_____

Appendix 2: Assessment checklists

DEPRESSION

	Moderate	Severe	Serious
Depressed mood	gloomy, sad	weepy, heavy	deep despair
Loss of interest	neglects usual interests	doing little, productivity down	rejects any enjoyment or satisfaction
Social withdrawal	neglects friends and social activities	actively avoids social contact	not responding to environment
Hopelessness	wonders if improvement possible	highly pessimistic about the future	sees no future for self, world, etc.
Suicidal feelings	feels life is not worth living	considers suicide	plans or attempts suicide
Sleep problems	hard to fall asleep, restless, wakes	wakes early a.m., can't get back to sleep	

SUICIDE RISK

General risk screening

- male
- high expectations of self
- chronic physical health problem / pain / disability
- substance abuse / addiction (self or family)
- history of psychiatric problems (self or family)
- current depression
- family history of suicide
- previous suicide attempts
- focus on themes of death
- suppressing emotions
- negative view of life/future
- social isolation
- poor family support
- in abusive relationship
- sudden loss (relationship, redundancy, bereaved, etc.)
- anniversary/reminder of loss

Continued overleaf

DEPRESSION

	Moderate	Severe	Serious
Retardation	slow thought, speech, activity; lacks energy	apathy	complete stupor
Appetite changes	appetite reduced – or overeating	weight loss	major weight loss, or stops eating
Physical symptoms	wind, indigestion, constipation, feeling of heaviness	cardiovascular, palpitations, respiratory, pains, headaches	
Sexual / Genital	loss of interest in sex	menstrual disturbance, erectile failure	
Diurnal variation	mood same through the day, but each day may be different	mood varies through the day, same pattern every day / gives up because of poor concentration	

SUICIDE RISK

General risk screening

- significant life changes
- intoxication
- *for adolescents*: family breakup, conflict; parents seen as hostile, indifferent, having extremely high expectations or highly controlling; poor communication skills, peer relationships, school achievement; antisocial behaviour; sexual or physical abuse; recent suicide by friend or relative.

Current risk assessment

- Thinking of suicide now?
- How lethal is the proposed method? (Higher – firearms, hanging, gassing, cutting wrists, pills – Lower)
- Any preparations? (giving away valued possessions, making a will, etc.)
- What situations trigger suicidal ideation?
- What positives/options seen in self or circumstances?

Concentration / Cognitive	hard to read, follow TV programme, etc	gives up because of poor concentration	disordered thinking, depersonalisation, derealisation
Health concerns	worries about health	preoccupied with health	hypochondriacal delusions
Guilt	self-reproach	sees depression as a punishment	delusions of guilt
Anxiety	restless, tense, irritable	apprehensive, fears, worries over trivia	highly agitated
Suspicious thinking	suspicious of others and their motives	ideas of reference	delusions of reference or persecution

Appendix 3: Useful organizations and websites

Aeschi Working Group
www.aeschiconference.unibe.ch/

American Association of Suicidology
4201 Connecticut Avenue, NW, Suite 408
Washington, DC 20008
USA
www.suicidology.org

American Foundation for Suicide Prevention
120 Wall Street, 22nd Floor
New York, NY 10005
USA
www.afsp.org

Australian Institute for Suicide Research and Prevention
Griffith University, Mt Gravatt Campus
Brisbane, Qld 4111
Australia
www.griffith.edu.au/aisrap

Befrienders Worldwide
International Officer, Samaritans
Upper Mill, Kingston Road
Ewell, Surrey
KT17 2AF
United Kingdom
www.befrienders.org

Centre for Research and Intervention on Suicide and Euthanasia
c.p. 8888, Succ. Centre-Ville
Montréal, Québec, H3C 3P8
Canada
www.crise.ca

Centre for Suicide Prevention
Suite 320, 1202 Centre Street SE
Calgary, AB T2G 5A5
Canada
www.suicideinfo.ca

Centre for Suicide Prevention
University of Manchester
Oxford Road
Manchester
M13 9PL
United Kingdom
www.centre-suicide-prevention.man.ac.uk/

Centre for Suicide Research
Department of Psychiatry
Warneford Hospital
Headington, Oxford
OX3 7JX
United Kingdom
www.psychiatry.ox.ac.uk/csr/index.html

Center for the Study and Prevention of Suicide
Department of Psychiatry
University of Rochester Medical Center
300 Crittenden Boulevard
Rochester, NY 14642–8409
USA
www.rochesterepreventsuicide.org/

Choose Life: Suicide Prevention in Scotland
Ground Floor, Europa Building
450 Argyle Street
Glasgow
G2 8LG
United Kingdom
www.chooselife.net/

European Network for Suicidology
Josephine Scott
St Mary's Hospital
Castlebar, Co. Mayo
Ireland
www.uke.uni-hamburg.de/extern/ens/

International Association for Suicide Prevention
Central Administrative Office
Le Barade
F–32330 Gondrin
France
www.med.uio.no/iasp/

Irish Association of Suicidology
16 New Antrim Street
Castlebar, Co. Mayo
Ireland
www.ias.ie

Mind
15–19 Broadway
London
E15 4BQ
United Kingdom
www.mind.org.uk

Ministerial Council for Suicide Prevention
Telethon Institute for Child Health Research
PO Box 855
West Perth, WA 6872
Australia
www.mcsp.org.au/

National Centre for Suicide Research and Prevention of
Mental Ill-Health
Box 230
SE–171 77 Stockholm
Sweden
www.ki.se/suicide/english/info_presentation_nasp.html

National Strategy for Suicide Prevention
c/o SAMHSA
PO Box 42557
Washington, DC 20015
USA
www.mentalhealth.samhsa.gov/suicideprevention/

National Suicide Research Foundation Ireland
1 Perrott Avenue
College Road
IRL–Cork
Ireland
www.nsrf.ie

Ontario Suicide Prevention Network
19387 Glen Road
Williamstown, ON K0C 2J0
Canada
http://zope.vex.net/%7Ewbell/OSPN/

Organization for Attempters and Survivors of Suicide in
Interfaith Services
OASSIS
211 Russell Avenue, Apt. 71
Gaithersburg, MD 20877
USA
www.oassis.org/

Samaritans
Upper Mill, Kingston Road
Ewell, Surrey
KT17 2AF
United Kingdom
www.samaritans.org

Suicide and Mental Health Association International (SMHAI)
PO Box 702
Sioux Falls, SD 57101–0702
USA
http://suicideandmentalhealthassociationinternational.org/

Suicide Forum
Online support group
www.suicideforum.com/

Suicide Prevention
156 Westcombe Hill
London
SE3 7DH
United Kingdom
www.freewebs.com/suicideprevention/

Suicide Prevention Action Network USA (SPAN USA)
1025 Vermont Avenue, NW, Suite 1066
Washington, DC 20005
USA
www.spanusa.org/

Suicide Prevention Information New Zealand
PO Box 10051
Dominion Rd
Auckland 1446
New Zealand
www.spinz.org.nz/

Suicide Prevention Resource Center
Newton, Massachusetts office
Education Development Center, Inc.
55 Chapel Street
Newton, MA 02458–1060
USA
http://www.sprc.org/

Suicide Prevention Resource Center
Washington, DC office
Education Development Center, Inc.
1000 Potomac Street NW, Suite 350
Washington, DC 20007
USA
http://www.sprc.org/

Suicide Research and Prevention Unit
University of Oslo
Sognsvannsvn. 21, Bygning 12
N–0320 Oslo
Norway
www.med.uio.no/ipsy/ssff/hovedengelsk.htm

Unit for Suicide Research
Department of Psychiatry and Medical Psychology
UZ Ghent
De Pintelaan 185 (K12F)
9000 Ghent
Belgium
http://users.ugent.be/~cvheerin/English/Presentation.html

World Federation for Mental Health
6564 Loisdale Court, Suite 310
Springfield, VA 22150–1812
USA
www.wfmh.org

World Health Organization (WHO)
Geneva
Switzerland
Suicide information
www.who.int/topics/suicide/en/
www.who.int/mental_health/prevention/suicide/suicideprevent/en/

Yellow Ribbon International
PO Box 644
Westminster, CO 80030–0644
USA
http://www.yellowribbon.org/

Appendix 4: Useful books on suicidology from 2000 onwards

Duffy, D. and Ryan, T. (eds) (2004) *New Approaches to Preventing Suicide: A manual for practitioners*. London: Jessica Kingsley Publishers.

Maris, R.W., Berman, A.L. and Silverman, M. (2000) *Comprehensive Textbook of Suicidology*. New York: Guilford.

O'Connor, R.C. and Sheehy, N.P. (2000) *Understanding Suicidal Behaviour*. Leicester: BPS Blackwell.

Rudd, M.D., Joiner, T. and Rajab, M.H. (2001) *Treating Suicidal Behaviour: An effective, time-limited approach*. New York: Guilford.

Simon, R.I. and Hales, R.E. (eds) (2006) *Textbook of Suicide Assessment and Management*. Washington, DC: American Psychiatric Publishing.

Williams, J.M.G. (2001) *Suicide and Attempted Suicide*. London: Penguin.

Yufit, R.I. and Lester, D. (2005) *Assessment, Treatment, and Prevention of Suicidal Behavior*. New York: Wiley.

Appendix 5: WHO ICD-10 codes

X60 Intentional self-poisoning by and exposure to nonopioid analgesics, antipyretics and antirheumatics

X61 Intentional self-poisoning by and exposure to antiepileptic, sedative-hypnotic, antiparkinsonism and psychotropic drugs, not elsewhere classified

X62 Intentional self-poisoning by and exposure to narcotics and psycho-dysleptics (hallucinogens), not elsewhere classified

X63 Intentional self-poisoning by and exposure to other drugs acting on the autonomic nervous system

X64 Intentional self-poisoning by and exposure to other and unspecified drugs, medicaments and biological substances

X65 Intentional self-poisoning by and exposure to alcohol

X66 Intentional self-poisoning by and exposure to organic solvents and halogenated hydrocarbons and their vapours

X67 Intentional self-poisoning by and exposure to other gases and vapours

X68 Intentional self-poisoning by and exposure to pesticides

X69 Intentional self-poisoning by and exposure to other and unspecified chemicals and noxious substances

X7O Intentional self-harm by hanging, strangulation and suffocation

X71 Intentional self-harm by drowning and submersion

X72 Intentional self-harm by handgun discharge

X73 Intentional self-harm by rifle, shotgun and larger firearm discharge

X74 Intentional self-harm by other and unspecified firearm discharge

X75 Intentional self-harm by explosive material

X76 Intentional self-harm by smoke, fire and flames

X77 Intentional self-harm by steam, hot vapours and hot objects

X78 Intentional setf-harm by sharp object

X79 Intentional self-harm by blunt object

X80 Intentional self-harm by jumping from a high place

X81 Intentional self-harm by jumping or lying before moving object

X82 Intentional self-harm by crashing of motor vehicle

X83 Intentional self-harm by other specified means

X84 Intentional sell-harm by unspecified means

Index